CHILTON'S
MORE MILES PER GALLON
GUIDE

Second Edition

CHILTON'S
MORE MILES PER GALLON
GUIDE

RONALD M. WEIERS, S.A.E

CHILTON BOOK COMPANY   RADNOR, PENNSYLVANIA

To the memory of my father,
whose inventiveness in the pursuit of efficiency
will always be a source of pride and inspiration.

All opinions expressed in this book are the opinions of the author. The editors at Chilton Book Company have not tested, nor does Chilton Book Company endorse any of the products specifically mentioned. All products mentioned are typical of high quality products available from many reputable manufacturers of similar equipment, and the exclusion of any company or product is purely unintentional; it would be impossible to list them all.

SAFETY NOTICE

Proper service and repair procedures are vital to the safe, reliable operation of all motor vehicles, as well as the personal safety of those performing repairs. This book outlines procedures for servicing and repairing vehicles using safe, effective methods. The procedures contain NOTES and CAUTIONS which should be followed along with standard safety procedures to eliminate the possibility of personal injury or improper service which could damage the vehicle or compromise its safety.

It is important to note that repair procedures and techniques, tools and parts for servicing motor vehicles, as well as the skill and experience of the individual performing the work vary widely. It is not possible to anticipate all of the conceivable ways or conditions under which vehicles may be serviced, or to provide cautions as to all of the possible hazards that may result. Standard and accepted safety precautions and equipment should be used when handling toxic or flammable fluids, and safety goggles or other protection should be used during cutting, grinding, chiseling, prying, or any other process that can cause material removal or projectiles.

Some procedures require the use of tools specially designed for a specific purpose. Before substituting another tool or procedure, you must be completely satisfied that neither your personal safety, nor the performance of the vehicle will be endangered.

Contents

Acknowledgments

The author and Chilton Book Company express appreciation to the following for their cooperation and assistance in the preparation of this book:

American Automobile Association, Falls Church, VA
American Motors Corporation, Southfield, MI
American Petroleum Institute, Washington, D.C.
Atlantic Richfield Company, Los Angeles, CA
Automotive Information Council, Southfield, MI
Auto World, Inc., Scranton, PA
Car Care Council, Dearborn, MI
Champion Spark Plug Company, Toledo, OH
Chevrolet Division, General Motors Corporation, Detroit, MI
Coleman Company, Somerset, PA
Cummins Engine Company, Columbus, IN
Firestone Tire and Rubber Company, Akron, OH
Kamei USA, North Haven, CT
Mercedes-Benz of North America Inc., Montvale, NJ
Motor Vehicle Manufacturers Association, Detroit, MI
National Public Services Research Institute, Alexandria, VA
Recreational Vehicle Industry Association, Chantilly, VA
Rubber Manufacturers Institute, Washington, D.C.
Shell Oil Company, Houston, TX
Ted McWilliams Motor City, Monroeville, PA
Tire Industry Safety Council, Washington, D.C.
United States Department of Energy, Washington, D.C.
United States Environmental Protection Agency, Washington, D.C.
VDO-Argo Instruments, Inc., Winchester, VA
Volkswagen of America, Englewood Cliffs, NJ

Special thanks to the
Society of Automotive Engineers (SAE), Warrendale, PA

Chapter I

How Much Can You Save?

In these times of soaring fuel prices and uncertain availability, we're all concerned about stretching every fuel dollar as far as possible. Buying gasoline has become an adventure instead of an errand, and we could all use a sizable discount when we line up at the service station.

Assuming that you are a typical driver, the U.S. Department of Energy has estimated that you can save a significant portion of the more than $800 you are probably spending each year for fuel. According to their estimates, careful buying, driving, maintenance, and planning can provide you with the equivalent of a 47¢ discount on each gallon of gasoline.[1] Their estimate assumes that you travel 11,000 miles each year in a car that gets 14 to 15 miles per gallon, and that gasoline costs one dollar per gallon.

As with so many other drains on your income, the amount you save will depend on how much you currently spend for owning and operating your car. So before proceeding to the main purpose of this book—helping you become a more fuel-efficient driver—let's take an overall look at the kind of expenses your car involves.

THE COSTS OF DRIVING

The costs of owning a car can be broken down into two categories—variable and fixed. Variable costs are directly related to the number and type of miles you drive, and include fuel, oil, maintenance, and tires. Fixed costs, on the other hand, don't change much regardless of the number of miles driven. They include insurance, license and registration fees, taxes, finance charges, and depreciation. Together, these costs can amount to a considerable total over the course of a year. As we discuss the various car ownership costs, you may wish to use Figure 1-1 as a worksheet to calculate the cost of owning and operating your car.

Variable Costs
Fuel

Whether your car's engine is a domestic V8 or a four-cylinder import, the more miles you drive, the more fuel your car will consume. Figure 1-2 is derived from data developed by Runzheimer and Company for a 1979 intermediate-size sedan equipped with a V8 engine, automatic transmission, power brakes, and power steering, and driven 15,000 miles per year. As this figure indicates, the cost of fuel is typically the biggest single variable cost you will encounter. If you happen to be driving that intermediate sedan today, you're probably spending close to a nickel every time you pass a mile marker on the interstate. With fuel prices likely to go nowhere but up, the odometer on your dashboard will increas-

FIGURE YOUR CAR COSTS

Fixed Costs	*Yearly Totals*
Depreciation (divide by number of years of ownership)	_____
Insurance	_____
Taxes	_____
License and registration	_____
Loan interest	_____
Total Fixed Costs	_____

Variable Costs	*Yearly Totals*
Gas and oil per mile	_____
Number of miles driven	_____
Cost per year (multiply miles driven by gas and oil per mile)	_____
Maintenance (use your own figures or average of 1.10 cents multiplied by miles driven)	_____
Tires (see note under Maintenance)	_____
Other costs (car wash, repairs, accessories, etc.)	_____
Total Variable Costs	_____
Total Driving Costs per Year	_____
Cost per Mile	_____
(divide yearly total by total miles driven)	_____

Fig. 1–1. Worksheet for figuring the costs of owning and operating your car.

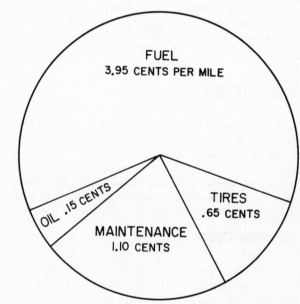

Fig. 1–2. Approximate breakdown of variable costs for the intermediate sedan described in the text. Skyrocketing gasoline prices have probably sent operating costs substantially higher than the 1979 figures indicated here.

ingly approach the day when it simultaneously reports both miles and dimes traveled.

You can estimate your fuel cost per year by using either the chart or the formula in Figure 1-3. To calculate your fuel cost per mile, just divide fuel cost

YOUR FUEL COST PER YEAR

Estimated MPG	$1.50	$1.40	$1.30	$1.20	$1.10	$1.00	$.95	$.90	$.85	$.80	$.75	$.70	$.65
50	$450	$420	$390	$360	$330	$300	$285	$270	$255	$240	$225	$210	$195
48	469	438	406	375	344	313	297	281	266	250	234	219	203
46	489	457	424	391	358	326	310	293	277	261	245	228	212
44	512	478	444	410	375	341	324	307	290	273	256	239	222
42	536	500	464	428	393	358	340	342	304	286	268	250	232
40	562	526	488	450	412	375	356	359	319	300	281	263	244
38	592	552	514	474	435	395	375	356	336	316	296	276	257
36	624	584	542	500	458	416	395	375	354	333	312	292	271
34	662	618	574	530	485	441	419	397	375	353	331	309	287
32	704	656	610	562	516	469	445	422	399	375	352	328	305
30	750	700	650	600	550	500	475	450	425	400	375	350	325
28	808	750	696	642	590	536	509	483	456	429	402	375	348
26	866	808	750	692	635	578	549	552	491	462	433	404	375
24	938	876	812	750	688	625	594	597	531	500	469	438	406
22	1022	954	886	818	749	681	647	613	579	545	511	477	443
20	1126	1050	976	900	825	750	713	675	638	600	563	525	488
18	1250	1166	1084	1000	917	834	792	750	709	667	625	583	542
16	1406	1312	1218	1126	1031	938	891	844	797	750	703	656	609
14	1608	1500	1392	1286	1178	1071	1018	964	911	857	804	750	696
12	1936	1650	1624	1500	1375	1250	1188	1125	1063	1000	938	875	813
10	2250	2100	1952	1800	1650	1500	1425	1350	1275	1200	1125	1050	975
8	2812	2626	2438	2250	2062	1875	1781	1688	1594	1500	1406	1313	1219

Fig. 1–3. This chart represents your fuel costs per year if you drive 10,000 miles per year. Your fuel cost per year can also be found using this formula:

$$\frac{\text{Miles driven per year}}{\text{Average mpg}} \times \frac{\text{Fuel cost}}{\text{per gallon}} = \frac{\text{Fuel cost}}{\text{per year}}$$

per gallon by the mileage your car delivers. For example, if you pay $1.10 per gallon and your car gets 15 miles per gallon, your fuel cost per mile is:

$$\frac{110\cent \text{ per gallon}}{15 \text{ miles per gallon}} = 7.33 \cent \text{ per mile}$$

Oil

Oil consumption, while not a major expense, also varies with the number of miles you drive. You can determine your oil cost per mile the same way you determined fuel cost. Just add up all you spend for oil, filters, and oil changes for the year, then divide by your annual mileage. Don't forget to include the one or two quarts which may be added between scheduled oil changes. While you should follow the specific recommendations of your car's manufacturer, keep in mind that the typical motorist will have the oil changed about every 6,000 miles.

In general, the per-mile cost of oil will represent approximately 3% of the cost per mile for gasoline. Don't let the low per-mile cost of oil mislead you into thinking that this is an unimportant item. Your car's health and efficiency depend very much on the oil you use and how often you have it changed.

Tires

As with oil, tires are a variable-cost item that can help raise or lower your fuel bill. As we'll see later, driving and maintenance practices that lead to more miles per gallon tend also to pay off in more miles per tire. As with oil, the importance of tires is often underestimated; their influence on other aspects of the car, especially fuel efficiency and front-end wear, cannot be ignored. If you drive with reasonable care and keep the wheels properly aligned, tire wear will be kept to a minimum. On the other hand, improper inflation, high speeds, hard cornering, rapid acceleration, and quick stops will all contribute to premature tire wear and a higher cost of vehicle operation.

You can estimate the cost per mile for tires either by dividing the cost of the tires by their actual or their expected lifetime in miles, or by including them in the estimate of maintenance expenses (see the following section).

Maintenance

Like fuel, maintenance makes up a major variable cost of operating your car. The "ounce of prevention" philosophy, though ignored by many, is a major key to lowering all of the variable costs discussed here. Reasonable maintenance combined with the efficient driving habits discussed later should help you to get not only the most miles per gallon from your car, but also the most miles per dollar.

The newer your car, the smaller your maintenance expenses are likely to be. However, even a very new car requires regular checkups and service. The only way to determine accurately the cost of maintenance is to keep a record of all expenditures. A glove compartment notebook is handy for this purpose. If you'd like a rough idea, use 1.1¢ per mile as an estimate of your maintenance expenditures. However, this is an average figure developed for a typical 1979 intermediate-size car and represents only routine maintenance.

Fixed Costs
Insurance

Your yearly insurance premium does not usually depend on the amount of driving you do. In many cases, the Sunday-mornings-to-church driver pays the same premium as the driver who logs 20,000 miles per year. Specific insurance costs depend on the amount of coverage, where you live, and the purpose for which the car is used. To determine your insurance costs, just add the premiums for all liability, property damage, comprehensive, and collision policies.

License, Registration, and Finance Charges

License and registration fees are due generally once each year and should be included in the fixed cost total. If you have a car loan, include the amount of annual interest in your fixed operating cost.

Taxes

Sales taxes or excise taxes are paid when you purchase your car, and once paid are gone forever. They should be considered part of the purchase price and included when you determine your car's depreciation.

Depreciation

Depreciation is the largest single expense in owning a car, and it is the difference between what you paid for the car and what you can sell it for now. To determine your annual depreciation expense, subtract the expected resale value of your car from the amount it cost in the first place, then divide by the number of years you plan to keep the vehicle.

Because cars depreciate at different rates depending on their style, mileage traveled, and overall appearance, depreciation is often difficult to determine.

Theoretically, the depreciation for a given year is the amount of value the car loses during the year. However, since the only way to be sure is to sell it twice—once in January, again in December—this is not a practical approach.

An approximation of your depreciation costs can be obtained by examining a used-car market value book (e.g., the NADA Official Used Car Guide, or the National Market Reports Inc. Red Book) published periodically and subscribed to by many libraries, banks, and auto dealerships. While depreciation is largely beyond your control, proper maintenance and care, along with good driving habits, can help to minimize its effect on your pocketbook.

Comparative Operating Costs

A breakdown of the driving costs for 1979 models of various sizes is presented in Figure 1-4, and it may be helpful in comparing your own driving costs with those of high-cost (metropolitan areas) and low-cost (small towns and rural locations) environments in the United States. The data in the figure assume that the car is owned for four years and driven 15,000 miles per year. The costs of insurance, license, taxes, loan interest, depreciation, gas, oil, tires, and maintenance are included in the total operating cost.

FUEL EFFICIENCY MEANS LOWER COSTS

According to the U.S. Department of Energy, an average family spending $800 per year on gasoline could keep 240 of these dollars each year by adopting the following fuel efficiency habits:[2]

Improved driving techniques:	$ 40 per year
Improved trip planning:	112
Use of properly inflated radial tires and high-mileage oil:	56
Regular tune-ups and adjustments:	32
Total annual savings:	$240 per year

	Variable Cost (¢ per mile)	Total Cost (¢ per mile)	Total Annual Cost
Subcompact (4 cyl)			
low-cost area	4.35	12.8	$1,923
high-cost area	5.05	16.4	2,462
Compact (6 cyl)			
low-cost area	5.55	14.6	2,190
high-cost area	6.70	18.7	2,808
Intermediate (8 cyl)			
low-cost area	5.65	16.6	2,486
high-cost area	6.95	21.1	3,170
Standard (8 cyl)			
low-cost area	6.00	17.7	2,659
high-cost area	7.40	22.6	3,391

Fig. 1–4. Typical costs for operating a 1979 model car in high- and low-cost areas of the United States. (*Source:* Runzheimer and Company, "Your Driving Costs," Falls Church, VA: American Automobile Association, 1979.)

Fig. 1–5. According to estimates by the U.S. Department of Energy, the average family spending $800 each year for gasoline could save $240 by adopting more fuel-efficient driving habits. If the family is in the 20% tax bracket, this is equivalent to a $300 raise in salary.

Income-Tax Bracket

		10%	20%	30%	40%	
	$ 0	$ 0	$ 0	$ 0	$ 0	
	40	44	50	57	67	
	80	89	100	114	133	
	120	133	150	171	200	
	160	178	200	229	267	
	200	222	250	286	333	
Annual	240	267	300	343	400	**Before-Tax**
Savings	280	311	350	400	467	**Equivalent**
on Fuel	320	356	400	457	533	**Savings**
	360	400	450	514	600	
	400	444	500	571	667	
	440	489	550	629	733	
	480	533	600	686	800	
	520	520	650	743	867	
	560	622	700	800	933	
	600	667	750	857	1000	

Fig. 1–6. Translating your annual fuel savings into equivalent before-tax income.

Money Saved is Better Than Money Earned

The well-known quote equating a penny saved to a penny earned undoubtedly was uttered before the income tax system came into being. Assuming that you are taxed 20%, that penny you earn ends up being only eight-tenths of a penny in your pocket. Thus, assuming the same 20% income tax rate, the family

If you take the steps in this column	... It's the same as saving about this much on each gallon of gasoline*	Savings on each gallon/cost per gallon
Purchase Decision		
Buying a vehicle that gets 10 mpg more than current vehicle	$.18	18.0%
Behind-the-Wheel Techniques		
30-second engine warmup		
Brisk and steady acceleration		
Anticipate traffic-use buffer zone		
Flow smoothly through traffic	.05	5.0%
Trip Planning and Alternatives		
Ridesharing	.09	8.8%
Combining trips	.05	5.0%
Car Care and Maintenance		
Using radial tires	.02	2.4%
Inflating tires to highest safe recommended pressures	.03	2.6%
Using high mileage/high fuel level oil	.02	2.1%
Regular tuneups and adjustments	.04	4.2% Total
The Bottom Line	$.47 Total	48.1% Total

*The savings are based on a gasoline price of $1 per gallon and assume that *all* of these items are accomplished together.

Fig. 1–7. According to U.S. Department of Energy estimates, adoption of these fuel-efficiency habits can provide the average motorist with the equivalent of a 47¢ discount on each gallon of gasoline. (*Source:* U.S. Department of Energy, Office of Conservation and Solar Applications.)

who is able to save $240 (after tax) on fuel each year is, in effect, adding the equivalent of $300 ($240 divided by .8) to its before-tax income. In other words, by saving $240 on fuel, the breadwinner has been provided with the equivalent of a $300 per year increase in salary. Depending on your fuel savings and your tax bracket, the annual before-tax equivalent of your savings may be calculated in similar fashion.

The table in Figure 1-6 shows sample calculations for after-tax savings up to $600 in various tax brackets. If you're presently a real gas guzzler, it's not impossible that you might save more than $600 on your fuel bill. If you save more than $600 on your fuel bill, divide your savings by .8 to calculate your before-tax equivalent. The tax brackets in the table go up to 40%. If you're in a higher bracket than that, you probably don't need to worry about the fuel efficiency of your Rolls, but feel free to enjoy the book anyway.

At the beginning of the chapter, the possibility of a 47¢ per gallon "discount" based on fuel efficient practices was mentioned. Figure 1-7 is a breakdown of how the U.S. Department of Energy arrived at this figure, and it also contains some useful general suggestions for obtaining your personal fuel discount. This book attempts to explain how these recommendations work, and contains many practical suggestions on how best to apply these and a lot of other fuel-efficiency strategies. You should find enough information to become as fuel efficient as your ability, concentration, and enthusiasm permit.

Becoming a more fuel-efficient motorist is not just a matter of memorizing a catchy jingle, buying some gadget, or installing a sail on top of your car. There are no magic formulas, but rather a large number of hints, tips, and strategies supported by logic, common sense, and the laws of physics. The emphasis in this book will be not only on what to do, but also on why the advice works. From time to time you may encounter a pep talk (to keep you thinking "efficiency") or a challenge (to persuade you to do something you didn't think you could do). Remember that how much you save is very much up to you—the tools are here for you to apply.

RECORDING YOUR FUEL EFFICIENCY

Before proceeding to become the most efficient driver on your block, there's one thing you need to do: prepare to keep accurate records of your progress. Forget that "I can drive to work for three weeks on a tank" chatter—think miles per gallon. For accurate measurements, keep the following in mind:

1. Record the mileage reading, to the nearest tenth if possible—otherwise you may be off by up to two miles in the distance covered between fill-ups.

2. Try to have the tank filled to the same level each time. Note that some attendants prefer not to make change and seem to squeeze fuel into (or in the vicinity of) your tank until they get to the nearest half-dollar, while others don't go more than a dime beyond the pump's automatic shut-off. Carrying loose change or a credit card tends to encourage sales of odd amounts of fuel.

3. If you drive a diesel-powered vehicle, keep in mind that diesel fuel "foams" as it enters your tank, and that only a slow and patient fill-up will ensure that the tank is really full. A rapid filling can lead to a tank that is a gallon or more away from really being full. You'll think it took less fuel to fill your tank, that you *used* less fuel on the last tank, and, as a result, you may calculate a fuel mileage that is much higher than what your vehicle actually delivered.

4. Try to have the car in the same position each time you fill up. For example, if the filler pipe is on the left and the car is leaning toward the left, an air pocket may remain at the right side of the "full" tank. Also, the more weight there is on the side of the car where the filler pipe is located, the better the chances of an air pocket in the tank and the better your latest fuel mileage will appear to be. If you are attempting to impress your economy-minded friends, take note of this and point 3, above.

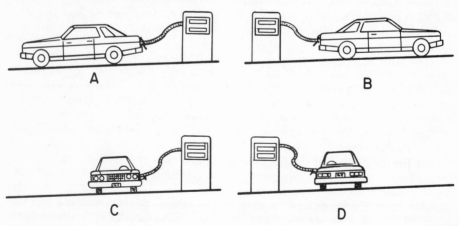

Fig. 1–8. Two of these vehicles are being short-changed with a less-than-full tank. See text for victims.

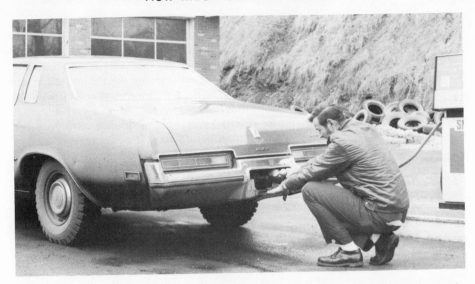

Fig. 1–9. This driver may not be getting a complete fill-up because his car is pointed up hill.

In order to have good drainage from their property, most filling stations have some degree of slope, generally towards the street or highway. In addition, many stations located on hills tend to have on upward or downward slope. Figure 1-8 shows four filling station scenes, with only two of the four vehicles really getting a complete fill-up. If you selected B and D as being short-changed, you're right. They will have air pockets instead of some of the fuel which could have been in the tank.

Unless your vehicle runs on air, try to notice the slope of the station island and position your car accordingly. This is especially valuable in a fuel-shortage situation where you may not be able to purchase fuel whenever you want. If your filler pipe is at the rear of the car, as in Figure 1-9, fill up with your car headed in the downhill direction. This station is located on a steep hill, and the driver may be losing a complete fill-up by having parked his vehicle with the filler pipe in a less than optimum position. (To position the fuel filler pipe as high

Speedometer Reading	Miles	Gals.	mpg	Avg. mpg, Last Two Fills	Comments
1400	—	—	—	—	just bought book and haven't had chance to keep records yet.
1652	252	11.9	21.2	—	turnpike.
1800	148	18.3	8.1	13.2	hauled anvils to auction.
2045	245	14.8	16.5	11.9	commuting.
2235	190	9.2	20.7	18.1	Sunday drive.
2447	212	15.2	13.9	16.5	"Moose" Edwards joined car pool.

Fig. 1–10. A format you may wish to use in keeping track of your fuel efficiency progress.

as possible, some drivers even go to the extreme of running their car onto a block of wood in order to raise the appropriate wheel three or four inches.)

5. To get a more accurate reading of the number of gallons you have just purchased, you can divide the cost of the fill-up by the cost per gallon. However, for most purposes, the tenth-of-a-gallon wheel on the pump should be sufficient.

6. Driving conditions have a lot to do with the fuel efficiency you will obtain. For example, open highway fuel mileage is generally much better than that obtained in slow-moving commuter or city traffic. If the driving conditions between this fill-up and the last were unusual in any way, it will add more insight to your fuel-efficiency records if you make note of this with a short comment.

Figure 1-10 is an example of a format you may wish to use in keeping track of your car's fuel consumption. Since fluctuations from fill-up to fill-up are bound to occur, you can make a little more sense from the figures if you also calculate the average miles per gallon for the two most recent fill-ups combined. Keep in mind that this is total miles divided by total gallons, not simply the average of the two mpg figures. In the records of Figure 1-10, the average of the first two fill-ups is $252 + 148 = 400$ miles divided by $11.9 + 18.3 = 30.2$ gallons, or 13.2 miles per gallon.

In keeping records of your fuel consumption, try to avoid reaching premature or unfounded conclusions regarding the cost or benefit of a particular device or strategy. With so many factors affecting your fuel efficiency, it's nearly impossible for you to detect the change brought about by one factor alone. For example, if you were to install fuel-efficient radial tires just before driving across your state with a 20-mph tail wind, you could wrongly conclude that the tires had increased your efficiency by 15 or 20%. They're good, but not quite that good. Of the suggestions in this book, many will involve fuel-efficiency improvements of 5% or less, with a lot being less than 1%. However, all those percents and fractions of a percent will add up to some very worthwhile savings.

CALCULATING YOUR SAVINGS

Depending on your present vehicle and how efficiently you drive and maintain it, applying the ideas in this book can reduce your fuel consumption by anywhere from 0% to 50%—0% if you're already a superstar who thinks and practices efficiency and 50% if you are presently a real leadfoot behind the wheel of a gas guzzler.

The fuel savings calculator in Figure 1-11 makes the assumption that improved planning, driving, purchasing, and maintenance habits will enable you to save 30% of the fuel you are now using. Let's say that you now drive 15,000 miles each year and get about 15 miles per gallon. A 30% reduction in fuel consumption will save you the cost of 300 gallons that you don't have to buy. The fuel savings calculator will tell you in an instant how many gallons you can save with a 30% reduction in your annual fuel consumption.

To use the calculator:

1. Place a dot on your present miles per gallon (scale at left side).
2. Place a dot on how many miles you would normally drive in a year (scale on right side).
3. Connect the two dots with a straight line.
4. Read your fuel savings at the center scale where the straight line has crossed it.
5. Multiply the gallons saved by the price you now pay for a gallon and find the number of dollars you'll save by reducing your fuel consumption by 30%:

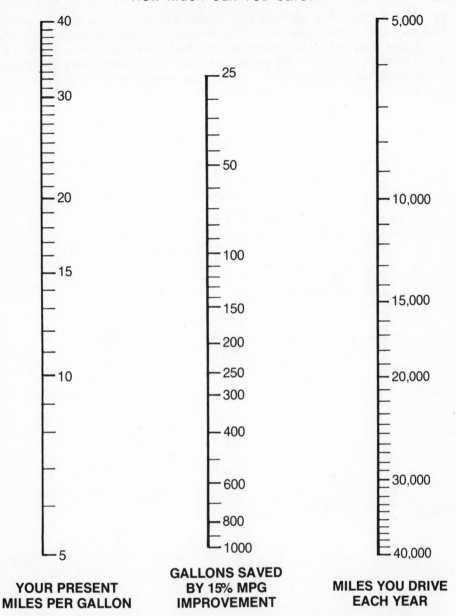

Fig. 1–11. Fuel savings calculator: Connect your present miles per gallon (left column) with the number of miles you average each year (right column) and see how many gallons you can save with a 30% reduction in fuel consumption.

Gallons saved x Price per gallon = Dollars saved

For example, if your present fuel efficiency is 14 miles per gallon, and you normally drive about 13,000 miles each year, a 30% reduction in fuel consumption will mean about 280 gallons that you won't have to buy. At $1.10 per gallon (if you can still find fuel priced that low), this translates into $308, which could buy a portable color TV, numerous cases of Michelob, several good bicycles, or a lot of other items that you've always wanted but never been able to justify. Perhaps a new AM-FM 8-track stereo cassette/radio to make driving and gas-line sitting a lot more enjoyable. Don't forget the motivation provided by Figure 1-6. If fuel costs $1.10 a gallon and you're in the 20% tax bracket, saving 280 gallons can translate into the equivalent of a $385 raise in your annual income.

Chapter 2
The Science of Saving

If you saw a midnight thief siphoning fuel from your tank, chances are that you would quickly do something about it. However, the pirates in this chapter are not people, but invisible forces. They are not armed with a siphon hose, but rather with the laws of physics. Though you won't see them, they can pilfer your fuel as surely as the best siphon thief in the business.

MAN AND MACHINE VERSUS NATURE:
2,300 MILES PER GALLON IN A MERCEDES!

Engineers and motorists have, for nearly a century, done battle against the forces of nature that will be discussed in this chapter. Of course, some attempts have been better than others. The best attempt ever was recently turned in by a group of young Mercedes-Benz apprentices who set a world fuel economy record

Fig. 2–1. These 2 photos show the effect of aerodynamics on fuel economy. Left, the 2,300 mpg vehicle that set the world fuel economy record. Right, the experimental Mercedes-Benz C-111/Ili (a record setter nine times over) flanked by the first-place economy vehicle and the second-place finisher, which achieved a respectable 2,275 miles per gallon.

by attaining the equivalent of nearly 2,300 miles per gallon during a mileage contest on a German race track.

The winning car, shown in Figure 2-1, was a three-wheeled vehicle weighing just 108 pounds and powered by a single-cylinder diesel engine of only ½ horsepower. The ten-foot-long fiberglass and aluminum creation used just under half an ounce of fuel (about .0039 gallon) to cover the 8.9-mile course. The car was two feet high, thirteen feet long, and had two of its twenty-four-inch bicycle tires mounted in front, outside the body, with the third enclosed behind the driver. This vehicle, designed for maximum aerodynamic efficiency, was operated at an average speed of 12 miles per hour by a seventeen-year-old driver, who eclipsed the previous fuel efficiency record by a comfortable margin—an *increase* of about 559 miles per gallon.

At today's prices, the fuel economy champ could have driven 2,800 miles—the distance from New York to Los Angeles—at a fuel cost of only $1.25. This is probably less fuel than some cars would require to start cold and be driven the length of a well-hit home run.

The second-place finisher in the event (the Kilometer Marathon, sponsored by Shell and a German auto magazine), was another diesel-powered creation. Compared to the first-place car, it was only slightly less fuel efficient—despite weighing 60% more and having an engine more than twice as powerful, it traveled the course at the frugal rate of 2,275 miles per gallon. The design of this vehicle was also quite novel, and featured an "outrigger" third wheel to complement the two bicycle wheels enclosed within the car's body. The second-place finisher, along with the record-setting 2,300 mpg car and an experimental Mercedez-Benz diesel car, is also shown in Figure 2-1.

While the two smaller vehicles would certainly have a great deal of difficulty keeping up with even the slowest traffic, the experimental Mercedez-Benz C-111/III certainly would not. This awesome machine has demonstrated the advantages of diesel power and state-of-the-art streamlining by breaking nine world records, including the feat of *averaging* 200 miles per hour over a distance of 310 miles (delivering almost 15 mpg along the way)!

While the three vehicles just discussed may seem a world apart from the conventional sedans and station wagons most of us drive, the fact is that their success in setting records involves overcoming the same forces of nature we face in trying to improve our own fuel efficiency. Such factors as air resistance, rolling resistance, acceleration resistance, gravity resistance, engine resistance, and weather and road surface conditions are constantly influencing your car's fuel efficiency, and your ability to become more fuel efficient will be enhanced if you have a better understanding of what these forces are and how they work.

WEIGHT

Weight, often referred to as mass, is the biggest contributor to poor fuel economy. But, unlike aerodynamics, which can be improved substantially by subtly reshaping body panels at reasonable expense, weight reduction is enormously expensive. In most cases, it involves redesigning entire portions or entire cars and using expensive lightweight metals and plastics.

Since the "energy crisis" of 1973, auto engineers have put their products on an energy diet to reduce the weight of cars and trucks. It is estimated that a reduction in weight of 100 pounds is equivalent to a 1% increase in fuel economy. The initial industry effort at "downsizing" lopped off about 900 to 1000 pounds per car, by reducing front overhang, reducing overall size, using lighter engines, eliminating the conventional spare tire, and a host of other weight-sav-

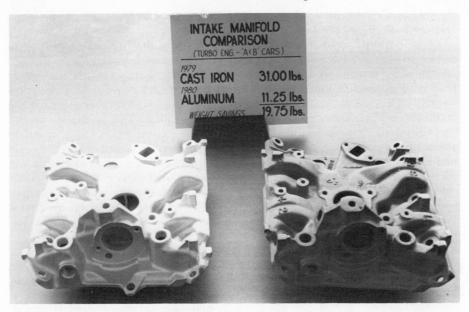

Fig. 2–2. These two intake manifolds from the 1980 GM turbocharged V6 engine demonstrate the weight savings from increased use of aluminum components.

Fig. 2–3. Smaller, lighter-weight components are a practical solution to the weight problem while maintaining excellent performance characteristics. The cast-iron rear brake was used on the 1979 Nova and was replaced on the 1980 Citation by the aluminum assembly on the right.

ing measures. But further efforts at weight reduction and application of the same ideas to smaller cars become increasingly difficult.

In the quest for greater fuel efficiency, much of the iron and steel used in earlier cars has already given way to thinner high-strength steel, plastic, and aluminum parts. Engineers are now working on exotic materials such as graphite fiber composites and thermoplastics which are attractive because of their low weight, high strength, durability, and resistance to corrosion, although their use is still limited because of cost, availability, and manufacturing methods.

Chrysler's Poly-car, dubbed the PXL for Polymeric Extra Light, is an example of the possible uses of high-strength, lightweight components that could find their way into cars of the future (see Figure 2-4). The car used twenty test parts manufactured from thermoplastic polymerics, including graphite composite driveshaft, leaf springs, and door hinges, and fiberglass reinforced wheels, door panels, bumpers, and structural members. The total weight savings over parts made from conventional materials was 160 pounds.

AIR RESISTANCE

Imagine an engine that produces less than 1 horsepower. Next, imagine this engine powering a vehicle to a level-road speed in excess of 138 miles per hour. Impossible, you say? No, it actually happened.

The "engine" in this case was a twenty-nine-year-old-man named Al Abbott. The "vehicle" was a *bicycle*. Mr. Abbott pedaled his bicycle at an average speed of 138.674 miles per hour.[1] Naturally, his bicycle was hardly the kind you'd ex-

Graphite Fiber

1. Engine Access. Bracket
2. Valve Pushrods
3. Door Hinges
4. Driveshaft
5. Rear Leaf Springs

W/Fiberglass

Thermoset

6. Bumper Energy Absorber
7. Grille Opening Panel
8. Wheels
9. Trans. Crossmember
10. Door Inner Panel

Thermoplastic

11. Fan
12. Oil Pan
13. Trans. Oil Pan
14. Heater Core Top
15. Window Handle

Non-Reinforced

16. Plastic Headlamp
17. Visor Bracket
18. Fixed Side Window

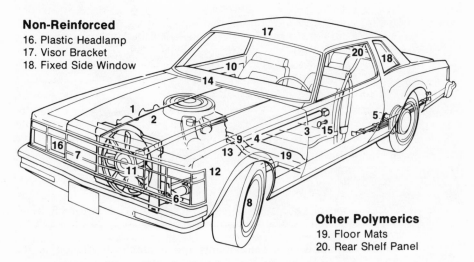

Other Polymerics

19. Floor Mats
20. Rear Shelf Panel

Fig. 2–4. Chrysler engineers were able to save 160 pounds on an experimental car using lightweight, high-strength materials.

Skylark Sedan
Weight (Mass) Reductions, 1980 vs. 1979

	lbs
New body design	− 205
Unitized construction	
High strength/low alloy steel usage	
Doors, seats and wiper system	
Semi-modular heating system	
Styled bumper fillers	
Front-wheel drive	− 185
MacPherson strut suspension	
Trailing arm rear suspension	
New brake system	− 49
Transverse mounted L-4 engine	− 84
Four-speed front-wheel drive transmission	− 22
New gas tank	− 60
Exhaust system sized to engine	− 04
Rack and pinion steering	− 22
P185/80R13 tires with 13″ wheels	− 40
Compact spare tire	
Cross flow radiator	− 07
One-piece aluminum bumpers	− 86
Local reinforcements	
Mini-energy absorber units	____
Total pounds reduction	763

Fig. 2–5. Buick engineers were able to save 763 pounds from the 1980 Skylark sedan in the areas shown. These weight reduction areas are typical of other manufacturers as well.

pect to find at your local store. Its front sprocket, in order to provide the necessary gear ratio, was nearly as large as the bicycle's wheels.

What was his secret? In addition to a high degree of strength and skill, this feat also required a pace car with a special box-shaped rear section to break a path through the air. By pedaling closely behind his pace car, the rider experienced practically no air resistance. A typical domestic sedan would require over 200 horsepower just to push its way through the air at 138 miles per hour. However, Mr. Abbott was able to attain the same speed with his body, capable of producing perhaps a single horsepower over a short period of time.

Note: "Horsepower" is the rate of doing work. One horsepower can move a 550-pound force one foot in one second. If you're so inclined, you can measure your own horsepower by running up a flight of steps. For example, if you weigh 150 pounds and can run up a 20-foot-high flight of stairs in 10 seconds, you've generated 150 x 20 divided by 10 x 550, or .55 horsepower. Remember that the height is measured vertically, and is less than the length of the stairway.

Air Resistance and Speed

If you've ever done a belly flop from the high dive, tried to carry a 4 x 8 sheet of plywood in a wind, or stuck your hand out the window of a fast-moving car, you've some appreciation of the fact that water and air resent your trying to move through them. And they return your movement with a force of their own.

At 55 mph, 60% of a car's power is used to overcome air resistance. When your car is traveling at even moderate speeds, the force exerted by displaced air

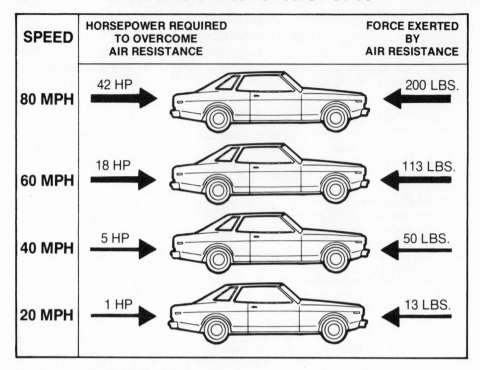

SPEED	HORSEPOWER REQUIRED TO OVERCOME AIR RESISTANCE	FORCE EXERTED BY AIR RESISTANCE
80 MPH	42 HP	200 LBS.
60 MPH	18 HP	113 LBS.
40 MPH	5 HP	50 LBS.
20 MPH	1 HP	13 LBS.

Fig. 2–6. Rapidly increasing air resistance is the reason higher speeds mean lower gas mileage. These figures are typical of a large sedan traveling at the speeds shown.

can be quite considerable. Figure 2-6 shows the air resistance that a typical full-size car encounters at various speeds.[2] As the figures indicate, the air reacts quite strongly to increases in speed. Doubling your speed from 20 mph to 40 mph actually quadruples the number of pounds of force which the air exerts against your car. (Note that the numbers in Figure 2-6 are rounded off.)

Also shown in Figure 2-6 is the horsepower it takes to overcome air resistance at the speeds shown. The horsepower required to overcome air resistance varies as the *cube* of your speed; so if you double your speed, you'll require eight times as much horsepower to overcome air resistance. The relationship is expressed as follows:[3]

$$\text{Horsepower Required to Overcome Air Resistance} = KDAEV^3$$

where:

K is a constant.

D is the vehicle's drag coefficient and is dependent on how aerodynamically efficient the car is. The more streamlined a car, the lower will be its drag coefficient and the better its fuel economy.

A is the frontal area of the car and is simply the area of a front view of the car. A rough approximation of your car's frontal area is 80% of its width times its height. Most passenger cars have a frontal area between 17 and 25 square feet.[4] Frontal area is one reason why low, narrow cars tend to get more miles per gallon—they don't need as much fuel to overcome air resistance.

Fig. 2–7. Passenger-car frontal areas don't vary much more than the three shown here. With other factors equal, the car with the smallest frontal area will get the best gas mileage.

E is the density of the air through which you're driving. The higher the altitude above sea level, the less air resistance you'll encounter at any given speed. Air density decreases by about 3% for every 1,000 feet increase in altitude and drops by about 1% for every 10°F rise in temperature.[5]

V is the speed at which you're traveling into the air around you. For example, you'll encounter the same air resistance driving 50 mph through calm air, or driving 40 mph into a 10 mph head wind, or driving 70 mph with a 20 mph head wind. In any of these situations, you'll be moving into the air around you at a rate of 50 mph.

Air resistance is caused not only by the flow of air around the vehicle, but also by the flow of air *through* it. Figure 2-8 shows how the total air resistance tends to be distributed among its principal components, which include the following:[6]

Form drag results from the basic shape of the vehicle body, and is the major source of air resistance.

Surface drag results from the actual friction between the body surface and the passing air that comes into contact with the surface. The greater the surface area of the vehicle, the more important this component will tend to be.

Lift drag is a function of body shape, and results from the energy generated

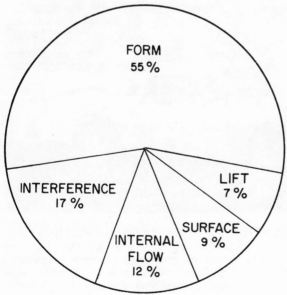

Fig. 2–8. A breakdown of total aerodynamic drag the typical vehicle must overcome. (*Source:* Kent B. Kelly and Harry J. Holcomb, *Aerodynamics for Body Engines*, SAE Paper 649A, January, 1963.)

as the passing air flow exerts a "lifting" force on the front and rear of the vehicle.

Interference drag occurs as the result of disturbances as air passes over the vehicle body. Such disturbances may include side-view mirrors, door handles, rain gutters, and radio antennas. Likewise, projections beneath the vehicle—engine pan, suspension parts, muffler and exhaust pipes, transmission and axle housings—contribute to interference drag, which is the second most important type of air resistance.

Internal flow drag results from the flow of air through the radiator and engine compartment, and through the interior of the vehicle by means of the ventilation, heating, and air conditioning systems.

Air Resistance and the Drag Coefficient

Of the variables in the air resistance equation presented in the previous section, the drag coefficient is the one about which you'll be reading more and more as automobile manufacturers try to win you over to their product. The drag coefficient is a measurement of the ease with which a vehicle slips through the air. The lower the number, the easier it moves through the air, and the better the fuel economy will be. The number (.417 for example) indicates the drag is 41% of the drag on a rectangular box of similar dimensions.

In the last few years, an increasing number of manufacturers have been using full-scale models in aircraft-type wind tunnels in order to design basic body shapes and "fine-tune" the aerodynamic details of their vehicles. The reason automotive engineers are placing such a heavy emphasis on aerodynamics is that it represents a relatively inexpensive method of substantially improving fuel economy. Each 10% gain in drag reduction is worth a 2% gain in fuel economy. Engineering a new engine or driveline to gain .1 to .2 mile per gallon can cost from $10 to $100 million, but bending a piece of sheet metal differently to improve aerodynamics can mean a 3% to 4% increase in fuel economy at very little cost.

Fig. 2–9. Automotive engineers are beginning to put into practice what NASCAR's race drivers and car builders have known for years. If you can alter the body shape, the car will slip through the air easier, which means less power is needed to overcome air resistance. Note the use of front and rear spoilers, filled-in areas around the windows and rear bumper, covered headlights, and filled body seams.

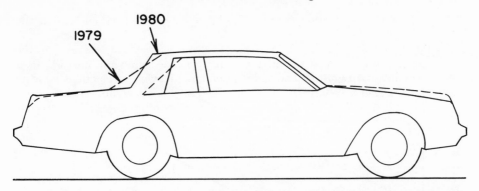

Fig. 2–10. The drag coefficient on this 1980 Buick LeSabre was reduced 14% by making the changes shown. This translates to a fuel economy improvement of about .5 mpg.

As the car moves through the air, the velocity of the air over the surface of the car changes and actually accelerates over the roof and hood. The changing speed of the air causes pressure differentials on the surface of the car, which, in turn, create aerodynamic drag or wind resistance. The greater the air drag, the more power required to propel the vehicle.

The auto industry has always known that aerodynamics were important when hurtling around a race track at 200 mph, but Volkswagen and Mercedes-

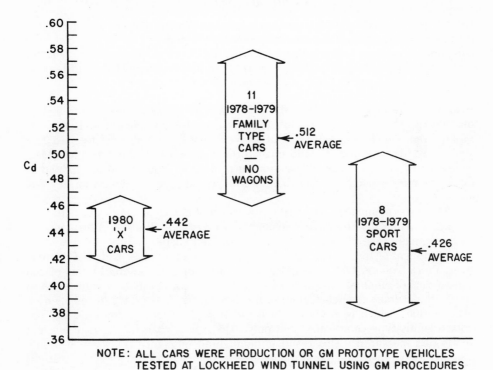

NOTE: ALL CARS WERE PRODUCTION OR GM PROTOTYPE VEHICLES TESTED AT LOCKHEED WIND TUNNEL USING GM PROCEDURES

Fig. 2–11. Aerodynamic drag coefficients of a sampling of family and sports cars compared to the 1980 GM X cars. (*Source:* Lloyd Nedley, *An Effective Aerodynamic Program in the Design of a New Car,* SAE Paper No. 790724, 1979.)

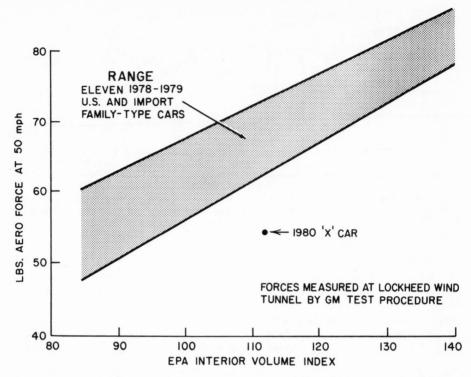

Fig. 2–12. A comparison of aerodynamic force at 50 miles per hour demonstrates the favorable drag coefficient of the 1980 X cars compared to other vehicles with comparable interior room. (*Source:* Lloyd Nedley, *An Effective Aerodynamic Program in the Design of a New Car,* SAE Paper No. 790724, 1979.)

Benz were the first to recognize the importance of aerodynamics on production model cars. During the coast-down tests used in the government fuel economy ratings, the vehicle is accelerated to a given speed, then allowed to coast to a stop. Volkswagen found it could coast further with better aerodynamics. Mercedes-Benz found that careful positioning of the body side moldings helped to direct air more smoothly along the sides of the car, creating less drag in those areas.

Domestic manufacturers were quick to adopt aerodynamic designs. In fact, the aerodynamically designed Oldsmobile Cutlass and Buick Century models were originally called "aerobacks" because of their shape.

In designing their 1980 "X" cars (the Chevrolet Citation and its GM relatives, Buick Skylark, Olds Omega, and Pontiac Phoenix), General Motors placed a great deal of emphasis on the aerodynamic properties of its new vehicles. As a result, the average drag coefficient of the 1980 X cars is just .442 (it ranges from .417 to .466), which is .07 lower than the average of eleven domestic and imported family-type cars tested, and only .016 greater than the average of eight sports cars measured.[7] This result is highlighted in Figure 2-11, which should also provide you with a general range of drag coefficient values for cars of various types. Family type cars marketed today have a drag coefficient around .459 to .578 with a few sports cars below .417. Compared to the 1979 Chevrolet Nova which it replaced, the 1980 Citation four-door hatchback had a drag coefficient which was nearly 21% less (.417 versus .525 for the Nova).[8]

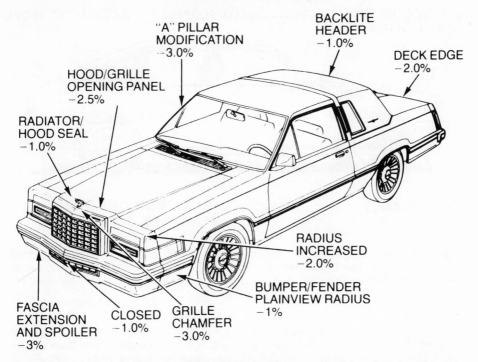

BACKLITE
HEADER
−1.0%

"A" PILLAR
MODIFICATION
−3.0%

DECK EDGE
−2.0%

HOOD/GRILLE
OPENING PANEL
−2.5%

RADIATOR/
HOOD SEAL
−1.0%

RADIUS
INCREASED
−2.0%

BUMPER/FENDER
PLAINVIEW RADIUS
−1%

FASCIA
EXTENSION
AND SPOILER
−3%

CLOSED
−1.0%

GRILLE
CHAMFER
−3.0%

Fig. 2–13. A breakdown of the 1980 Thunderbird aerodynamic improvements that totalled 19.5%—almost 2 miles per gallon.

Figure 2-12 shows how air resistance at 50 miles per hour tends to increase as the EPA Interior Volume Index increases, and illustrates the success of GM in providing its X cars with generous interior room without the penalty of high aerodynamic drag paid by many cars with the same amount of passenger space. While the other models tested must overcome about 62 to 73 pounds of air resistance at 50 mph, the X car finds its travel through the air to be about 10 pounds easier, which certainly has a positive effect on its fuel efficiency advantage in the marketplace.

As an example of the fine-tuning which leads to lower drag coefficients, Volkswagen was able to reduce the drag coefficient of its Rabbit from .48 to .42 by revising only slightly the original shape of the car's front end.[9] Likewise, GM found that a slight change in the hood edge configuration was able to provide a .02 reduction in the drag coefficient of the X car family.[10] Ford engineers improved the drag coefficient of the 1980 Thunderbird by 19.5% over 1979 models by careful attention to body shapes dictated by wind tunnel tests.

Prior to carrying out these kinds of "optimization" changes, GM engineers had already integrated drag reduction with principal styling features such as those shown in Figure 2-14. Ford, in designing its Fairmont/Zephyr series, spent over 320 hours testing these models in the Lockheed wind tunnel, in the process making minor styling revisions which reduced the drag coefficient by 13% compared to the original design. Ford estimates that a fuel economy increase of about 6% at 50 miles per hour can be attributed to these aerodynamic changes.[11]

When you are confronted with drag coefficient numbers, whether in advertisements or technical reports and articles, remember that a drag coefficient is

HOOD HEIGHT
AND SLOPE   WINDSHIELD SLOPE   BACKLIGHT SLOPE

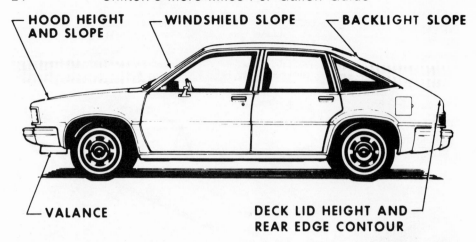

VALANCE   DECK LID HEIGHT AND
REAR EDGE CONTOUR

Fig. 2–14. These and other aerodynamic drag reduction features were integrated into the styling of the 1980 Chevrolet Citation and its GM relatives. (*Source:* Lloyd Nedley, *An Effective Program in the Design of a New Car,* SAE Paper No. 790724, 1979.)

typically determined with the car headed straight into the air (i.e., there is no crosswind). However, in the real world, some vehicles suffer more than others when there is a crosswind, and the effective drag coefficient rises drastically as the result of adverse air flow patterns, which depend on the individual vehicle and its design. A car can have a very low drag coefficient whenever there is no cross wind, but may become an aerodynamic slab when it is meeting the air slightly sideways instead of directly head-on.

Likewise, depending on the type of wind tunnel used and whether the prototype tested is complete with radiator and other necessary equipment, the drag

Fig. 2–15. Wind tunnel photograph of Omni 024 demonstrates the slippery aerodynamic design of the vehicle, which has a drag coefficient of .395, the lowest of a domestically produced U.S. car.

Fig. 2–16. Tires can exhibit air resistance as well as rolling resistance, as demonstrated in this wind tunnel photograph. As does any object passing through air, this tire has made a "hole" bigger than its own size. Note how the air flow is disturbed at a height nearly twice that of the tire itself. (Photo courtesy of the Society of Automotive Engineers.)

coefficient of a given vehicle may vary. It is unusual for two wind tunnels to arrive at precisely the same drag coefficient value for a vehicle, since measurement techniques vary and some tunnels are larger than others. A larger tunnel provides more room for air to pass around the vehicle, resulting in a different measurement than might be obtained in a smaller facility.

Some vehicles look very streamlined, but have a relatively high drag coefficient. Others look rather boxy, but are really quite aerodynamic—the Volkswagen Rabbit is a good example. Still others are aerodynamic in both looks and drag measurements—the Dodge Omni/Plymouth Horizon fit into this category. Examine Figure 2-15, which shows lines of smoke streaming past the Omni in the wind tunnel. The vehicle disturbs the air only slightly on its way past, as is demonstrated in the photograph by the lack of turbulence and the resulting smooth lines of flow.

Effects of a Crosswind

Let's look at the effect of air on a certain import as it travels 75 miles per hour (a legal speed at the time of the study) through a 20 mph crosswind. The air is subjecting the car to three different forces: [12]

1. A backward force of 106 pounds due to air resistance at this very high speed.
2. An upward force (the same kind that makes airplanes fly) of 186 pounds. Most cars tend to get "lighter" as their speed increases, but stay grounded because they weigh much more than the lifting force.

3. A sideward force of 166 pounds which tends to push the car toward one side of the road. This must be counteracted by steering against the wind, and involves additional friction between the tires and the road. A cross-wind, even though it would not seem to be a factor in your fuel efficiency, will actually reduce your mileage slightly.

ROLLING RESISTANCE

Whoever invented the wheel probably discovered rolling resistance shortly thereafter. Your tires' reluctance to roll is another important factor that affects your fuel efficiency. As a tire rolls, it squirms and flexes. This creates heat plus rolling resistance, which forces your engine to work harder and use more fuel. According to the Firestone Tire & Rubber Company, 5% to 10% of the fuel fed to the engine is used in overcoming tire rolling resistance.[13]

A great deal of attention has been devoted to tires to improve operating efficiency. The results can be seen in the introduction of low rolling resistance, high pressure tires using the latest rubber compounds and construction techniques.

The difference in operating efficiency between conventional radial ply tires and the new low rolling resistance tires, operating at the same tire pressure, can

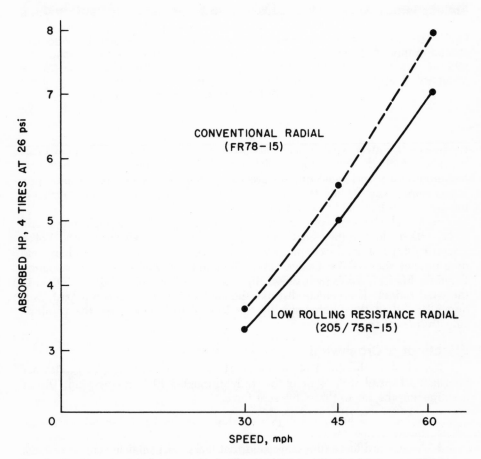

Fig. 2–17. Absorbed horsepower of the new low-rolling-resistance radial tires compared to that of conventional radial tires.

be seen in absorbed horsepower. This is the amount of horsepower lost due to friction between the tire and the road. At 30 miles per hour, the low rolling resistance tire absorbs about 3.33 horsepower, compared to more than 3.66 horsepower absorbed by conventional radial ply tires. At 60 miles per hour, the difference is even more significant—7 horsepower versus 8 horsepower for the conventional radial tire.

The difference in absorbed horsepower generally represents about a 10% improvement, which means that the car rolls easier. An additional 5% to 6% improvement in rolling resistance is gained by increasing the tire's operating pressure to 30 psi from the standard 26 psi operating pressure of a conventional radial ply tire.

Depending on the type of construction and the load it is supporting, a passenger car tire may exert a resistance of 10 to 30 pounds which must be overcome just to keep it rolling at highway speeds. That means that your engine has to fight between 40 and 120 pounds of rolling resistance from all four tires.

In the 0 to 55 mph range where most of our driving takes place, the force required to keep a tire rolling is relatively independent of speed. Tests by Firestone provide the data presented in Figure 2-18. At 50 mph on a standard-size car, the steel-belted radial construction kept total rolling resistance for all four

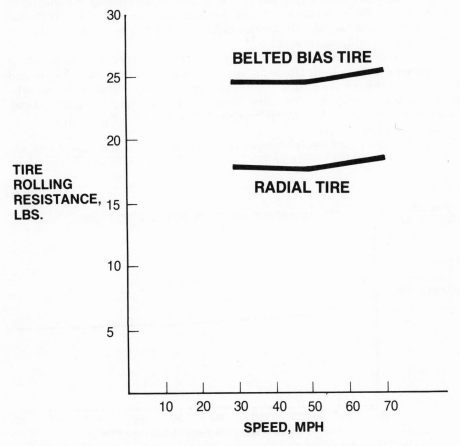

Fig. 2–18. Besides lasting a long time, radial tires save fuel by rolling a lot more easily. Data are based on a standard-size car. Rolling resistances would be less if the tires were installed on a lighter vehicle.

tires to 70 pounds, while four bias-belted tires were found to have a combined resistance of 98 pounds (40% more) at the same speed.[14] More recent developments by Firestone and other manufacturers have led to a new generation of metric-sized radials specially designed to accommodate higher inflation pressures and produce even less rolling resistance. With increased emphasis on fuel-efficient design, we can expect engineers to develop ways to further reduce the rolling resistance of the tires we buy.

Uniroyal, in its quest for a low rolling resistance tire for the GM X cars, developed a tire that has a rolling resistance of only 7.94 pounds.[15] (Since rolling resistance is proportional to the weight supported by the tire, the resistance would be higher if this tire were installed on a vehicle heavier than the Chevrolet Citation and other X car models. For example, if this tire were to support 10% more weight, its rolling resistance would be 10% greater. In comparing this figure to the data in Figure 2-18, remember that the resistances in the figure are the result of tests involving a relatively heavy standard-size automobile.)

Rolling resistance is much higher when a tire is cold. Test results have shown that the average tire demands 10% more energy during the first few miles of a trip than it will require during steady cruising on the highway. During stop-and-start conditions, cold tire rolling resistances will be even greater and may involve rolling losses 26% to 47% higher than during steady cruising.[16] Figure 2-19 shows how the rolling resistance of a tire tends to decrease as it is driven. As the figure indicates, it can take 30 minutes before the tire warms up and reaches its minimum level of rolling resistance.[17]

Once your tires are warmed up, they will have a practically constant rolling resistance for a given load. However, since horsepower is a function of force and speed, not just force alone, they will require more horsepower at higher speeds. Figure 2-20 combines air resistance horsepower and rolling resistance horsepower into a common chart involving six-cylinder cars from the compact, intermediate, and full-size classes.[18]

To determine how much horsepower is required for you to cruise at a steady speed, add the rolling resistance horsepower to the air resistance horsepower.

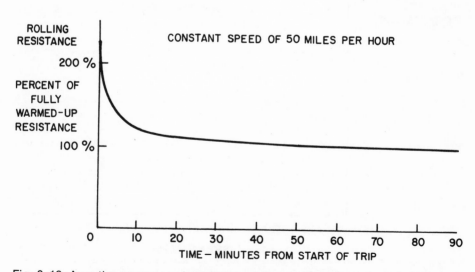

Fig. 2–19. As a tire warms up, its rolling resistance decreases. As the chart indicates, it can take 30 minutes or more until the tire reaches its minimum rolling resistance. This is one reason why short trips are not energy efficient.

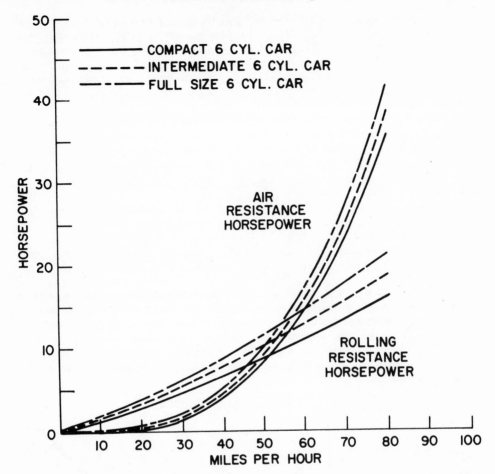

Fig. 2–20. Air and rolling resistance take their horsepower toll as speed goes up. When speed doubles, your engine must generate eight times as much horsepower to fight air resistance. (*Source:* Jack C. Cornell, *Passenger Car Fuel Economy Characteristics on Modern Superhighways,* SAE Report No. 650862, 1965.)

For example, for the compact car to cruise at 40 mph, approximately 10 horsepower is required—3 to overcome air resistance and 7 to overcome rolling resistance.

Your car's total resistance to rolling includes other parts of the drive train, such as the transmission, driveshaft, universal joints, rear axle, and wheel bearings. At lower speeds, automatic transmission torque converter slippage is also a factor. However, the primary component of rolling resistance is the combined reluctance of your tires to roll.

ACCELERATION RESISTANCE

Acceleration resistance is really no more than your car's reluctance to change its momentum. Changes in momentum use up energy, whether the direction of change is acceleration or braking. However, since properly operating brakes don't directly consume gasoline, we'll be concerned here with the effect of acceleration on your gasoline bill.

In the urban driving cycle of the Environmental Protection Agency tests, acceleration energy consumption accounts for about 17% to 23% of the total fuel energy use.[19] There's only one way to avoid this: never accelerate. However, this remedy isn't practical. A very good second-best strategy is never accelerate when you don't have to, and, when necessary, accelerate moderately. The amount of horsepower it takes to accelerate your car depends on three things:[20]

$$\text{Horsepower Required to Accelerate} = KVWC$$

where:

K is constant

V is how fast you're going when you decide that you'd like to be going faster. The higher your speed, the more horsepower (and gasoline) you're going to need for acceleration.

W is how much your car weighs. Accelerating a Cadillac is naturally going to be more expensive than accelerating a Volkswagen.

C is the rate at which you want to accelerate. Rather than blast from 40 mph to 60 mph in 5 seconds, your gas mileage will improve measurably if you have the patience to wait a little longer.

Figure 2-21 shows the general relationship between how fast you accelerate and the horsepower it will take to do the job. The graph holds true for any vehicle weight and any speed. The point is that horsepower required is directly proportional to the rate of acceleration and that an acceleration rate of zero will require no extra horsepower. Remember that we're talking about *extra* horsepower requirements, since your engine is already working to overcome air and rolling resistance.

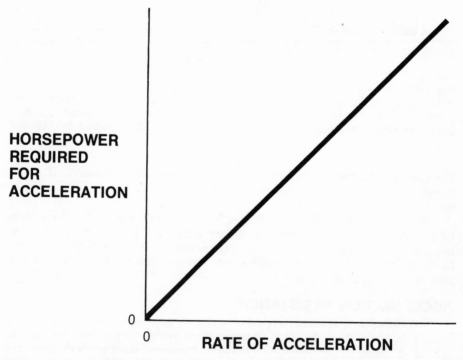

Fig. 2–21. This relationship between horsepower required for acceleration and rate of acceleration holds true for any vehicle weight at any speed.

An object that's moving tends to continue moving and one that's stationary tends to remain stationary. This applies to bowling balls, rubber ducks, and automobiles equally. It might take some gasoline to accelerate your car to 60 mph, but once you settle upon this, or any other constant speed, your only gasoline consumers are air and rolling resistance. When you keep your speed (and momentum) constant, you're eliminating acceleration resistance as a drain on your fuel supply. That's why the cruise control feature is so effective in improving fuel economy. It keeps acceleration at a minimum.

GRAVITY RESISTANCE

If you've ever driven up Pike's Peak or followed a loaded coal truck up a Pennsylvania hill, you know that fighting the effects of gravity takes horsepower. On a mere 5% grade (5 feet of rise over 100 feet of travel), a 3,000 pound automobile will experience a force of .05 × 3000, or 150 pounds. Assuming that this automobile is climbing the grade at 55 miles per hour, 22 horsepower will be necessary just to offset the effect of gravity. Add to this approximately 26 horsepower to overcome air and rolling resistance, and you'll need 48 horsepower to make it up the grade without losing speed. On the other hand, if the same car were coming down this grade, the driver would need to apply just a touch of throttle in order to maintain 55 mph.

The maximum grade on most interstate highways is about 5% to 7%. To determine how much gravity resistance force your car must overcome in climbing a given grade, just multiply the operating weight of your car times the percentage of the grade. For example, a 7% grade will exert a force of 280 pounds on a 4,000 pound automobile.

Climbing a hill is like loaning energy to an old friend (gravity). You pay on the way up, but receive your repayment on the way down in the form of kinetic energy. Attacking hills is an important segment of the efficient driving strategies we'll explore in a later chapter.

ENGINE RESISTANCE

In the preceding sections, we've seen how outside forces make your engine work harder and consume more fuel. Add engine mechanical friction, air, fuel, and fluid flow resistance, the power necessary to turn the cooling fan, water pump, and alternator, and you have still more invisible thieves anxious to steal your fuel. These drains can consume 10% or more of the energy contained in each gallon of gasoline.[21] Within the engine itself, seemingly countless moving parts come into contact with one another and with stationary bearing surfaces. One prime source of mechanical friction within the engine occurs at the pistons and rings. This single component can account for 65% of the mechanical friction in an engine.[22]

As we will discuss later, it is very important to minimize sources of friction by proper attention to the engine lubricating system, including the use of high-quality oil, preferably of the new fuel-efficiency type. Since the amount of fuel energy contained in each gallon is converted to useful work at the driving wheels at a relatively low rate of efficiency, this makes it even more important that we drive, maintain, and equip our vehicles in an intelligent and efficient manner.

WEATHER CONDITIONS

Colder weather lowers fuel efficiency by increasing the length of time it takes the various moving parts of your car to warm up. Four such parts are the tires, the warm-up requirements of which we've already discussed. In general, lubricants don't flow easily when the temperature is low, even when the lubri-

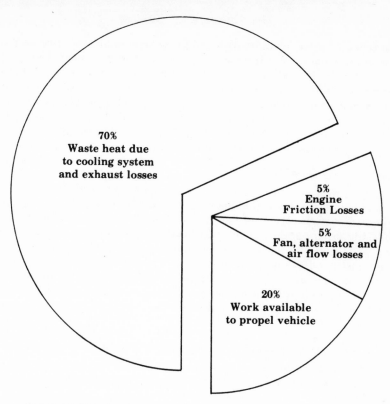

Fig. 2–22. This is what happens to the energy in your gasoline when your engine is operating at wide-open throttle. At part-throttle, this distribution changes and an even greater proportion of energy is lost to the cooling system and exhaust. (*Source:* Carl E. Burke, *et al.,* "Where Does All the Power Go?" *SAE Transactions,* 65 [1957].)

	Test Temperature, °F			
Test Cycle	20	45	70	100*
FTP Fuel Economy, Miles Per Gallon				
City	12.9	13.9	14.8	13.1
City/Highway	15.5	16.3	17.1	15.1
Highway	20.6	20.9	21.2	18.6
FTP Fuel Consumption, Gallons/100 Miles				
City	7.79	7.20	6.76	7.65
City/Highway	6.47	6.12	5.84	6.62
Highway	4.85	4.80	4.72	5.38
FTP Fuel Consumption, % Increase Over 70° Test				
City	15	7	Base	13
City/Highway	11	5	Base	13
Highway	3	2	Base	14

*With air conditioner in operation.
FTP = Federal Test Procedure

Fig. 2–23. As ambient temperatures increase, your car's fuel efficiency will also tend to go up, as these test data indicate. (*Source:* B. H. Eccleston and R. W. Hurn, *Ambient Temperature and Trip Length—Influence on Automotive Fuel Economy and Emissions,* SAE Paper No. 780613, 1978.)

cant is as warm as it's going to get. Cold weather fuel efficiency also suffers because of the cool air entering the engine. Some cars feed heated air to the air cleaner under certain conditions, but this only reduces the effects of the lower temperatures—it does not eliminate them.

At 50 miles per hour, each 10° F drop in temperature will lower your fuel mileage by about 2%.[23] As indicated in Figure 2-23, fuel efficiency increases significantly as higher temperatures help vehicle parts and lubricants to move more easily. The data are based on tests involving four vehicles driven according to the 1975 Federal Test Procedure trip cycle.[24]

Note how the trend is reversed at an ambient temperature of 100° F, with the vehicle air conditioning system in operation. Based on the highway portion of the test, use of the air conditioner at 100° F required nearly two-thirds of a gallon more per 100 miles than the four-car average at 70° F without the air conditioner in operation. However, if you have an air conditioner and can drive in 100° temperatures without using it, you must have a great desire for efficiency and little need for comfort.

Wind can increase or decrease fuel economy depending on whether it is a tailwind, crosswind, or headwind. For a car that normally gets 20 mpg:

> 18 mph tailwind = 12% gain in fuel economy (+2.4 mpg)
> 18 mph crosswind = 1% loss in fuel economy (− 2 mpg)
> 18 mph headwind = 10% loss in fuel economy (−2 mpg)

Precipitation of any kind (rain, snow, sleet) can cause as much as a 10% loss in fuel economy. This translates to a 2 mpg loss for a car that gets 20 mpg.

ROAD SURFACE CONDITIONS

Poor road surfaces will increase your car's rolling resistance far beyond the smooth-road resistances already discussed. At a speed of 40 mph, a patched-up

Fig. 2–24. A gravel road can reduce your fuel mileage by 35%. In off-road driving, the penalty can be even greater, but may be cheap entertainment if your vehicle is up to it.

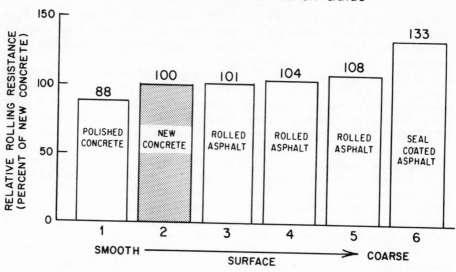

Fig. 2–25. Relative rolling resistances associated with various road surfaces compared to new concrete. A tire will have about 33% more rolling resistance when traveling over seal-coated asphalt than on new concrete. (*Source:* L. W. DeRaad, *The Influence of Road Surface Texture on Tire Rolling Resistance,* SAE Paper No. 780257, 1978.)

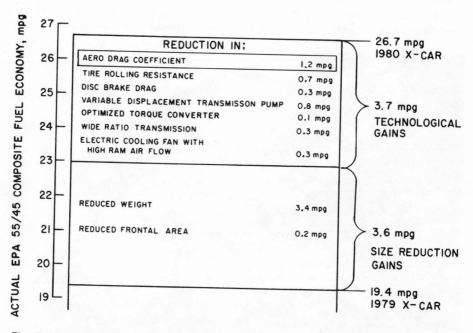

Fig. 2–26. A breakdown of the components that make up the 37% improvement in fuel efficiency for the 1980 X cars compared to their 1979 counterpart. The result of this attention to engineering detail is a vehicle that requires only about 12 horsepower when cruising at 50 mph. (*Source:* F. C. Porter, *Design for Fuel Economy—The New GM Front Drive Cars,* SAE Paper No. 790721, 1979.)

asphalt road will reduce your fuel mileage by about 15%, a gravel road by 35%, a sandy surface by 45%, and a dirt road by 15% to 35%.[25] A road that is covered with water or snow also increases rolling resistance and reduces your fuel efficiency by as much as 1 mile per gallon.[26]

Figure 2-25 presents a common variety of road surfaces which you are likely to encounter in your everyday driving. While they may seem very similar from the vantage point of your driver's seat, they can be extremely different in terms of their effect on your car's fuel efficiency. As Figure 2-25 shows, the most coarse surface (seal-coated asphalt) is accompanied by a rolling resistance that is 51% higher than that of the smoothest (polished concrete). Later in the book we'll explore the possibilities of achieving better fuel efficiency by responding appropriately to the types of surfaces you are encountering in various lanes or on parts of a single lane.

YOU AND THE ENGINEER

Just as an overall efficiency gain of 37% is comprised of a number of components, some major, others minor, the improvements you can make in your own fuel efficiency also vary in their importance. In the next chapter, we'll discuss what is likely to be one of your biggest potential areas for improvement—the selection of a fuel-efficient vehicle. Figure 2-26, for example, describes the contributions various design strategies have made toward raising the fuel efficiency of the 1980 GM X car over that of the 1979 series.

If you are not yet ready to purchase a new car, your efficiency gains will have to result from more efficient driving, maintenance, and planning with regard to your present vehicle. In either case, it is important to realize that your overall savings will be the sum total of your use of many different fuel-efficient practices and habits, some of which may not seem very important at the time. Chances are that your next car will be a lot more fuel efficient than your last one—and by understanding the principles and following the advice in this and later chapters, you should be able to follow through on the engineers' hard work and save yourself many fuel dollars at the same time.

Chapter 3
Buying for Efficiency

With the possible exception of the expectant mother, no one receives more advice than the new or used car buyer. In this chapter, you'll find plenty of advice, but all of it will be directly or indirectly connected with the aim of this book—to stretch your fuel dollar. Although selection of a vehicle is not a frequent decision, it is the most important long-term factor in determining how much of your income you will be spending for fuel.

At first glance, it would seem that shopping for a fuel-efficient car is an easy task—just buy the smallest car you can find and get more miles per gallon than you ever dreamed possible. However, as with most decisions, there are other things to consider.

EVALUATING YOUR NEEDS

Before rushing to the dealer to buy a car that you can fill up with an eyedropper, you must really ask: Do I need a car at all? Perhaps a bicycle, moped, small motorcycle, or even a new pair of walking shoes will suffice. If you live in an area with good public transportation, a car may be a needless luxury, as well as a nuisance to look after and to park in a congested environment.

If you decide you do need a car, then consider how many passengers the car will normally be a carrying, how much luggage or storage space you will need, what level of comfort is desired by you and your passengers, and the functions the car will be called upon to serve. For example, a car which is a superstar in commuting or running errands may literally fall flat on its face when called upon to haul a family and camping trailer on an extended vacation.

If you already have a larger car to carry your family and its cargo, the decision to complement it with a small and efficient vehicle for short trips may be a good one. On the other hand, if you need room for six people and their luggage only once or twice a year, you'd probably be better off to sell your gas guzzler, buy a smaller, more practical vehicle for everyday use, and rent a larger model to use on those exceptional occasions when a much greater capacity is required.

In selecting a car based on your transportation needs, *always* make your decision based on the *everyday* needs your car must satisfy—after all, it is in everyday driving that most of your fuel dollars are consumed. Buying for that occasional use is likely to cost you a lot of money during the rest of the year. In addition, be sure to consider how a proposed additional car will fit into your present vehicle fleet, how many miles you will be driving it, and what levels of safety and performance you will require.

Until someone comes up with a car that delivers 50 miles per gallon and holds seventeen people and their luggage, some degree of compromise will always be necessary. However, such compromises can best be made if you keep in mine your *real* transportation needs and how they will be best satisfied through your purchase of a particular model.

After you've analyzed your needs and narrowed down the list of purchase candidates, stick to your guns when you enter the showroom. Don't buy on impulse and don't be talked into something you don't really want—the more expensive or fancy model may lead to a great deal of dissatisfaction in your bank account when you have to pay for the extra fuel to keep it going over the years ahead. Avoid being stricken with "showroom fever" and you will already have gone a long way toward achieving your fuel efficiency goal without unduly sacrificing your transportation needs.

THE BASIC VEHICLE
Size and Interior Room

In the past, we've often identified the size of a car in terms of its overall length or its wheelbase. Things have changed, though, and cars are now categorized by interior measurements (a combination of front seat, rear seat, and trunk space) so that you can make a more informed purchase decision. The Environmental Protection Agency (EPA) has divided passenger cars and station wagons into the interior-size classes shown in Figure 3-1. This and other information is contained in the *Gas Mileage Guide*, prepared annually by the EPA and published and distributed by the U.S. Department of Energy. This booklet

Vehicle Class	Cubic Feet of Passenger and Luggage Volume	Examples of 1979 Models in Category
Sedans		
Minicompact	less than 85	Honda Civic Renault Le Car
Subcompact	85 to 100	Volkswagen Rabbit Ford Mustang
Compact	100 to 110	AMC Pacer Ford Granada
Mid-Size	110 to 120	Chrysler Cordoba Ford Fairmont
Large	more than 120	Chevrolet Impala Ford LTD
Station Wagons		
Small	less than 130	Datsun 810 wagon Chevrolet Monza wagon
Mid-Size	130 to 160	Ford Fairmont Buick Century
Large	more than 160	Chevrolet Impala Mercury Marquis

Fig. 3–1. Environmental Protection Agency grouping of sedans and station wagons into size classes is based on interior room for passengers and luggage or cargo. (*Source: 1979 Gas Mileage Guide,* U.S. Environmental Protection Agency, 1979.)

is readily available in new car showrooms and from other sources, and will be discussed further later in this chapter.

In considering which classification best fits your needs, keep in mind the number and size of passengers the car will normally be carrying. For one or two adults, a minicompact or subcompact will generally be best, even if one or two small children are to be carried in the rear seat. A compact model will be required for three or four adults for whom comfort is important. If five or six adult passengers are normally carried, a mid-size or large-size vehicle will probably be needed.

Weight

The most important factor in your new car's fuel consumption will be how much it weighs. The heavier the car, the more energy it requires to climb hills, accelerate, and overcome rolling resistance. In addition, the greater frontal area of a larger, heavier car will mean more horsepower needed to fight air resistance at highway speeds. Figure 3-2 describes the relationship between weight and fuel economy as determined by the EPA for automobiles of a recent model

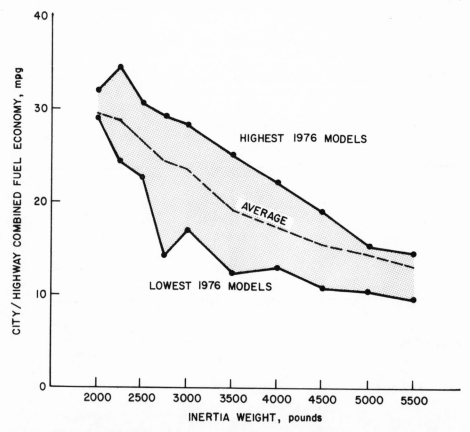

Fig. 3–2. While your car's weight is the most important factor in determining how many miles per gallon it will deliver, fuel efficiency will tend to vary within any given weight category. Differences in engine sizes, emission control systems, and drive trains contribute to the wide ranges shown here. (*Source:* T. C. Austin, R. B. Michael and G. R. Service, *Passenger Car Fuel Economy Trends through 1976,* SAE Paper No. 750957, 1975.)

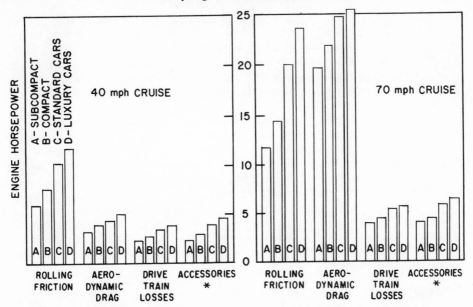

* INCLUDING FAN AND ALTERNATOR FOR ALL CAR SIZES, POWER STEERING FOR TWO LARGEST CARS;
DOES NOT INCLUDE AIR CONDITIONING.

Fig. 3–3. The effect of car size on engine power requirements. Note that most of the power to move the car is used to overcome weight (rolling resistance) and aerodynamic drag.

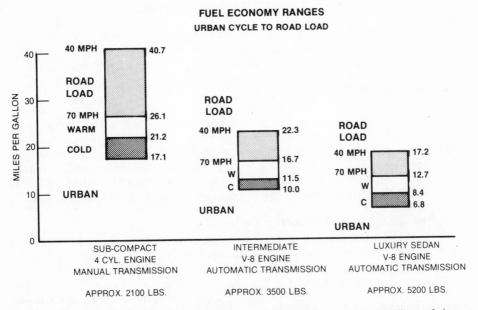

Fig. 3–4. Driving conditions can affect the gas mileage of any car, regardless of size. (*Source:* G. J. Huebner, Jr., and D. J. Gasser, "General Factors Affecting Vehicle Fuel Consumption." Paper presented at National Automobile Engineering Meeting, Society of Automotive Engineers, Detroit, Michigan, May 15, 1973.)

year.[1] The curve shows that a 500-pound gain in weight tends to reduce fuel economy by 2 to 5 miles per gallon. Likewise, a 2,500-pound car will tend to get twice the gas mileage of one weighing 5,000 pounds.

The penalty for buying a larger, heavier car will be less severe if most of your driving is at highway speeds with relatively little stop-and-go operation. At these higher and more constant speeds, the acceleration resistance we discussed in the previous chapter will have less influence.

Besides their weight disadvantage when stripped, heavier cars also tend to be equipped with larger engines and power-robbing equipment which are often necessary to offset their greater bulk. Figure 3-4 summarizes the miles per gallon achieved by typical subcompact, intermediate, and luxury cars under various driving conditions.[2] The subcompact model tested achieved 40.7 miles per gallon at a steady road speed of 40 mph, 26.1 at a steady speed of 70 mph, 21.2 when warmed up and operated in a typical urban driving cycle, and 17.1 when operated from cold in the same urban driving cycle. Comparable figures are presented for the intermediate and luxury models. Weight effect on gas mileage is the most important reason for buying the smallest and lightest car that will satisfy your driving needs.

Body Style

Choice of body style will depend largely on your individual requirements for carrying people and things. Again, keep in mind that the smallest car that meets your carrying requirements will generally be the most efficient one for you to drive. My own choice is the subcompact or compact station wagon with its combination of versatility, economy, and load-carrying ability. This size wagon has about the same weight and frontal area of the sedan with which it is related, yet can haul more goods when the need arises. In a later chapter, you'll learn how the author, plus wife, three kids, and large German shepherd managed to get 55 miles per gallon (with the dog riding, not pulling) from a subcompact wagon.

Hatchback sedans are also handy, but they sacrifice a bit of carrying ability because of their sloped rear deck. Naturally, if you intend to travel light, go the sedan or sports car route and get the same economy with a little more flair.

Exterior Dimensions

Besides the obvious need for your new car to fit into your garage, there is another reason for checking the exterior dimensions of the models from which you're trying to choose—frontal area. With other factors equal, the car with the smallest frontal area is going to have the easiest time slipping through the air that surrounds it. You can get a fair approximation of a car's frontal area by calculating width $\times$ height $\times$ .8. Longer, narrower cars will tend to have less frontal area than shorter, wider cars containing the same cubic footage inside.

Engine Size and Location

Your fuel efficiency will depend more on your car's weight and frontal area than on the size of its engine. With other factors equal, a 10% increase in the displacement of an engine will result in only a .1 mpg drop at high cruising speeds and a .2 mpg reduction in a typical urban trip.[3] Figure 3-5 illustrates the steady-speed miles per gallon of comparable cars equipped with a small six-cylinder engine, a large six-cylinder engine, and a V8.[4] At higher speeds, where air resistance becomes the major force resisting progress, the various engines produced nearly the same number of miles per gallon.

When two cars are otherwise equal, the one with the smaller engine will generally be more economical because conventional internal combustion engines

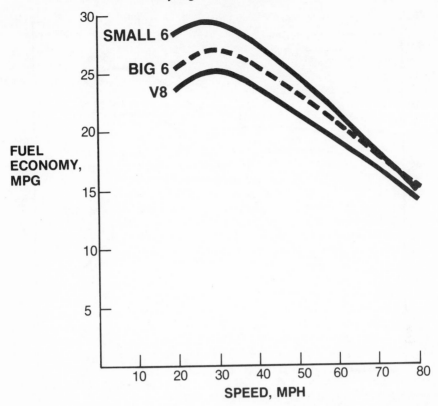

Fig. 3–5. At higher speeds, engine size has relatively little influence on gas mileage. (*Source:* J. J. Cornell, *Passenger Car Fuel Economy Characteristics on Modern Superhighways,* SAE Paper No. 650862, 1965.)

are more efficient when operating closer to their full power capabilities. However, when compared to weight and frontal area, engine size is not a highly significant factor in determining the fuel economy you'll experience in everyday driving.

For most of us, a standard engine will provide all the power we need. However, if you plan to pull a trailer or carry heavy loads, a larger engine may be required just to keep up with traffic under certain conditions. While you may sometimes need a larger engine, consider how much extra fuel you're going to use during the majority of miles when you're not climbing 14,000-foot mountains or helping your neighbor pull out tree stumps. Except for very special needs, fight temptation and settle for a standard engine.

Even if you need a larger engine, you may have to be content with a smaller one. It's no secret that the larger V8's (and maybe all V8's) are being phased out of use. Engines, like cars, are being downsized. As an example, notice how Chrysler's engine line-up has changed in the last five years:

Engine	1975	1979
4 cylinder 86–156 cu. in.	3.9%	30.9%
6 cylinder 225 cu. in.	34.3	28.0
8 cylinder 318 cu. in.	23.8	27.3
8 cylinder 360 cu. in.	21.2	13.8
8 cylinder 400 cu. in.	12.0	—
8 cylinder 440 cu. in.	4.8	—

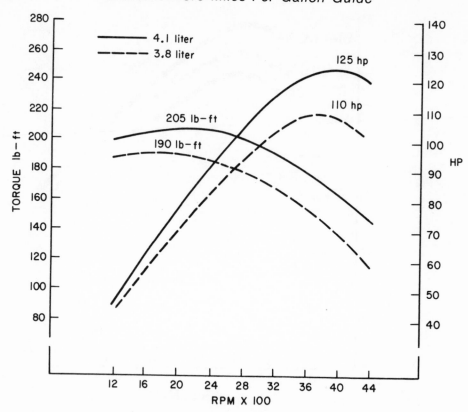

Fig. 3–6. Comparison of the power output of GM's 1980 3.8 liter V6 and a 1980 4.1 liter V6. Fuel economy is about the same and the larger 4.1 liter engine is actually 11 pounds lighter than the 3.8 liter engine.

Engine location may have a slight effect on your fuel economy if you live in an area where snow is a problem. If the engine is located over the drive wheels (for example, front-engine/front-wheel-drive or rear-engine/rear-wheel-drive), you may not require the use of chains or snow tires as often as the person who owns a car with less inherent traction. The relationship of this to your fuel mileage is that snow tires and tires with chains tend to have very high rolling resistance compared to warm-weather tires.

Location of Parts

Good fuel efficiency depends heavily on routine tune-ups and maintenance. Whether you perform the work yourself or hire someone you trust, easy accessibility to the distributor, spark plugs, lubrication fittings, and oil, air and fuel filters will tend to make your work less difficult or your mechanic's work less expensive. And the easier it is to do something, the greater the chance that it will be done right.

ENERGY-EFFICIENT ALTERNATIVE ENGINES

Most of today's cars are powered by the conventional internal combustion engine. It has been around for more than eighty years, and during this time, it has provided dependable service and reached a very high state of development. However, increasingly tight emission control requirements, combined with the

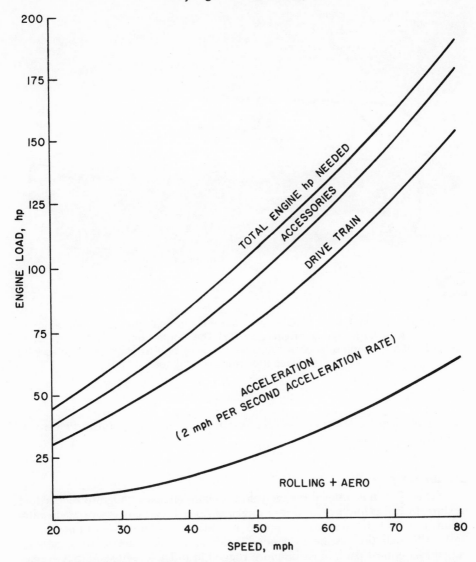

Fig. 3–7. The chart shows the engine horsepower requirements for an acceleration rate of 2 mph/second, equivalent to accelerating from 0–60 mph in 30 seconds. Even at this relatively sedate pace, power requirements are triple that of steady speed cruising.

constraints of weight, efficiency, and driveability, have led to the development of increasingly competitive alternative sources of automotive power.

Whether in the form of a 4, 5, 6, V6, or V8 engine, the principal alternatives to a conventional engine are largely based on the four-cycle principle of the conventional engine, shown in Figure 3-9. During the intake stroke, the intake valve opens and the moving piston draws an air-fuel mixture into the cylinder. As the crankshaft continues to rotate, the intake valve closes and the piston moves upward to compress the air-fuel mixture for improved burning. The power stroke occurs after the mixture explodes, forcing the piston downward. Fi-

Fig. 3–8. The 4 wheel drive AMC Eagle station wagon can provide a fuel efficient alternative to a larger truck or off-road RV. The Eagle combines 4-wheel drive with a 6-cylinder engine to offer the pulling power and traction of vehicles with larger, less fuel-efficient engines.

nally, the exhaust valve opens and the piston moves upward to push the exhaust gases from the cylinder.

Diesel Engine

While the conventional engine relies on ignition spark to ignite the air-fuel mixture in the cylinder, the diesel engine uses a very high compression ratio (often over 20:1) to squeeze the intake air until it can ignite fuel from its own heat. Although the engine is generally similar in construction to a gasoline engine, its critical parts must be more rugged in order to withstand the greater loads and rougher combustion imposed by the high compression pressures. As Figure 3-10 indicates, the modern diesel engine is quite similar in construction to its gasoline counterpart. The VW diesel portrayed here, though beefed up in many areas for greater durability, looks very much like the gasoline version found in the Rabbit and some other Volkswagen models.

Since the diesel engine has no carburetor to premix air and fuel, air comes in through a normal intake manifold and the fuel enters by way of an injector in the cylinder head. This allows fuel entry to be carefully timed, thus preventing pre-ignition. An injector sprays fuel into the combustion chamber or precombustion chamber just as the piston is nearing its uppermost position during the compression stroke.

Figure 3-11 shows the cycles of operation of a diesel engine, in this case the Volkswagen model. On the intake cycle, fresh air is drawn into the combustion chamber, than is compressed as the intake valve closes and the piston begins to squeeze the air to about one twenty-third its original volume. Towards the end

THE FOUR-STROKE CYCLE

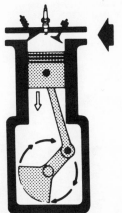

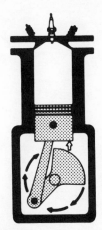

1. INTAKE

The intake stroke begins with the piston near the top of its travel. As the piston begins its descent, the exhaust valve closes fully, the intake valve opens, and the volume of the combustion chamber begins to increase, creating a vacuum. As the piston descends, an air/fuel mixture is drawn from the carburetor into the cylinder through the intake manifold. The intake stroke ends with the intake valve closed just after the piston has begun its upstroke.

2. COMPRESSION

As the piston ascends, the fuel/air mixture is forced into the small chamber machined into the cylinder head. This compresses the mixture until it occupies ⅛th to 1/11th of the volume that it did at the time the piston began its ascent. This compression raises the temperature of the mixture and increases its pressure, increasing the force generated by the expansion of gases during the power stroke.

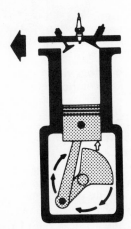

3. IGNITION

The fuel/air mixture is ignited by the spark plug just before the piston reaches the top of its stroke so that a very large portion of the fuel will have burned by the time the piston begins descending again. The heat produced by combustion increases the pressure in the cylinder, forcing the piston down with great force.

4. EXHAUST

As the piston approaches the bottom of its stroke, the exhaust valve begins opening and the pressure in the cylinder begins to force the gases out around the valve. The ascent of the piston then forces nearly all the rest of the unburned gases from the cylinder. The cycle begins again as the exhaust valve closes, the intake valve opens, and the piston begins descending and bringing a fresh charge of fuel and air into the combustion chamber.

Fig. 3–9. The four-stroke cycle of a gasoline-powered, spark ignition engine.

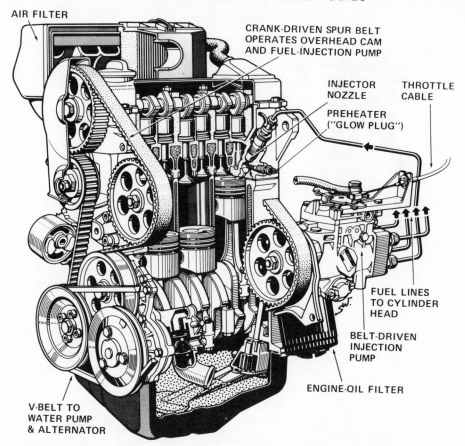

AIR FILTER

CRANK-DRIVEN SPUR BELT
OPERATES OVERHEAD CAM
AND FUEL-INJECTION PUMP

INJECTOR   THROTTLE
NOZZLE   CABLE

PREHEATER
("GLOW PLUG")

FUEL LINES
TO CYLINDER
HEAD

BELT-DRIVEN
INJECTION
PUMP

ENGINE-OIL FILTER

V-BELT TO
WATER PUMP
& ALTERNATOR

Fig. 3–10. Phantom view of the fuel-efficient Volkswagen Diesel engine shows a number of key components, including the "glow plug" which heats up to assist starting when the engine is cold.

of the compression stroke, fuel is injected into the swirl-type precombustion chamber and ignites in the hot air. Turbulence assures that the fuel is thoroughly mixed. Combustion begins in the swirl chamber, then spreads downward to completely burn the fuel and exert pressure on the piston. On the exhaust cycle, the piston simply pushes out the burned gases like the conventional engine.

The biggest advantage of the diesel engine is its superior fuel efficiency. According to the EPA, a diesel will obtain from 40% to 70% better fuel mileage than a gasoline engine.[5] Since the diesel has a much higher compression ratio, it will burn fuel more completely and convert more of the available fuel energy into horsepower. An additional advantage is that a gallon of diesel fuel contains more energy than a gallon of gasoline—an average of 137,750 BTU per gallon compared to only 123,500 for gasoline.[6]

The Cummins Engine Company has estimated the diesel versus gasoline "savings ratio" for various types of truck operation. Either the number of no-load to full-load (idle to acceleration) cycles per day or the percent of time spent idling can determine the fuel savings of a diesel compared to a gasoline engine as estimated in the following table:[7]

Diesel Fuel Saving Ratio	No Load/ Full Load Cycles per Day	(or)	% Time Spent Idling
1.5	0–50		Under 20%
1.5–2.0	50–100		20%
2.0–2.5	100–125		40%
2.5–3.0	125–150		60%
3.0–4.0	over 150		80%

Thus, if a diesel engine were to completely start and stop 150 times a day, it would get between three and four times the fuel mileage of a gasoline engine operated under the same conditions. Low speed operation makes the diesel's advantage even greater.

Because the diesel has neither ignition system nor a carburetor, there are no spark plugs, contact points, condensers, coils, or ignition wires to replace or maintain. The fuel injection system that replaces the carburetor is, like the rest of the engine, relatively maintenance-free. Other diesel advantages are improved durability and driveability. With emission controls making other engines balk and run unevenly, the diesel's high compression design and controlled distribution of fuel enables it to meet current emission standards with ease.

Disadvantages of the diesel engine for passenger cars include low horsepower per weight and displacement, relatively slow acceleration, occasional hard-starting in sub-zero temperatures, a greater need for quality oil (diesel fuel often contains sulphur), an inherently noisy combustion process, exhaust smoke under certain operating conditions, and a slightly higher initial cost.

However, for the individual truly interested in fuel efficiency, the diesel is well worth the minor inconveniences it may involve. I own a VW Rabbit Diesel that has *averaged* over 50 miles per gallon during the first 2,000 miles of ownership—and 60 to 65 miles per gallon on highway trips at 55 mph has not been uncommon. If this seems like bragging, it isn't. Anyone who can hold a steering wheel and press a gas pedal could do the same. Actually, through very careful driving on rural roads at average speeds of 30–35 mph, the author has achieved fuel-efficiency figures in excess of 85 miles per gallon without coasting, shutting off the engine, or breaking any laws.

A challenge to the diesel engine of the future will be to control some combustion products which are presently unregulated (particulate emissions in the form of smoke or soot) and to accommodate tighter restrictions on other emissions already under federal regulation (such as nitrous oxides). Hopefully, the technical expertise of such manufacturers as Mercedes-Benz, General Motors, Volkswagen, and Peugeot will combine with reasonable and sound regulatory judgment to enable the fuel-efficient motorist of the 1980s help ease our energy burden while enjoying the fuel savings provided by the diesel engine.

Turbocharged Engine

In the past, turbocharging has generally been considered a high-performance device for increasing the output of an engine. In a turbocharged engine, greater efficiency is obtained by using the energy of the exhaust gas (energy which would otherwise be wasted) to spin a turbine, which in turn compresses the air being fed into the engine. Normally, the engine must suck in its own air, using up energy in the process. However, with turbocharging, a plentiful supply of air is not only "force-fed" to the engine, but it also becomes possible to in-

THE DIESEL FOUR-STROKE CYCLE

1. AIR INTAKE
Rotation of the crankshaft drives a toothed belt which turns the camshaft, opening the intake valve. As the piston moves down, a vacuum is created, sucking fresh air into the cylinder, past the open intake valve.

2. AIR COMPRESSION
As the piston moves up, both valves are closed and the air is compressed about 23 times smaller than its original volume. The compressed air reaches a temperature of about 1650°F, far above the temperature needed to ignite diesel fuel.

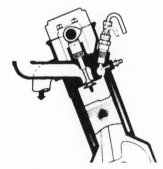

3. FUEL INJECTION AND
    COMPRESSION
As the piston reaches the top of the stroke, the air temperature is at its maximum. A fine mist of fuel is sprayed into the prechamber where it ignites and the flame front spreads rapidly into the combustion chamber. The piston is forced downward by the pressure (about 500 psi) of expanding gasses.

4. EXHAUST
As the energy of combustion is spent and the piston begins to move upward again, the exhaust valve opens and burned gasses are forced out past the open valve. As the piston starts down, the exhaust valve closes, the intake valve opens, and the air intake stroke begins again.

Fig. 3–11. Operating cycle of VW's diesel is basically similar to that of a conventional engine, but it ignites fuel by heat of compression instead of requiring spark plugs. Note in step 3 how tightly the air has been compressed compared to its original volume during the intake cycle. The combination of lots of air and high compression helps the diesel engine operate at a very efficient level.

troduce a greater quantity of air/fuel mixture into the combustion chamber, thereby obtaining more power from an engine of a given size. In addition, turbocharging allows a leaner mixture (higher ratio of air to fuel) to be burned efficiently in the combustion chamber.

In essence, turbocharging allows a very small engine to produce the power normally expected of a larger engine without losing its fuel efficiency advantage

Fig. 3–12. The combination of turbocharging and diesel power can provide both high performance and outstanding fuel efficiency. The Mercedes 300SD has been rated at 24 mpg (city) by the EPA, and can do much better on the highway. Mercedes has been the pioneer of automotive diesels in the U.S. and has delivered over two million diesel-powered vehicles worldwide since 1936.

under normal driving conditions. In a way, it's the best of both worlds—the economy of a small engine combined with the performance of a much larger one. Turbocharging is an especially attractive addition to the passenger car diesel engine, which tends to suffer from a relatively low power output for its size and displacement. A small diesel engine, when turbocharged, is capable of producing the same amount of power as a conventional diesel that is 40% larger, thus providing savings of weight and space for about the same cost as its nonturbocharged counterpart.[8]

Stratified Charge Engine

The stratified charge engine is generally similar to the conventional engine, but with one important difference. In an emission-controlled conventional engine, a lean mixture (high ratio of air to fuel) is desired in order to reduce the output of carbon monoxide and hydrocarbons. On the other hand, a relatively rich mixture (high ratio of fuel to air) is desirable in order to reduce emissions of nitrous oxides. Since a conventional engine can't have a rich mixture and a lean mixture at the same time, the result is the multitude of hang-on emission control pumps, hoses, and other gadgets you see in your engine compartment. The stratified charge engine does the one thing that a conventional engine can't do— have a rich mixture and a lean mixture at the same time.

One type of stratified charge approach is that used by Honda in its CVCC engine, which has a third valve that introduces a rich mixture into a small prechamber, where ignition takes place. Once ignited, the contents of the prechamber in turn ignite a much leaner mixture in the main combustion chamber. The second approach to stratified charge engine design is represented by Ford's PROCO (programmed combustion) engine, in which the dynamics of the com-

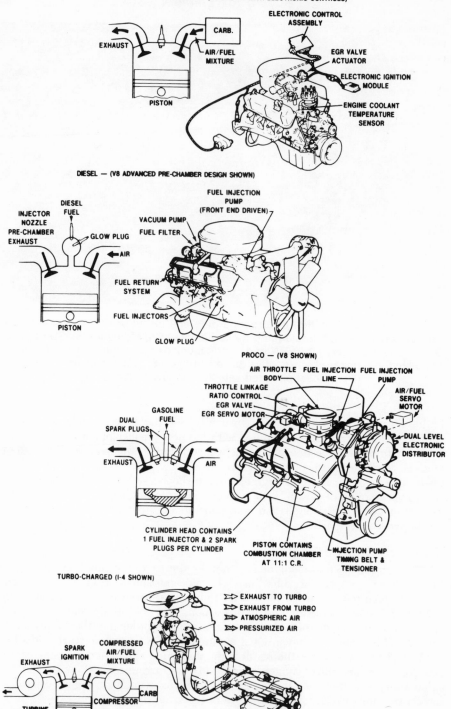

GASOLINE — (V8 SHOWN WITH ELECTRONIC CONTROLS)

EXHAUST
CARB.
AIR/FUEL MIXTURE
PISTON

ELECTRONIC CONTROL ASSEMBLY
EGR VALVE ACTUATOR
ELECTRONIC IGNITION MODULE
ENGINE COOLANT TEMPERATURE SENSOR

DIESEL — (V8 ADVANCED PRE-CHAMBER DESIGN SHOWN)

INJECTOR NOZZLE
DIESEL FUEL
PRE-CHAMBER
EXHAUST
GLOW PLUG
AIR
PISTON

FUEL INJECTION PUMP (FRONT END DRIVEN)
VACUUM PUMP
FUEL FILTER
FUEL RETURN SYSTEM
FUEL INJECTORS
GLOW PLUG

PROCO — (V8 SHOWN)

DUAL SPARK PLUGS
GASOLINE FUEL
EXHAUST
AIR
CYLINDER HEAD CONTAINS 1 FUEL INJECTOR & 2 SPARK PLUGS PER CYLINDER

AIR THROTTLE BODY
FUEL INJECTION LINE
FUEL INJECTION PUMP
THROTTLE LINKAGE
RATIO CONTROL
EGR VALVE
EGR SERVO MOTOR
AIR/FUEL SERVO MOTOR
DUAL LEVEL ELECTRONIC DISTRIBUTOR
PISTON CONTAINS COMBUSTION CHAMBER AT 11:1 C.R.
INJECTION PUMP TIMING BELT & TENSIONER

TURBO-CHARGED (I-4 SHOWN)

EXHAUST
SPARK IGNITION
COMPRESSED AIR/FUEL MIXTURE
TURBINE (DRIVES COMPRESSOR)
COMPRESSOR
CARB.

EXHAUST TO TURBO
EXHAUST FROM TURBO
ATMOSPHERIC AIR
PRESSURIZED AIR

Fig. 3–13. A summary of the engine alternatives discussed in this section. This diagram was originally intended to express possible engine alternatives for light trucks, but its general principles and descriptions may also be applied to auto engines you are likely to see in the 1980s. PROCO is Ford's approach to the stratified charge engine design. (*Source:* D. J. Bickerstaff, *Light Truck Fuel Economy by Design Efficiency,* SAE Paper No. 781063, 1978.)

bustion chamber are combined with other controls to properly separate the rich and lean mixtures within the cylinder. This latter approach is known as the open chamber design, while the former is of the pre-chamber type.

While the pre-chamber design is currently on the market, the open chamber, PROCO design is not available at this writing. However, don't be surprised if you have the opportunity to purchase such an engine sometime in the early 1980s. With fuel costs, technology, and emission regulations constantly changing, such an appearance is not unlikely. According to the EPA, the pre-chamber stratified charge engine will deliver fuel efficiency at least equivalent to conventional engines, while the open chamber design is expected to provide a 12% improvement.[9] Figure 3-13 shows the conventional engine and its likely alternatives for the 1980s.

OPTIONAL EQUIPMENT
Automatic Transmission

The fuel efficiency impact of an automatic transmission is negative, but perhaps not as serious as you may think. The loss will depend largely on the rear axle ratio and the kind of driving conditions you normally encounter. With other factors equal, the use of an automatic transmission can reduce fuel mileage by up to 15%.[10] However, the automatic has some advantages that can make its efficiency more comparable to that of a manual transmission, and in some cases better. First, most cars equipped with an automatic transmission are provided

Weights of Optional Equipment

The following chart lists the approximate weights of optional equipment installed at the factory or available as dealer-installed options. These weights must be added to the weight of the car to realize the total weight.

Equipment	Weight (lbs)	Equipment	Weight (lbs)
Power steering		Rear window air deflector	5
4-cylinder	20	Automatic level control	10
8-cylinder	25	Trunk trim package	10
Radio		T-bar roof	40
AM	6	Bumper guards (front	
AM/FM	7	& rear)	15
AM/FM/Tape	12	Heavy duty battery	7
Sunroof		Vinyl roof (full vinyl)	6
Glass	25	Undercoating	25
Steel	35	Rear wiper/washer	10
Electric door locks		Floor mats	10
2-door	7	Heavy duty suspension	15
4-door	12	Wood grain applique	
Power seat	20	(station wagon)	13
Power windows	22	Power brakes	12
Wire wheel covers	20	Front console	10
Roof luggage carrier	15	Conventional spare tire	25
Air conditioning	75–100	Folding rear seat	35
Heavy duty radiator	9	Styled steel wheels	8
Cruise control	5	Luxury interior	9

Fig. 3–14. Since weight is one aspect over which you have some control in your purchase of a new car, consider the typical weight of popular options and weigh their advantages and disadvantages.

with a lower, more economical rear axle ratio than their manually shifted counterparts. Second, because the throttle movement in shifting a manual transmission tends to increase hydrocarbon emissions, it is easier for a car with automatic transmission to meet EPA exhaust standards. At a given level of emission control, the car with manual transmission requires more strict engine adjustments, often in the form of a more retarded ignition spark.

When climbing hills or traveling at lower speeds, the torque converter of the automatic transmission will have more slippage and cause lower fuel mileage. However, at steady highway speeds, the torque converter will tend to lock up and deliver economy closer to that of an identical car equipped with manual transmission. Tests involving an intermediate size car have shown that automatic transmission costs between .5 mpg (steady 70 mph speed with a lower rear axle ratio than the manual model) and 1.8 mpg (urban travel cycle with equal rear axle ratios).[11]

If you lean towards the automatic as your choice, try to get one with a locking device that eliminates torque converter slippage above certain speeds. In conventional torque converters, slippage can absorb about 6% of the system's efficiency at a 55 mph highway speed.[12] A lockup can improve city fuel efficiency by 2% and highway efficiency by 6%.

As with other automotive components, transmissions are becoming more fuel efficient as the combination of technology and fuel savings motivation makes higher efficiency more attractive to both buyers and manufacturers. For example, in designing the 1980 X car series, GM engineers were able to increase overall drive train efficiency significantly compared to the previous model, especially at lower speeds. Figure 3-15 shows the difference in drivetrain configuration between the two models along with a chart describing the efficiency advantage of the new transmission at various road speeds.

The slippage and loss usually associated with the automatic transmission are also overcome by the new Ford AOT (automatic overdrive transmission). It has three features that provide fuel savings: (1) a mechanical lock-up device that eliminates slippage in the fluid coupling, (2) a fourth gear, overdrive gear ratio, and (3) a redesigned torque converter blade that improves fuel efficiency at idle. The AOT increased the fuel mileage of a 1980 Mercury Marquis by 24% in overdrive, compared to the same car in third gear. Ford engineers predict the transmission will deliver a three-to-four-mile-per-gallon improvement in typical customer usage.

When everything else is equal, the manual transmission may be more efficient than an automatic, but recent improvements in automatic transmission efficiency mean that if you are not very proficient in driving a manual or if you drive mostly in commuter traffic, the automatic transmission may be your best bet. In addition, if you aren't a very good manual shifter, your automatic car will require no clutch replacements and fewer transmission, engine, and drivetrain repairs than will your misused manual.

Optional Rear Axle Ratio

The rear axle ratio is simply the number of times your driveshaft must rotate in order to make the rear wheels rotate once. Since top gear in domestic cars is usually direct-drive, the rear axle ratio is also the number of times your engine has to rotate in order to make the rear wheels turn one time. In general, a numerically low (for example, 2.53) rear axle ratio means less engine wear, slower acceleration, and more miles per gallon than a numerically high ratio (for example, 4.11).

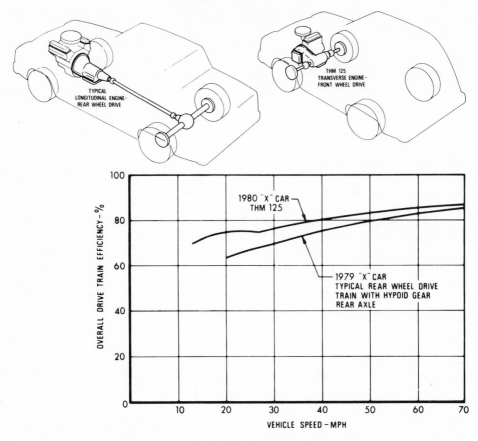

Fig. 3–15. Drivetrain layout sketches show the difference between the 1980 GM X car series (below) and the models they replace. The graph shows how the combination of front wheel drive and high-efficiency Turbo Hydra-Matic 125 automatic transmission increase drivetrain efficiency at highway speeds. (*Source:* E. A. Koivunen and P. A. Le Bar, Jr., *A New Automatic Transmission for Improved Fuel Economy—General Motors THM 125,* SAE Paper No. 790725, 1979.)

Some cars have an indirect-drive top gear, in which case the rear axle ratio must be multiplied by the high gear ratio in order to compare different cars. For example, one Porsche model has a rear axle ratio of 4.43 and a fifth gear ratio of .76 which, when multiplied together, result in what amounts to a 3.36 rear axle ratio. This ratio can then be compared to those of standard cars.

Standard axle ratios are, at best, a compromise. The 3.73 ratio that provides good hill-climbing ability in the mountains of West Virginia may be a little too short-legged for cruising the plains of Nebraska. For this reason, it is to your advantage to specify an optional (usually between $20 and $30) economy axle ratio which will allow you to maintain highway speeds while using fewer engine revolutions. Tests have shown that reducing the rear axle ratio by 10% (for example, from 3.00 to 2.70) can improve your fuel economy by 2% to 5%.[13]

The following table compares the engine speed (revolutions per minute) necessary to propel two cars at various speeds in high gear. The vehicles are equal except for their rear axle ratios.

Road Speed (mph)	Car A (2.29 axle) (rpm)	Car B (3.90 axle) (rpm)
30	960	1630
35	1120	1900
40	1280	2170
45	1440	2440
50	1600	2710
55	1750	2990

At 55 mph, the engine in car A will be turning more slowly than that of car B when car B is traveling only 35 mph. Don't forget that the axle ratio effect is most important when other factors, such as weight, engine efficiency and design, and frontal area, are equal. For example, a small sports car with a 3.90 rear axle will easily exceed the miles per gallon achieved by a luxury sedan with a ratio of 2.73.

Be wary of the linguistics used by auto salesmen and mechanics: some mistakenly refer to the economy ratios as "high" and the stump-pullers as "low." A ratio is a numerical expression and should always be given as such. If it's an economy ratio that you want, be sure that it is numerically low, not just verbally described as "low."

Five-Speed or Overdrive Transmission

Early overdrive transmissions consisted of an add-on section at the rear of the transmission that provides an extra gear ratio to reduce the speed of the driveshaft to about 80% of the speed of the engine. In other words, it's rather like a transmission behind the transmission. With the overdrive in operation at cruising speeds, your miles per gallon can increase by 10% or more.[14]

Because of high initial cost, lack of usefulness in low-speed driving, and competition from low rear axle ratios and five-speed transmissions which accomplish the same purpose, the overdrive transmission in this form is somewhat of a relic from the past. However, you may see the word "overdrive" used in conjunction with a four- or five-speed transmission. In this sense "overdrive" means the ratio of the top (or top two) gears is below a numerical ratio of one to one.

In deciding whether or not to opt for the five-speed transmission, find out whether its top gear will provide a numerically lower overall drive ratio than the top gear in the four-speed version of the transmission. In some cases, the fifth gear may be an overdrive, but the manufacturer has raised the numerical ratio of the rear axle and left you with the same number of engine revolutions at 55 mph as the individual who bought the four-speed. While some may advise not to purchase a five-speed transmission unless a great deal of your driving is on the highway, through intelligent driving techniques and proper gear selection you can make it pay in all but the most extreme stop and go driving conditions.

Power Accessories

Accessories such as power steering, power brakes, power seats, power windows, and power sunroof reduce fuel mileage due to the extra weight (up to 30 pounds for each) that they add to the car. In addition, they consume mechanical power directly from the engine or electrical power indirectly supplied by the engine through the alternator.

The mileage loss because of power steering tends to decrease as you travel at higher speeds, and the friction of the engine-driven hydraulic pump becomes less important relative to air resistance and other forces trying to impede your

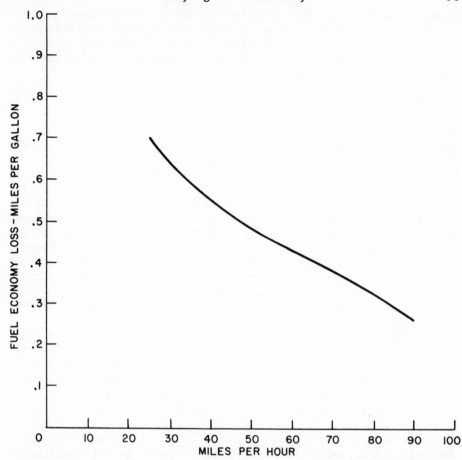

Fig. 3–16. While the fuel efficiency penalty of power steering will be less at higher speeds, you'll still lose about one-half mile per gallon at the 55 mph national speed limit. (*Source:* J. J. Cornell, *Passenger Car Fuel Economy Characteristics on Modern Superhighways,* SAE Paper No. 650862, 1965.)

car's progress. You can expect power steering to reduce economy by about .7 mpg at a steady speed of 25 miles per hour.[15] Despite its fuel penalty, power steering may be necessary in a heavy car that is frequently used in low-speed maneuvering in which the steering wheel would otherwise be difficult to turn, or in highway driving where the quicker response of power steering provides better evasive ability in avoiding an obstacle. This is a case where the weight factor hits you twice—once for the weight itself, again for the power steering which you may need to handle it. Many smaller cars don't even offer power steering as an option. With lighter front ends and quicker steering, they can get along without it.

If you're strong enough to open your car door, chances are you've got more than enough strength to step on the brake pedal hard enough to stop your car with all the deceleration of which it is capable. The point is, power brakes are a needless luxury for most of us. The same applies to electric motors that raise and lower our windows, adjust our seats, and open our sunroofs.

Any electrical accessory will require power that must come from the engine by way of the alternator. Tests on an intermediate car with automatic transmission showed that, with the alternator operating at its maximum output of 40 to 50 amperes, fuel mileage suffered by between .9 and .5 miles per gallon.[16] As would be expected, lower electrical demands resulted in smaller reductions in efficiency.

Air Conditioning

Whether cooling or sitting idle, an air conditioning system adds about 75 to 100 pounds of weight to your car. In urban driving, this extra weight can be expected to decrease gas mileage by about .4 mpg for a subcompact car and about .1 mpg for a standard-size model.[17] As with any other source of weight, there is a larger penalty during stop-and-go driving than in steady-speed highway operation.

When the air conditioning unit is being used, power must be provided to drive the compressor and fan, thus leading to even greater losses in gas mileage. In one test, at an ambient temperature of 85° F, use of the air conditioner reduced economy by about 2.5 mpg at 20 miles per hour and by about .5 mpg at a speed of 80.[18] In another test of fuel efficiency at 50 miles per hour, it was found that economy dropped by about .4 mpg when the windows were rolled down, while having the windows up and the air conditioner turned on reduced efficiency by more than 2 miles per gallon, a decrease of about 10%.[19] See Figure 3-17.

Depending on the aerodynamics of your particular vehicle, and how much drag is produced by rolling down the windows to keep cool, it is possible that turning the air conditioner to a low setting at highway speeds may be more efficient than holding the car back by lowering the windows. However, in general, it is more efficient to not purchase the air conditioner in the first place.

As with other accessories, the mileage penalty of air conditioning is less at higher speeds because of the rapidly increasing resistance of the air through which the car is moving. It's like forgetting about your toothache after you've dropped a bowling ball on your foot. At higher speeds, air resistance tends to overshadow all other sources of resistance and cause them to be relatively less important.

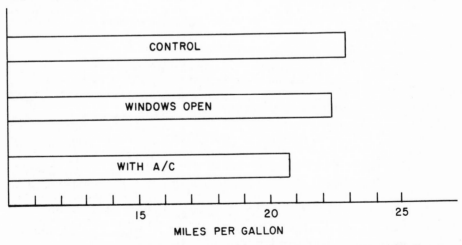

Fig. 3–17. Tests of a compact vehicle at a steady 50 mph showed that lowering all the windows was about 2 mpg more efficient than using the air conditioner. (*Source:* R. W. Donoho, *EPA MPG—How Realistic?*, SAE Paper No. 780866, 1978.)

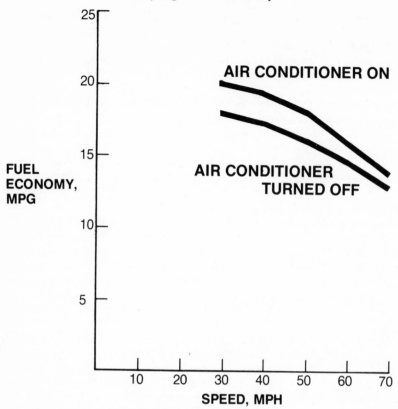

Fig. 3–18. As with most power accessories, the fuel economy penalty is less at higher speeds than at low speeds. But at lower speeds the penalty for operating the air conditioner is still considerable.

Automatic Speed Control

A speed "thermostat," this option will maintain any constant speed you desire without your having to touch the gas pedal. Because there is a minimum of acceleration when the device is in operation, the amount of fuel consumed by acceleration resistance will be minimized. The heavier your car, the more you can benefit from this option. The disadvantages of the device are its initial cost, generally around $100, and the possibility of your becoming inattentive from not having anything to do while you're driving.

Another consideration is that such an option is not useful during urban driving, suburban driving, or any type of operation in which speed must vary or where interaction with other vehicles is frequent. In addition, the driving techniques described in the next chapter should enable you to get enough miles per gallon in steady-speed driving that such a device will become unnecessary.

However, if a great deal of your driving is over long, uncongested stretches of interstate highway, and you use the speed control device properly, the result could well be more comfortable and efficient driving at little or no loss in safety.

Disc Brakes

Front disc brakes are superior in so many ways—including directional stability, fade and moisture resistance, and ease of service—that it's difficult to evaluate them on a fuel efficiency basis. However, the disc brake pads do press lightly against the rotor (disc) at all times instead of retracting as do the shoes of properly adjusted drum brakes. To this extent, frictional losses on the road can be slightly greater than with drum brakes. It has been estimated that the normal level of disc brake drag is sufficient to reduce fuel efficiency by up to .5 miles per gallon.[20]

One possible compensating factor is that the front wheel bearings need not be disturbed during the annual or semiannual safety inspection required in some states. In order to inspect the brake linings of a front drum brake, it is necessary to partially dismantle the hub and wheel bearing assembly—a procedure which, if carried out by a careless mechanic in untidy surroundings, might result in a faulty wheel bearing adjustment or dirt entering the bearing lubricant. Besides wearing out rather quickly, a dirty or binding front wheel bearing isn't good for your health or your gas mileage.

The brake pads on disc brakes are very simple to replace and can be moved very slightly away from the rotor by a simple driving strategy (included in next chapter's discussion of driving for efficiency). For this and the reason previously mentioned, my vote goes to the ordering of front disc brakes if they're optional and using them without regret if they're standard.

Radio and Sound Equipment

It would seem that optional equipment in this category is more hedonistic than economical. Naturally, a car radio can be useful in receiving helicopter reports of fuel-consuming traffic jams between you and the destination to which you may be commuting. However, a radio, tape deck, or short wave adapter has other advantages as well. To the extent that driving efficiently depends on your patience and state of mind, entertainment equipment, commercial-free music, and short-wave broadcasts can help take the urgency out of your driving and the lead out of your foot. Long trips won't seem quite so long, traffic jams won't be as frustrating, and the kids can listen to music instead of fighting or playing count-the-cows.

Whether for information, entertainment, or communication, a Citizens Band (CB) radio can be invaluable on a long trip. Shortly following the lowering of the national speed limit to 55 mph, the public became aware of the many advantages of CB, including tracking the movements of "Smokey Bear" and his radar set-ups. Since then, CB has grown in popularity to the point that it is second only to the telephone as a means of two-way electronic communication. Many CB owners would not drive without their radio, claiming it keeps them more alert, helps them pass the time on a long trip, and alerts them to radar traps and road hazards. The author has avoided at least a few major traffic jams by simply listening to the CB chatter on his radio.

Other practical uses for the CB radio include asking for local information regarding best routes to travel, where to eat, or where to stay overnight or camp, thus avoiding a bad experience or the waste of time and fuel dollars in a do-it-yourself search. In addition, garages and law enforcement personnel frequently monitor emergency channel 9 in order to respond quickly to an accident or breakdown. With a CB, your travel can be a lot more efficient, safe, and enjoyable. Don't hesitate to buy one. It's well worth the extra weight.

Although this arrangement will not always provide optimum range for CB broadcasting, the combination AF/FM/CB antenna is a good idea for the fuel efficient CB'er to consider—with only one antenna mast disturbing the air flow, there will be slightly less air resistance than with a separate antenna for the CB. However, if you do wish to have a separate CB antenna (the combination units can be pretty expensive), the magnetic mount and rain gutter clip-on are good possibilities to keep in mind. They are easily removed for such occasions as when you are not using the CB or have parked and left the car. In the latter situation, the removable antenna is useful for its theft-avoidance value, since the presence of a CB is not so obvious when there is no tell-tale antenna.

Instrumentation

Like the radio, dashboard instruments can be a source of entertainment and encourage alertness and patience. In addition, they are sources of useful information on what's happening (or about to happen) in your engine or electrical system. While most new cars tend to have "idiot lights" instead of gauges, it's not a bad idea to consider the purchase of additional instrumentation at the time you buy your car. In considering possible gauges for your car, put the following at the top of your list:

Fig. 3–19. These and other conventional dashboard instruments can take the place of your "idiot lights" and provide information on fuel efficiency and mechanical well-being.

Water Temperature

This gauge monitors the temperature of your engine coolant. As the engine warms up, the temperature should rise to somewhere in the 180° to 200° F range, perhaps higher depending on your particular model. Once you've determined the normal readings for your car—stop-and-go driving temperatures will tend to be high, interstate cruising somewhat lower—you can keep alert for unexplained changes in the gauge reading. For example, if you discover that your gauge reading is too cool for a given driving condition, your thermostat may not be working properly, thus depriving you of the good fuel efficiency that a fully warmed-up engine will deliver. Likewise, if the temperature is too hot, this can indicate low coolant level, a defective radiator cap, incorrect ignition timing, slipping drive belts, or other problems that might mean that your engine is not functioning efficiently.

Ammeter

The ammeter indicates the condition of the charging system. It will show charge (+) when the battery is being charged and discharge (−) when the battery is releasing more current than it is receiving from the alternator. After you've started your car, the rate of charge should be high, then taper off after the engine has run for a short time. If the ammeter continues to indicate a high rate of charge under conditions when you are not using much electricity, this may indicate a weak battery that is incapable of storing electricity efficiently. In this instance, your alternator may be pouring electricity into a battery that cannot hold it effectively. This wastes fuel, since the alternator receives its own energy from the motion of the engine. Another possible cause for continued high ammeter readings is a defective voltage regulator, which will also cause the alternator to be overworked, the battery to be overcharged, and your fuel bill to be higher than it should.

Voltmeter

Some drivers prefer a voltmeter instead of an ammeter because it gives a more complete picture of the battery's condition. Even though the vehicle uses a 12-volt electrical system, the voltmeter should typically read between 13 and 15 volts. As on the ammeter, consistently low or high readings indicate a malfunction that is very likely to affect your fuel efficiency.

Vacuum Gauge

A vacuum gauge is a good measure of your car's fuel consumption rate. This instrument measures the vacuum that exists in the intake manifold during part-throttle operation. The vacuum gauge registers between 0 and 30 inches of mercury and can help you to achieve more economical driving habits and speeds. By keeping the vacuum gauge needle in the upper ranges (actual numbers will vary depending on your car), you'll be getting as much fuel efficiency as your car can deliver. (How to use the vacuum gauge when driving is discussed in Chapter 3.)

Vacuum gauges have been sold under exotic names that imply they indicate your miles per gallon rather than your intake manifold vacuum. However, they are still vacuum gauges. Some cars may be equipped with an "idiot light" that is activated whenever the vacuum falls below a selected level. Instead of constantly telling you the intake manifold vacuum, this arrangement activates a warning light to remind you that you're wasting gas.

By keeping the vacuum in your mind, you'll be better able to think economy on the road.

Tachometer

Although the tachometer, which registers engine rpm, is often thought of as a high-performance instrument used by drag racers, its importance lies in helping you keep the engine from turning too slowly or too quickly. For most engines, there is a range of speeds (rpm's) in which they operate most efficiently, i.e., using the smallest amount of fuel per unit of work performed. The most efficient range is generally slightly less than the rpm at which the engine produces its maximum torque. For example, if an engine produces its maximum horsepower at 5,000 rpm and its maximum torque at 3,000 rpm, it is likely that the greatest efficiency will occur around 2,000 to 3,000 rpm, and that 2,500 rpm may be highly desirable as a guide to selecting the gear to be used in a particular situation.

Use of the tachometer is discussed in more detail in Chapter 3.

Fuel Consumption Meter

The ideal way to lighten both your foot and your fuel bill is to have a gauge or instrument that tells you exactly how many hundredths of a gallon you've used since resetting the device. Such gauges are available at relatively low cost, although they are more expensive than the simple vacuum gauge. There are several different kinds.

A *fuel totalizer* reports only the number of tenths or hundredths (better, if available) of a gallon used since resetting the instrument reading. This is a useful device for practicing fuel-efficient driving techniques and evaluating your success and improvements. Because it tells you exactly how much fuel has been consumed, it is also valuable in deciding between alternate routes for trips you frequently make, such as commuting to work.

A *miles-per-gallon gauge* reports your instantaneous mpg rate, which increases or decreases from one moment to the next. Its usefulness lies in promoting awareness of fuel efficiency and allowing you to view current performance while it's happening, but is best when combined with a fuel totalizer so that you can measure how well you're doing.

A *trip computer*, in addition to instantaneous mpg data, will tell you how much fuel is left in your tank, how many miles per gallon you've averaged since your last fill-up, how long it will take to get to your destination, and just about everything except whether you'll need a rest stop along the way.

Of these three instruments, I recommend the use of a fuel consumption totalizer as the best information value for the money.

Limited-Slip Differential

The limited-slip differential sees to it that both rear tires do their share when you're faced with a slippery road surface. While it is helpful in getting you to your destination under adverse traction conditions, and while it involves no added weight to the car, this is not an option that will save you fuel. A possible exception would be if it decreases your need for snow tires by providing the same advantage as having the engine over the drive wheels.

Trailer-Towing Package

The trailer-towing option generally includes a number of heavy-duty and durability items, such as heavy-duty springs and shock absorbers, larger radiator, and special automatic transmission oil cooler. However, these are accompanied by larger tires and a numerically higher rear axle ratio. The larger tires won't hurt much, but if you're primarily interested in fuel efficiency, you may have to specify an economy axle ratio, if available, and try to get your heavy-duty and durability features separately so you can purchase only those that you need or want. Naturally, if you plan to pull a heavy trailer, follow the manufacturer's recommendations and opt for the entire package. Like the limited-slip differential, this isn't an option that is generally useful in improving fuel efficiency.

Permanent Roof Rack

In addition to its usual role as shiny dead weight, a permanent roof rack does nothing to aid your car's fight against air resistance at high speeds. If you must use a rack often, its permanence will not be a disadvantage. However, if you rarely need to carry roof-top items, consider a suction-cup or gutter-clamp removable rack instead. If at all possible, make do with the interior of the car as a storage location for bulky items, as rooftop loads tend to give your car the air resistance of a two-story bus when traveling at highway speeds.

Electronic Ignition

The electronic ignition system is generally thought of as a performance item rather than an aid to gas mileage. By either eliminating the ignition points or reducing the current they carry, the electronic ignition system can extend the interval between tune-ups. This can be an advantage for do-it-yourselfers who don't have the time or ability to do their own tune-ups. As your engine gets further away from its last tune-up, performance and gas mileage decrease. A principal advantage of an electronic ignition is not so much that performance and economy are increased, but that a given level of performance and efficiency can be maintained over a longer period of time without the necessity of a tune-up along the way. Some cars have electronic ignition as standard equipment. If you tend to be rather lax about periodic tune-ups, and if my pleas in Chapter 5 don't sway you, you may be a candidate for an after-market electronic ignition system.

Keep in mind that some electronic ignition systems are highly geared for performance in the form of strong ignition sparks supplied all the way up to the uneconomical speeds of 6,000 RPM and beyond. As a good economy-minded driver, you won't benefit greatly from the performance capabilities of such high-powered systems. Electronics, consumer, automotive enthusiast, and do-it-yourself magazines carry detailed tests and technical information on various systems that are available. Look before you leap.

ENERGY-EFFICIENT TIRE SELECTION

Tire selection has come a long way from the days when the only choice was whitewalls versus blackwalls. Next to the selection of the vehicle itself, tires are probably the next most important decision you'll make when buying your car.

Tire Types

Bias-ply is the conventional tire design which has been around for about half a century. This type of construction is low-priced but wears out the quickest at the highest tire cost per mile. The bias-ply construction, illustrated in Figure 3-20, shows the criss-crossing cords that make up the tire body. The tire cords are in two, four, six, or eight layers and at a 30°–40° angle to the center line of the tire. Although its many plies result in a relatively stiff sidewall and tread, a bias-ply tire will squirm and run hotter than either a belted bias tire or a radial. Because of these contortions and self-generated heat, its high rolling resistance will hold you back when you're trying for those all-important miles per gallon.

Belted bias tires, shown in Figure 3-21, also have their body cords arranged in a criss-cross pattern and are really just an improved version of the conventional tire. In addition to its conventional body, the belted bias tire also has

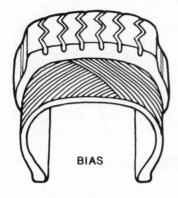

BIAS

Fig. 3–20. Cross-sectional view of a conventional bias-ply tire. (Courtesy of Rubber Manufacturers Association.)

BELTED BIAS

Fig. 3–21. Cross-sectional view of a belted bias-ply tire shows the tread stabilizing belts that give it longer life and lower rolling resistance. (Courtesy of Rubber Manufacturers Association.)

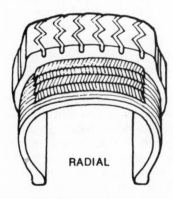

RADIAL

Fig. 3–22. Inflexible tread belts and radial body plies enable the radial tire to have lower rolling resistance than either the conventional or belted bias types. (Courtesy of Rubber Manufacturers Association.)

special layers or "belts" under the tread. With this construction, a stiff sidewall is combined with increased strength and stiffness in the tread. Having less tread squirm, the belted bias tire runs cooler, lasts longer, and has lower rolling resistance than a conventional tire.

Radial-ply construction, illustrated in Figure 3-22, includes a body with cords running at a 90° angle to the center line of the tire. These body cords may be arranged in as many as three plies, or layers. The radial-ply tire also has between two and four very strong tread belts, which may be made of steel, fiberglass, or rayon. Because of its radial body and belted tread, the radial tire has a flexible sidewall and an extremely stiff tread. The bulging sidewall will cause a radial to look underinflated even when it isn't. The practically inflexible tread reduces squirming to a minimum, resulting in cool running, very long tread life, and sharply lowered rolling resistance.

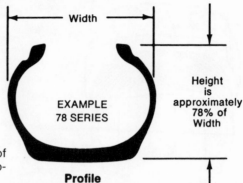

Fig. 3-23. A tire's "profile" is the ratio of its height to its width. (Courtesy of Rubber Manufacturers Association.)

Tire Profile

The profile of a tire is the ratio of its height to its width, and is shown in figure 3-23. The "78" series tire shown is 78% as high as it is wide. The lower the profile number, the fatter the tire. Wider tires will improve stopping and cornering by putting more tread in contact with the road. However, this larger "footprint" can make your car harder to steer and, with other factors equal, may have more rolling resistance than a narrower tire.

For Top Efficiency: The Radial Tire

If you can handle the higher initial cost of the radial tire, you'll be repaid with lower tire cost per mile as well as from 3% to 10% more miles per gallon. My personal choice is the steel-belted radial, on which I've been riding for most of my driving life. (The same steel-belted radials were once transferred from their original car to two subsequent vehicles over a total distance exceeding 60,000 miles.) Whether on the road or pushing the car back and forth to get through your crowded garage, the low rolling resistance of the radial tire will be evident to you and your fuel bill.

The rolling resistance of the radial design has been shown in various tests to be only about three-fourths that of a belted bias tire and about two-thirds that of a conventional bias tire. In one study, the use of steel-belted radials reduced 50 mph rolling resistance by 28 pounds when compared to belted conventional tires.[21] Although 28 pounds doesn't seem like much, depending on the frontal area of your car, this can make a big difference. For example, let's say that a standard sedan is cruising at a steady speed of 50 mph. Its engine is pushing against about 170 pounds of combined resistance from air and rolling. If the switch to radial tires takes away 28 pounds of that force, the resistance the engine must fight is down to only 142 pounds, a reduction of 16%. Because of resistance in and around the engine itself (fan, alternator, etc.), the car's fuel consumption won't go down by 16%, but fuel mileage will still increase by between 1 and 1.5 miles per gallon at that steady speed.

The effects of giving your car a 28-pound pat on the back are evident in the chart in Figure 3-24, based on data collected by the Firestone Tire and Rubber Company during testing of their original-equipment steel-belted radial tire against its comparable belted bias model.[22] The test involved a standard size domestic sedan driven at the steady speeds shown.

Other studies and estimates of the advantage of equipping your car with radial tires include miles-per-gallon increases of 3%, 6%, and 5–10%, depending on the source and the driving conditions assumed. The greatest mpg increase

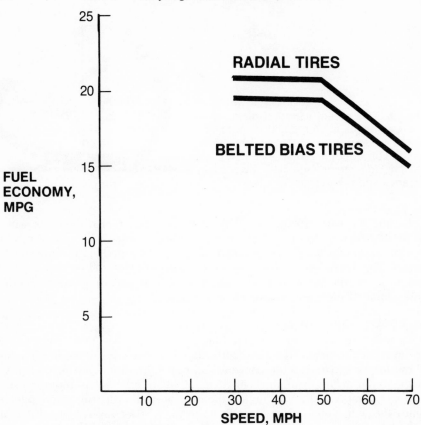

Fig. 3–24. Radial tires have less rolling resistance and can increase your fuel mileage, as shown in tests by Firestone Tire and Rubber Co. on a standard size sedan.

with radials will be evident at moderate, steady speeds during which rolling resistance is the main force holding you back. The smallest increases will be at high speeds, when air resistance is your main obstacle, and during stop-and-go driving, during which acceleration resistance is your biggest enemy.

The New High-Pressure Radials

Current developments in tire technology promise even greater fuel efficiency than the conventional radial has been able to deliver. For example, some of the new P-metric-sized radials have construction refinements that make it possible to inflate the tires to higher pressures without sacrificing comfort and tire life, while at the same time delivering lower rolling resistance and improved fuel efficiency. A number of manufacturers have come out with these tires and they are well worth your consideration, especially in view of the skyrocketing fuel prices we are likely to face in the 1980s.

Figure 3-25 shows a cross-sectional view of a new generation radial tire, illustrating how its sidewall forms a greater curve than the conventional design at left. The greater curvature allows the sidewalls to flex sufficiently to absorb shocks and to ride comfortably despite the much higher inflation pressures (up to 50% more than normal) which are used.

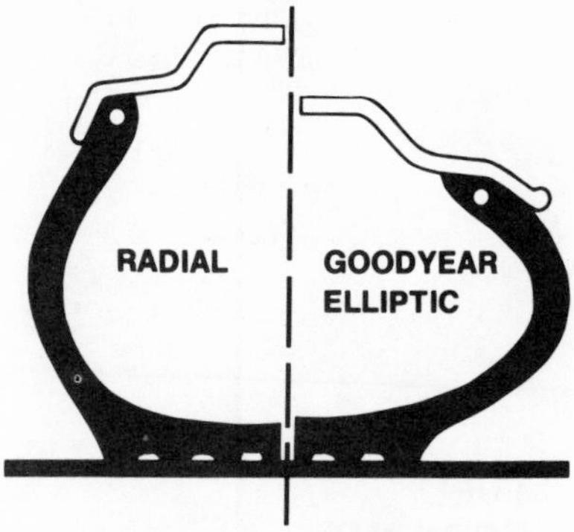

Fig. 3–25. This recent variation of the radial tire has an elliptical cross section and allows inflation pressures as much as 50% higher than the conventional radial. As a result, this type of design can provide even lower rolling resistance and greater fuel efficiency.

During the early 1980s it is likely that most major manufacturers will be able to offer high-pressure and other radial designs which will significantly improve your fuel efficiency. Technology is moving very rapidly in this area and, as you read this, there may well be tires on the market that roll even more easily than those available at this writing. Try to stay aware of new developments—some of them may really pay off.

The Space-Saver Spare

By selecting one of the available temporary-usage spare tires, you can have more space in your trunk as well as better fuel efficiency due to the lower weight of these tires compared to the conventional spare tire. Some are smaller in size and are stored in the trunk in an inflated condition; others may require a small canister of compressed air to unfold them to normal size; still others offer efficiency through their thinner size. By choosing a space-saver spare if it is not standard on your car, you may save about five to fifteen pounds—that's weight your engine won't have to work to haul around.

OTHER NEW CAR FACTORS TO CONSIDER
Color

Light colors tend to reflect heat and keep your car cooler. The choice of a lighter color should be considered if you live in a warm climate, regardless of whether you're equipping your new car with air conditioning. If you have air conditioning, a lighter color will help reduce the amount of cooling that the air conditioner must do, the proportion of time that it is operating, and the horsepower drain resulting from its operation. If you don't have air conditioning, a lighter color will make it less necessary to pay the air resistance penalty of lowered windows when traveling at highway speeds, and increase the probability that the flow-through ventilation will be able to keep you comfortable while cruising.

Dark colors tend to absorb heat and will help keep your car warmer in cold weather, thus reducing your use of the heater and its blower fan. Whereas light colors and tinted windows may be desirable in reducing the heat absorbed by an air-conditioned car, they can work against you in colder weather.

Seating Comfort

Like the radio equipment described earlier, seating comfort seems at first glance to be a luxury. After all, a car would be much lighter and more economical if it were equipped with orange crates instead of plush seats. Not quite true. You won't get good fuel efficiency while you're speeding in an attempt to reach your destination before your back breaks. While most cars you are considering will likely have comparable seating, be sure that your prospective model has enough leg and head room, and that the seat back, if not adjustable, is fixed at a comfortable angle for you. Since your foot will spend a lot of time on the gas pedal, be sure that the angle is not awkward when the accelerator is pressed through its range of motion. Likewise for the clutch in a manual-transmission car—is it easy for you to depress it fully?

When you're sitting at home in your easy chair, you normally have the footrest in front of the chair, not offset to the right. Make sure that you won't require a knee operation in order to sit straight ahead and still be able to step on the throttle. On some smaller cars, the pedals may be drastically to the right of the straight-ahead position in which you're sitting, a fact that becomes more noticeable after 6 hours on the road than it may have been during the 10 minutes in the showroom.

Be sure you know whether you prefer the Italian-style arms-straight driving position or the steering-wheel-under-the chin stance. In some cars, you may not be able to easily reach the steering wheel when your legs are comfortable. A reasonable degree of comfort will aid your gas mileage by helping you enjoy the ride instead of clock-watching along the way. While you needn't sit in the showroom all day, don't be afraid to spend a few extra minutes trying on the seating package of each model you're considering.

Fuel Tank Size

If your trips are primarily short and local, a relatively small fuel tank may not be a handicap. However, if you often drive long distances, especially through areas where fuel is not in plentiful supply, the number of gallons your tank holds will be rather important. Determine the cruising range of a car you have in mind by multiplying its expected trip miles per gallon times the number of gallons the tank holds. Before making this calculation, you may wish to subtract one or two gallons from the tank size in order to allow for a safety margin. Unlike some older models, modern cars don't have a reserve tank to use as a crutch. When you run out today, you're out.

As an example of generous cruising range, consider the AMC Spirit, which has a fuel tank capacity of 21 gallons and probable fuel mileage of 25 mpg or more. This combination would enable the car's driver to travel over 500 miles between fill-ups. On the other hand, another small car of equal economy may have only a 10-gallon tank. Even the most daring driver would have to shop for gas every 200 miles. An optional, oversize fuel tank is offered on some vehicles, and they may provide a capacity of 30 gallons or more, depending on the size of the vehicle and its normal fuel consumption. While the use of such a tank will greatly extend your range of operation, remember that you'll be increasing the weight of your car and thereby reducing its fuel mileage. Not only will the larger fuel tank weigh more than a standard tank, but the extra gasoline it holds (assuming you use the extra capacity) will further add to the vehicle's weight. Every 10 gallons of gasoline you carry adds about 60 pounds to the weight, decreasing your gas mileage by about .2 miles per gallon—not much, but consider that it costs fuel to haul fuel.

Aerodynamic Drag Reduction Devices

Aerodynamic drag reduction devices, generally referred to as "spoilers," have been used in racing for many years. However, their effectiveness in reducing the drag coefficient of a vehicle may be applied to production cars as well,

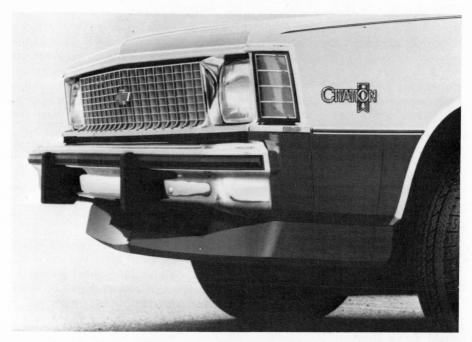

Fig. 3–26. By smoothly directing air over and around the vehicle, a standard or optional front spoiler beneath the bumper will reduce aerodynamic drag and provide increased fuel efficiency at highway speeds.

thus improving fuel efficiency at highway speeds. The purpose of a front spoiler is to help air smoothly over and around the vehicle in order to reduce the turbulence that results when air is buffeted about beneath the car. Likewise, the rear spoiler is intended to help the vehicle leave a cleaner "wake," that is, to minimize the amount of turbulence and suction which occurs in the air stream after the vehicle has passed through it.

Depending on the basic design of a vehicle, the installation of these aerodynamic aids can be effective in improving fuel efficiency by roughly 2%. In some cases the improvement will be less, while in others a greater increase will result. Based on wind tunnel tests, Kamei USA reports that installation of a front spoiler on the Volkswagen Rabbit resulted in a 4% reduction in the drag coefficient, an increase of 6% in top speed and a 1.4% decrease in fuel consumption under combined driving conditions.[23]

While the effect of aerodynamic drag reduction devices will be negligible in city driving, if your driving is mostly at highway speeds in the 55 mph range, the addition of aerodynamic aids could pay off in fuel savings. Some vehicles may have spoilers as standard equipment, or they may be incorporated into the basic shape of the vehicle.

In addition to reducing drag, the installation of a spoiler on the front and/or rear of the vehicle can provide improved handling, since the resulting alteration of the airflow around your car will reduce the amount of natural "lifting" that tends to reduce the weight on the driving wheels. This effect of the airflow on the vehicle was discussed in the preceding chapter, and is related to the lifting forces that act on the car at highway speeds.

THE EPA AND YOUR CAR-BUYING DECISION

Beginning with the 1976 model year, the U.S. government required that a fuel efficiency label be attached to all new cars sold in the United States. In addition, the efficiency figures for various models had to be made available at all new car dealerships at no cost to the consumer. The resulting booklet, the *Gas Mileage Guide*, contains fuel efficiency information on all new cars and allows you to compare the models you are considering for purchase. In addition to reporting on cars, the *Guide* also contains fuel efficiency data on station wagons, vans, and light trucks, and provides information on engine size, number of cylinders, transmission type, fuel delivery systems, body types, and interior room.

How the Mileage Figures are Obtained

The fuel efficiency values in the *Gas Mileage Guide* are obtained from laboratory tests in which each vehicle is tested under highly controlled conditions on a dynamometer. The dynamometer is a stationary device with rollers beneath the driving wheels, and it simulates the operation of the vehicle under various driving conditions. To ensure comparability between vehicles, each vehicle is "driven" through a standard driving cycle which describes very exactly the speed to be observed at various points in time.

For example, the EPA urban driving cycle, shown in Figure 3-27, involves a distance of 7.5 miles at an average speed of 19.7 miles per hour for a duration of 22 minutes and 52 seconds.[24] As indicated in the figure, there are a great many stops (mph = 0) along this simulated route, and the result is a great many accelerations and decelerations during the nearly 23 minutes of testing. The fuel mileage for this cycle is reported in the *Gas Mileage Guide* as the "city" mileage for 1978 and earlier vehicles, and is listed as the "estimated mpg" for 1979 and later vehicles.

Earlier *Guides* also included the results of a highway driving cycle, but the results of the urban cycle are now the only figures reported, as the EPA feels

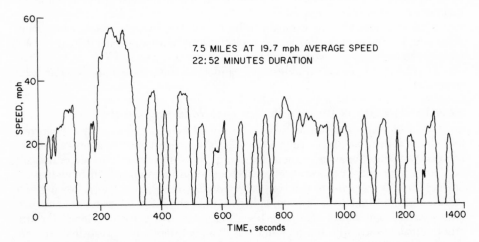

Fig. 3–27. A speed-versus-time description of the EPA Urban Driving Cycle on which the *Gas Mileage Guide* estimates are based. Note the very high number of stops (0 mph) and the numerous accelerations and decelerations which hold the average speed to less than 20 miles per hour. (*Source:* Bain Dayman, Jr., *Realistic Effects of Winds on the Aerodynamic Resistance of Automobiles,* SAE Paper No. 780337, 1978.)

that these mileages are a better estimate of the average fuel consumption the consumer will experience in average driving. According to the EPA, this format is an interim measure that will be observed until technical changes can be made to improve the accuracy of the fuel economy numbers being generated. (When comparing the values in 1979 or later *Guides* with those in 1978 or earlier editions, use the "city" figures from the older *Guide*.)

How Realistic Are the EPA Figures?

How realistic are the EPA mileage estimates? There is no question that fuel consumption in a particular car will vary widely depending on the driver. Complicating the estimate is the fact that cars are even more variable than drivers.

There has been considerable public criticism of the EPA fuel consumption figures as being too optimistic. However, the EPA tests are useful as a simplified representation of the wide variety of conditions that affect fuel consumption. In addition to the driving cycle itself, the test establishes many standard test conditions for variables, such as type of fuel, ambient temperature, and "soak time" (elapsed time since the vehicle was last operated, which affects warm-up conditions). Though the standard test conditions are meant to be representative, each introduces a variable into the measurement of fuel consumption which tends to make it higher or lower than actual customer usage indicates.

As an example, look at the dynamometer tests. Tire rolling resistance is affected by vehicle weight distribution and tire pressure, among other factors. But only one pair of tires is cradled on the dynamometer roller, to simulate motion over the road during the test. Because of this, front-wheel-drive cars can experience higher losses due to tire rolling resistance than rear-wheel-drive cars. Tire pressure also influences rolling resistance and the EPA tests specify an artificially high tire pressure to increase durability during the tests.

Many other factors also contribute small biases toward the final EPA economy number. Road surface type, road state of repair, wind, weather conditions, altitude, engine accessory loads, and customer maintenance will all affect the actual in-use fuel economy number.

Fuel economy labels are meant to be useful in comparing *relative* economy of cars and in *estimating* the actual fuel consumption experienced in use. Obviously the, in-use fuel economy obtained by any given driver/vehicle combination is subject to many variables and cannot be determined by standardized tests.

How to Use the Numbers in the *Gas Mileage Guide*

The test conditions under which the fuel efficiency figures have been obtained are similar for every car and are fairly representative of average driving conditions. While for your particular driving circumstances the numbers may all be a little high or a little low, you can be confident in comparing the *relative* efficiencies of the vehicles in the size range which you require. If you buy a given vehicle and find that your mileage is higher than the EPA estimate, chances are that your mileage would also have been higher than the EPA estimate for any other vehicle. Naturally, the fuel efficiency you get depends a great deal on your driving habits, the condition of your vehicle, and the type of roads and traffic conditions your driving involves.

Because there will be a wide range of fuel efficiencies in any given size range, you should take these into consideration and lean toward purchasing the most efficient vehicle available within the size range you need.

As an example of the variations within vehicle size classes, consider the following differences which are based on a recent *Gas Mileage Guide:*

Compact: 130% difference in mpg between highest- and lowest-mpg vehicle.
Mid-Size: 136% difference between highest- and lowest-mpg vehicle.
Large-Size: 100% difference between highest- and lowest-mpg vehicle.[25]

As an incentive to make do with a compact instead of a mid-size, it may be interesting to know that this same issue of the *Guide* reports a 163% difference in fuel efficiency between the highest compact versus the lowest mid-size. Likewise, if you're able to satisfy your needs with a mid-size instead of a large-size, you may benefit from the 116% difference between the highest mid-size and lowest large-size.[26]

For best results, you should combine the information from the *Gas Mileage Guide* with the information contained in the earlier parts of this chapter, then make your choice based on long term efficiency in *everyday* use. After a bit of calculation, you may even find that by driving a more efficient vehicle during everyday travel, you'll be able to rent a luxury limousine for several days a year and still come out way ahead.

TRY A TRAILER

If the main thing holding you back from buying a really small and fuel efficient car is a frequent need to haul fertilizer, bricks, 4-by-8 panels, trail bikes, bicycles, logs, tree stumps, topsoil, lawnmowers, or vacation and camping gear, seriously consider the small utility trailer as a means to fill the gap between the fuel efficient car you want and the inefficient hulk you sometimes need. Such a trailer may weigh only 250 pounds empty, but can have a capacity in excess of 900 pounds, hold 18 (without top) or 36 (with top) cubic feet of cargo, and carry 4-by-8 building panels without your having to fold them up to get them home. Once the panels are home, you can unhitch the trailer and take your high ef-

Fig. 3–28. A small utility trailer, like the Coleman Versatrailer shown here, can enable you to purchase an economy car and still handle the occasional bulky load.

ficiency car on a 40 or 50 mile per gallon trip without carrying along the extra space you needed to carry the panels. For the price difference between a highly efficient small car and a bigger, less efficient wagon, you can probably buy a utility trailer and have enough cash left over to buy a good set of stereo components or enough fuel to drive for a year or so. In tests conducted by the author, the utility trailer shown in Figure 3-28 required extra fuel at the miserly rate of just one-half gallon per 100 miles of travel, which means that the trailer can be pulled about 200 miles for each gallon of fuel it causes the car to consume. Not bad. Where else can you find something that gets 200 miles per gallon and has the ability to handle 4 x 8 panels lying flat?

BUYING A USED CAR

When shopping for a used car, you should look for the same characteristics, features, and options you would want in a new car. The only problem is that there is very little chance that you'll find everything you're looking for in a single used car. However, you should still keep in mind the advice offered earlier so that you can better estimate the probable fuel mileage of an individual used car with its particular combination of options, accessories, dimensions, and weight.

A very important consideration in the purchase of a used car is the mechanical soundness of the car you have in mind. Whereas a new car has a reasonable warranty, a used car bought from a dealer may have only a short guarantee period, and one purchased from an individual owner will have none at all.

Most of the mechanical factors that can significantly affect gas mileage can be checked by you, if you're mechanically-inclined, by a mechanic in whom you have great faith, or by a diagnostic clinic. My recommendation is to take a proposed used-car purchase to a diagnostic clinic. Whether you're buying from a dealer or from an individual, if the car is as good as he or she says it is, the seller shouldn't mind your having a diagnostic center check it out.

At a diagnostic center—the Mayo clinic of the automotive world—technicians will connect everything but an IBM computer to the car in order to give it a complete "physical," determine what work may be necessary to bring it up to snuff, and advise you of the costs and consequences involved. Considering the benefits, the cost of having the used car checked at a diagnostic center is an excellent investment. Modern diagnostic equipment has the advantage of being able to test a car's key components while they are actually performing their critical jobs.

If there are no diagnostic centers in your area, the best alternative is to bring the prospective purchase to a *trusted* mechanic who you know will give you a reliable soundness report.

Armed with the center's test report or a mechanic's evaluation, you will be in a better position to decide whether the chariot you are considering is a gem or a lemon. If the tests uncover an expensive defect in the car, turn it down and you've saved a bundle of repair money, not to mention the substandard fuel mileage its mechanical problems may have caused. If the tests are favorable, buy the car, then drive and maintain it intelligently to keep it in the good shape it's in.

If you're buying (or have already purchased) a used car, you may wish to call the NHTSA (National Highway Traffic Safety Administration) hotline to find out what, if any, safety recalls have been undertaken since the car was manufactured. All you have to do is call the toll-free number (800-424-9393) and give the clerk the year, model, and serial number of the vehicle. You can then find out if the car has ever been included on a manufacturer's recall list, the reason for any recalls, and correct any problems that may not have been taken care of by the previous owner.

Chapter 4
Driving for Efficiency

Whether you drive a Cadillac, a Volkswagen, a moving van, or a milk truck, you can improve your fuel efficiency by remembering a few basic rules and applying them to the driving situations you encounter. While short formulas never tell the whole story, here is one to keep in mind the next time you fill up:

Travel at low, steady speeds
+ Maintain your car's momentum
+ Anticipate conditions ahead
+ Accelerate moderately
+ Be patient
= More miles per gallon

Fig. 4–1. Regardless of your present vehicle and the driving conditions you face, chances are you can get between 5% and 10% more miles from each tankful just by adopting fuel-efficient driving habits. If you really try, you should be able to do even better, with 20% not unlikely.

The forces you're up against don't know or care how much money you spend for gasoline. They've been described in Chapter 2 and are listed below to refresh your memory:

Air resistance
> + Rolling resistance
> + Acceleration resistance
> + Gravity resistance
> + Engine resistance
>> = Fewer miles per gallon

Besides knowing the facts and opposing forces, inspiration will also be important. Like pole-vaulting, in which one's opponent is the crossbar, or sprinting, where the runner fights a stopwatch, driving for efficiency is an individual event in which you're competing both with yourself and with the miles per gallon figure calculated from the odometer and gas pump. By approaching driving for efficiency as a challenge, and not as drudgery, your fuel mileage may even exceed that of less-inspired friends who happen to own smaller cars. Economy-run reporters who confide that "you won't approach the fuel mileage of Mr. XYZ, but here are some little tips for you" imply that Mr. XYZ has some magical abilities you lack. Don't believe it—give that little extra effort and you'll see.

SMOOTH AND STEADY WINS THE FUEL EFFICIENCY SWEEPSTAKES
Low Speeds Save Fuel

The expense of driving at higher speeds is evident in Figure 4-2. When traveling at a constant speed, each model was most efficient at about 30 to 40 miles per hour.[1] At speeds over 40 mph, higher air resistance attacks a car's frontal area and causes efficiency to drop sharply. When you double your speed, you need eight times as much horsepower to fight air resistance. At speeds below 40, tire rolling resistance is the major factor causing low gas mileage. Another study revealed that a car getting 19.7 miles per gallon at 40 mph delivered only 18.3 at 50 mph, 16.2 at 60 mph, and just 14.2 at a speed of 70.[2]

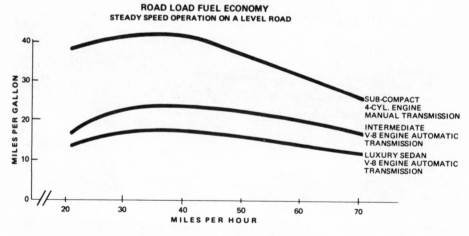

ROAD LOAD FUEL ECONOMY
STEADY SPEED OPERATION ON A LEVEL ROAD

Fig. 4–2. Speeds of 35–40 mph are best for maximum economy. (*Source:* G. J. Huebner, Jr., and D. J. Gasser, "General Factors Affecting Vehicle Fuel Consumption." Paper presented at National Automobile Engineering Meeting, Society of Automotive Engineers, Detroit, Michigan, May 15, 1973.)

Your car will deliver its best fuel mileage at moderate speeds in the neighborhood of 35–40 miles per hour. When it's not possible to maintain this most efficient speed, do the next best thing and travel as slowly as possible without becoming a safety hazard. A 10% increase in your speed (e.g., from 50 to 55 mph) will require a 33% increase in the horsepower you need to overcome air resistance. Greater increases are even more costly, as shown in the following table:

Increase in speed	10%	33%	Increase in horsepower
	20%	73%	required to overcome
	30%	120%	air resistance
	40%	175%	
	50%	240%	
	60%	310%	

When higher air resistance is translated into reduced fuel efficiency for a typical automobile, the results may be predicted by using the California Highway Patrol data contained in Figure 4-3. For example, if you drive an average vehicle and reduce your speed from 65 miles per hour to the national speed limit of 55, you can expect to save 12% on the amount of money you're spending for fuel.[3]

Regardless of the vehicle, higher speeds will mean less efficiency. However, don't feel too sorry for the driver of a diesel-powered car. For example, the driver of diesel-engined Volkswagen Rabbit may find his or her fuel efficiency dropping from 65 miles per gallon at 40 mph down to a mere 50 mpg at a speed of 55.[4] (Actually, with the five-speed option, both of these efficiency figures are likely to be a bit higher than for the four-speed transmission with which the vehicle was equipped in these tests.)

Maintain a Constant Speed

By keeping your speed as steady as possible, you'll conserve your car's momentum and reduce its fuel consumption. Unnecessary changes in speed can be quite wasteful. For example, by letting your speed fluctuate between 55 and 65 mph, instead of maintaining a constant 60, you can lose between 1 and 1.5 miles per gallon.[5] When you're traveling at a steady speed, acceleration resistance isn't present and it doesn't matter as much how heavy your car is.

Another reason why constant speeds are best is that air resistance increases far more rapidly than your increase in speed. Remember that doubling your

Initial Speed

	70	65	60	55	50	45	40	
70	0							
65	6	0						
60	12	6	0					**Percentage**
55	18	12	6	0				**of**
50	23	17	12	6	0			**Fuel**
45	27	22	17	11	6	0		**Saved**
40	31	27	22	16	11	6	0	
35	34	30	25	20	15	10	4	
32	34	30	25	20	15	10	4	

Reduced Speed

Fig. 4–3. This table shows the approximate percentage of fuel saved by reducing speed on a typical car. For example, by lowering your speed from 65 mph to 50 mph, fuel consumption will go down by about 17%. (*Source:* California Highway Patrol.)

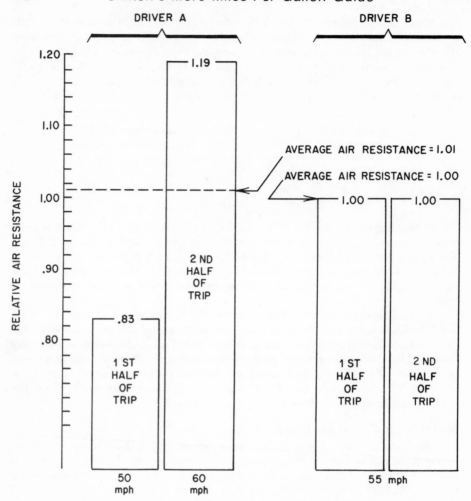

Fig. 4–4. Because air resistance increases faster than your speed, driver B, who drives a constant speed during two halves of a trip, will encounter less air resistance than driver A, who has traveled at two different speeds along the way. While the 1% difference is not dramatic, it's just one more reason why steady speeds are best.

speed quadruples the air resistance you will encounter. In Figure 4-4, driver B has driven an entire trip at a steady 55 miles per hour, while driver A drove at 50 miles per hour for the first half and at 60 mph during the second half of the trip. As a result, driver A will encounter an average of 1% more air resistance during the trip, which will contribute to his achieving lower fuel efficiency along the way.

If your car doesn't have a cruise control device, you can practice until you can do almost as well as the machine. When driving on an open highway, glance at your speedometer every ten seconds or so. If your spot-checks show, for example, readings of 57, 60, 65, 59, 56, you're not doing very well. Keep practicing until the readings are very nearly constant, for example: 60, 60, 61, 59, 60. This type of practice is an excellent application of the little extra effort we talked about earlier.

Accelerate Moderately

A jackrabbit start may be good for hares, but it's very expensive for your car. A rapid getaway can use twice as much gasoline as a more moderate, gradual start. In moving off from a stop, try to get into a high gear as soon as the engine will accept the load. With an automatic transmission, this means a very light foot on the throttle so that high gear will be chosen as early as possible. With a manual transmission, don't over-speed the engine in the lower gears—learn to shift up at the minimum speed the engine will accept in the next higher gear.

If you drive an emission-controlled car equipped with a transmission-controlled spark (TCS) retard mechanism (see Chapter 5), it's even more important for you to get into high gear as soon as possible. In these cars, unnecessary use of the spark-retarding lower gears will keep your engine running without spark advance (inefficiently) for a longer period of time.

Brake Sparingly

The world's most expensive magic trick is the one you perform when you change gasoline into brake lining dust. Every time you step on the brake, you're dissipating momentum that the engine worked hard to build up. Don't use the brake more often than is really necessary. Just as a polite cowboy might tip his hat to ladies on the street, some drivers touch their brake at practically every turn in the road.

Frequent panic stops are a sign that you aren't driving as economically as you could. While panic stops are necessary at the time they're made, most of them reflect that the car was traveling too fast in the first place. Although you don't hear much about "jackrabbit stops," they aren't economical either. Some of the worst braking offenses include charging a stop sign only to screech to a halt; braking unnecessarily while traveling uphill; rushing into a turn, then applying the brake; not releasing the handbrake completely; and "riding" the brake.

As an indication of how little the brakes can be used, consider that two men once drove from Detroit to Los Angeles without once touching their specially sealed brake pedal.[6] While you needn't go to this extreme, remember that hitting the brake isn't free—it's paid for by your fuel dollar.

Pass Smoothly

If you're driving for maximum fuel efficiency, you probably won't be passing anything except gas stations. However, when you must pass, accelerate as gradually as possible and increase speed only to the level that safety requires. This may be difficult to do, as we all have a bit of race-driver within us that tempts us to whip right out there and show the other guy what a real car can do. Making an impression on the person you're passing will also make an impression on your fuel bill.

Merge Smoothly

We've all been in the sidewalk or doorway situation where we meet another person and play the guessing game of who goes first. When merging onto an interstate or other major highway, the same thing happens. Interaction with other cars tends to upset the smoothness of your driving. If you simply blast onto the highway with eyes straight ahead, you've wasted fuel as well as risked your neck. If you timidly creep up to the highway itself, you'll be forced to accelerate for all you're worth just to keep your car from becoming a hood ornament on a Kenworth. Either strategy will reduce your fuel efficiency.

By trying to "fit in" with the traffic with which you're merging, and by making use of the full acceleration distance provided by the highway engineers, you

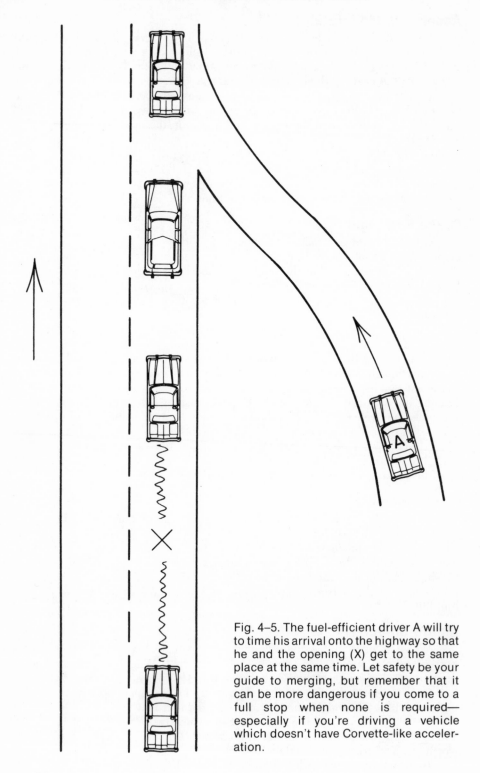

Fig. 4–5. The fuel-efficient driver A will try to time his arrival onto the highway so that he and the opening (X) get to the same place at the same time. Let safety be your guide to merging, but remember that it can be more dangerous if you come to a full stop when none is required— especially if you're driving a vehicle which doesn't have Corvette-like acceleration.

can maintain your momentum, speed up at a more gradual rate, and save fuel. Figure 4-5 shows how the fuel efficient driver should merge onto a limited-access highway with fast-moving traffic. The same basic strategy applies to any merging situation—anticipate the opening *before* it becomes available to you.

SOME LITTLE THINGS THAT MEAN A LOT
Steady at the Wheel

By keeping the steering wheel as motionless as possible, you'll minimize the side-to-side movement that increases both the distance you must travel and your tires' rolling resistance along the way. Each little change in direction interrupts your car's considerable momentum and the front tires will demand just a little more horsepower for their work.

A Drag Eraser

If your car is equipped with disc brakes, and if you sometimes drive for long distances on a very straight road, here's a tip that can make a slight reduction in your rolling resistance. Disc brake pads, instead of retracting away from the rotor, will drag lightly against it after you've released the brake pedal. Your front wheel bearings, if adjusted properly, will have a very small amount of looseness, or "play." If you keep your foot off the brake, then make a left turn followed by a right turn, play in the wheel bearings will move the rotor just enough to push the brake pads very slightly back into their housings and reduce their drag on the rotor. Once you're on that straight piece of road, the normal act of passing and returning to your lane can provide enough sideward force to retract the pads ever so slightly.

Don't Pump the Gas Pedal

It wouldn't help your fuel mileage if the neighborhood kids decided to refill their squirt guns from your tank. However, every time you press down on the gas pedal, you activate a squirt-gun-like device called the accelerator pump. Thinking that you want to accelerate, the faithful gadget shoots some raw gasoline into the engine to smooth the transition from steady speed to acceleration.

Some economy-run drivers have been known to disconnect the accelerator pump in order to avoid the squirt-gun effect. However, this is neither necessary nor safe for everyday driving purposes. By moving the gas pedal very slowly when you accelerate, you can fool the accelerator pump and save the gas it would otherwise squirt into the engine. To see for yourself how much gasoline is wasted by this pump, turn the engine off, remove the air cleaner, hold the choke valve open, and manipulate the throttle. With the help of someone observing the carburetor throat, you can even practice pressing on the gas pedal until you have a better feel for how fast it can move before the accelerator pump goes into action. For safety, make sure you have the engine turned off and are not smoking when either observing or practicing. Because raw gasoline squirted into a stopped engine will thin the oil, it's also advisable to do your accelerator-pump practicing just before you change oil.

Rule Out That Barrel

On most later model cars equipped with a two-barrel carburetor, one will do the work under normal conditions and the second will operate only at high speeds or when extra power is needed. When in the same gear, pressing to a certain point of the acclerator pedal movement will cause a slight surge in the engine's power and a change in the sound it's making. By becoming familiar with the point at which your second barrel is activated, you can avoid the drop in economy that accompanies its use. This advice goes double for readers driving four-barrel carburetors.

However, many older domestic cars with two barrel carburetors do not have this progressive opening sequence. Therefore, both barrels are always operating, which requires the driver to have a very light foot.

Open Windows Waste Fuel

At highway speeds, a fully open window will increase your car's air resistance and lower your miles per gallon. On a warm day, it's better to crack the vent windows slightly and use the flow-through ventilation with which your car may be equipped. If you don't have flow-through ventilation, crack open as many windows as necessary and use cool air from the conventional heater-defroster air system. If your car has flip-open rear windows, as shown in Figure 4-6, your conventional venting or flow-through system will be able to move more air through the car if these back windows are opened slightly.

Economy-run drivers have been known to swelter inside their cars in order to avoid opening a window and suffering the penalty of increased air resistance. At very low speeds, air resistance is less important and it's not as expensive to lower the windows. However, you can leave them up and your friends will think you have air conditioning.

Turn Off the Heater Fan

When traveling at speeds over 40 miles per hour, you're wasting fuel by turning on the heater-defroster fan. At these speeds, normal air resistance will force plenty of air through the intake of your heating-ventilation system. Unnec-

Fig. 4–6. If your car has flip-open rear windows, opening them slightly can make it easier for fresh air to enter and flow through the vehicle, reducing the need to fully open the front windows or to use the air conditioner or ventilation fan.

essary use of the fan places an extra load on the alternator, which in turn places an extra load on the engine. The electric fan, depending on its size, design, and running speed, may consume between 4 and 24 amperes of electrical current. An alternator forced to supply 40 to 50 amperes will lower gas mileage by .5 to .9 miles per gallon.[7] As with so many other consumers of your gasoline dollar, the electric fan should be used only when you need it.

Spare the Air

If your car has air conditioning, use it sparingly. The fan in an air-conditioned car will tend to draw electrical currents in the higher end of the 4 to 24 ampere range mentioned above. Use of the air conditioner will also require engine horsepower to operate the compressor unit and to activate the magnetic clutch which keeps the compressor engaged.

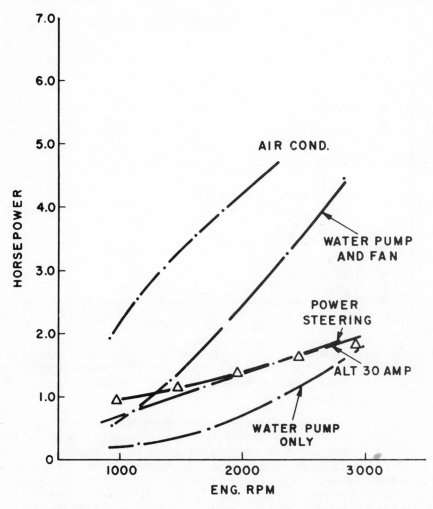

Fig. 4–7. Power requirements for engine-driven accessories increase as the engine runs at higher speeds. For the large size vehicle in this test, the air conditioner compressor required more than four horsepower at an engine speed of 2,000 rpm. (*Source:* C. W. Coon and C. D. Wood, *Improvement of Automobile Fuel Economy*, SAE Paper No. 740969, 1974.)

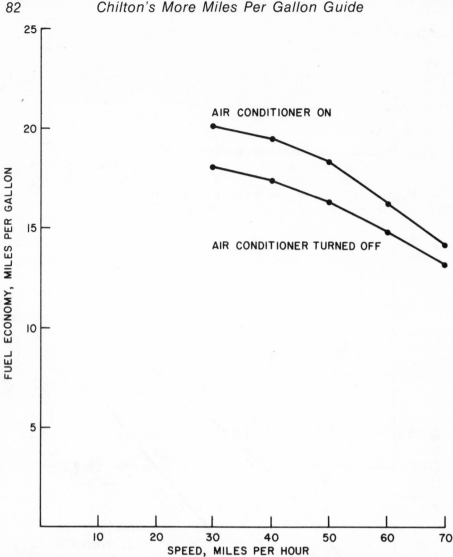

Fig. 4–8. In this test, use of the air conditioner reduced efficiency most in the moderate speed range. When traveling at higher speeds or into stiff headwinds, the fuel efficiency difference will tend to be less.

Figure 4-7 shows the number of horsepower required to operate the air conditioning compressor and other engine-powered accessories in tests conducted on a standard size vehicle.[8] At an engine speed of 2000 RPM, operation of the air conditioning compressor required over four horsepower. Figure 4-8 compares the average fuel efficiency of test vehicles with and without their air conditioning units in operation at steady speeds.[9] Depending on the speed traveled, drivers lost between 1.0 and 2.2 miles per gallon by turning on the air conditioner. While 1.0 miles per gallon difference at 70 mph may seem irrelevant because of the 55 mph national speed limit, remember that the important factor is your car's speed relative to the air. For example, driving 55 miles per hour into a 15 mph headwind will provide about the same effect as 70 mph through still air.

In Chapter 3 it was stated that it may be more efficient in some vehicles to use the air conditioner with the fan on a low speed instead of driving with the windows fully open. While this may be true for some vehicles that lose a great deal of aerodynamic advantage with the windows fully lowered, that have a small passenger compartment volume to cool, or that are being driven into a stiff headwind at highway speeds, it is generally advisable to avoid using the air conditioner unless you are in extreme physical distress and are willing to trade fuel efficiency for personal comfort.

Avoid Idling

That breakfast-table warm-up might make your car warm and toasty by the time you've finished your pancakes, but you've been getting zero miles per gallon in the process. It's much more efficient to start out from cold and warm up the entire car at the same time—at least you'll be getting miles from gasoline otherwise wasted in a standing car. The same advice applies to drive-in banks, movies, ice-cream stands, hamburger stands, and gas stations. If you know that you're going to be stationary for more than a minute, you'll save fuel by shutting off and restarting instead of allowing the engine to idle.

One situation in which idling is preferable to restarting your engine is whenever you arrive home and prepare to put the car into the garage. If you have no automatic garage door opener, or if it is impossible to easily remove the garage door key from your key ring, you'll have to shut off the engine, open the garage door, then restart the engine to put the car into the garage. By having an automatic door opener or using a more handy key ring, you can avoid the fuel and wear penalties of a restart.

While Your Car Warms Up

Any professional athlete knows that it takes a gradual warm-up before going full tilt. Arm-conscious baseball pitchers don't take all those warm-up tosses just so the management can sell more popcorn. Your car also needs to warm up before it can run most efficiently, which in cold-weather driving may take over five miles.

After sitting in the driveway during a wintry night, your car is as stiff as an arthritic statue. Engine oil is like molasses, wheel bearing grease has the consistency of window caulking, and other lubricants are also too thick to properly flow between the moving parts. After you've started the engine, wait until the oil pressure warning light goes off, then move off and drive more slowly than usual for the first few miles. Rolling resistance during this period will be very high, and you'll save fuel by going slower against the extra drag.

When starting a cold engine, don't speed it up to the point where it sounds like pistons are about to come bursting through the hood. Besides wasting fuel, this can damage moving parts that are not yet fully lubricated. Instead of racing a balky engine, let it idle for half a minute or so until it is smooth enough to move the car.

Remember that a prolonged warm-up in the driveway is needless idling and a waste of fuel. If you limit your stationary warm-up to no more than half a minute, you'll be rewarded in two ways: first, you will obtain more miles from the fuel you buy; second, your engine will last longer, since an idling engine will warm up more slowly and incur more wear than one which is gently driven for the first few miles.

When You're Going the Wrong Way

When you're traveling down a busy two-way road and discover that you're headed in the wrong direction, there's a fuel-efficient answer to your problem. Figure 4-9 shows two ways of handling this dilemma. You can turn right, as

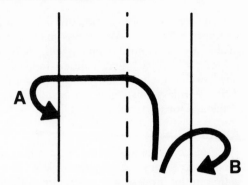

Fig. 4–9. Two possible ways to turn around when you discover you're headed in the wrong direction on a busy two-way road. Text tells why driver A saves fuel.

driver B did, then attempt to turn left in order to get going in the desired direction. However, driver B has a problem: before he can turn back onto the highway, he must wait until two lanes of traffic are clear—a long wait on many busy roads. Driver A, on the other hand, drove a little further in the wrong direction until he could make a convenient turn into a parking lot or street on the left side of the road. Once there, he only needed to wait until one lane of traffic was clear, which is more probable than two lanes being clear at the same time. If the road is very crowded, driver A will be headed in the proper direction while driver B is still back there playing the "It's-OK-to-the-left-what-about-the-right?" game and idling away his fuel.

Making That Difficult Left Turn

It's all but impossible to turn left onto a four-lane road that is crowded with cars but uncontrolled by a stop light. Yet many drivers sit at the intersection and waste their fuel while praying for an opening that stretches across all four lanes at the same time. A safer and more efficient approach is to turn right and go a short distance until you can turn left into a street or lot, then come back in the direction you wanted to go in the first place. Through a little creative thinking and going with the flow of traffic, you can often find more efficient ways of getting to your destination. It can often be more economical to "use" the traffic flow instead of fighting it.

When You Reverse

When you want to back up, use the brakes to stop the car completely, then shift into reverse and apply the gas. It's more efficient to stop the car with the brakes than it is with the engine. Likewise, if you're already traveling backward, use the brake to stop before you shift into first or drive and step on the gas. Reversing a car's momentum in either direction takes energy, of which the engine is an expensive source. With today's automatic and synchromesh transmissions, it's all too easy to use the engine to do a job more efficiently done by the brakes.

If you have enough room, and if laws and safety conditions permit, making a U-turn will help you maintain your momemtum and use less fuel than would be required by a back-and-forth reversing maneuver. Since highway U-turns are almost universally illegal, U-turns can save you fuel primarily in parking lots, service stations, and other similar areas.

TAKING TO THE HILLS

In getting the best fuel mileage your car and driving conditions can deliver, hills can be very important. Like the stock market, they either go up or down—

and, as the successful stock trader knows, each direction calls for a different strategy.

The Down Start

When starting from rest on your way down a hill, let gravity give you a hand. With a manual shift, allow the car to drift a few feet before you engage the clutch. Depending on your car and the steepness of the hill, you may even be able to start off in second gear instead of first. Allowing gravity to change your momentum from stopped to moving will mean less wear on your clutch and more miles to your gallon. If you drive an automatic, you can also make use of gravity's pull on your car. Just keep a soft touch on the gas pedal and gravity will help you get into your economical high gear in a very short time.

The greater ease of accelerating downhill is one reason why it's a good idea to stop on the right side of a downhill road whenever you need to read the map or stop for fuel, food, or whatever. Your engine is at its thirstiest when you ask it to accelerate up a hill.

Skipping a Gear

Though skipping a gear is a common fault of novice drivers, skipping a gear when accelerating downhill can reduce wasteful throttle manipulations (remember the accelerator pump) involved in the ritual of shifting through all the gears when they're not really necessary. Going from first to third or from second to fourth can save fuel when you're accelerating downhill—but be careful not to lug the engine (drive in too high a gear for your speed).

The Up Start

Starting from rest on an uphill road calls for your foot on the brake until the very instant that you begin to accelerate. Otherwise the engine will have to reverse the car's momentum from downhill drift to uphill acceleration. For an automatic transmission, this is relatively easy—all you have to do is keep your left

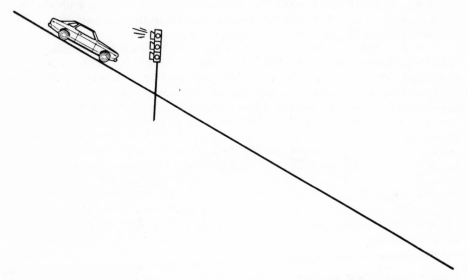

Fig. 4–10. When you're accelerating away from a downhill stop sign or red light, you may be able to save fuel by skipping one or more gears if you drive a manual transmission.

foot on the brake until your right foot has begun to press the gas pedal. With a manual transmission, the problem can be a little harder on both your clutch and your fuel mileage.

If you're driving a stick shift, keep the handbrake applied until the clutch is almost engaged and the engine is just starting to move the car. With a little practice, you should be able to start on a hill without drifting back at all. The secret is correct timing in releasing the handbrake—too soon and you'll drift, too late and you may stall the engine. Needless to say, the stick driver is going to waste both fuel and clutch lining if he rides the clutch in order to hold his position on a hill.

Driving the Ups and Downs

Except for the most extreme circumstances, don't ever accelerate while climbing a hill. You'll be using fuel far out of proportion to the little speed you may pick up. If acceleration is inefficient on a level road, it's downright wasteful on the way up a hill.

If you drive a heavy car, especially one with an automatic transmission, don't poke along on your way up a hill. Gradually press the gas pedal in order to maintain your momentum before you reach the hill, but remember not to accelerate too much. Automatic transmissions tend to "lock up" and become more efficient at higher speeds, so it pays to climb quickly. Learn not to approach a hill with any more initial speed than you need in order to easily maintain momentum on the way up. Likewise, don't put your foot to the floorboard in an impossible attempt to maintain speed on a very steep grade. If a hill starts to win the momentum contest, be a good loser—slow down as it dictates and continue climbing at a rate that feels comfortable.

In a small car, allow your speed to drop slightly as you climb. Keep the gas pedal steady if you're not slowing down too quickly, press down gradually if you are. If you're driving a manual transmission, don't be afraid to downshift if necessary—you'll get better fuel mileage by allowing the engine to run at a more efficient speed. Don't worry about traveling slowly as you reach the peak. This speed is easily picked up as you gradually accelerate on the way back down.

Regardless of the car you're driving, let gravity help you gain speed on the downhill side. Any extra fuel you use here may well be wasted by a sharp curve on the way down or by a stop sign at the bottom. Follow the stock trader's example and don't invest expensive fuel into a hill that's on its way down.

If your car is relatively low-powered and has a manual transmission, you will probably find yourself traveling in a lower gear as you reach the peak of a hill. If

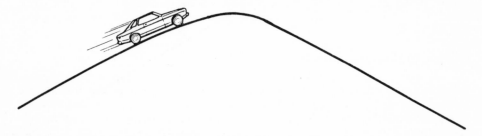

Fig. 4-11. If you drive a low-powered car with manual transmission, shift into a higher gear just *before* you reach the peak of a hill. By the time you complete your shift, you will be on the way down and your acceleration will be assisted by gravity.

the road heads downward at the top, you can save fuel by shifting into a higher gear just before you reach the peak. In this way, you will have already reached the peak and started down by the time you have completed your shift. This helps in two ways. First, by shifting into a higher gear earlier, you have reduced the number of engine revolutions (and engine friction) during this distance. Second, you will top the hill at a slightly lower speed and may not have to brake as often or as hard on the way down (remember that the brakes are indirect consumers of fuel).

For some drivers, placing the transmission in neutral and coasting downhill may be a strong temptation. Don't do it—for a number of good reasons:

1. It's illegal in many places.

2. In today's steering-lock-equipped cars, a driver coasting with the engine off might remove the ignition key by force of habit, thus locking the steering wheel when the car is moving at high speed.

3. It can damage the internal parts of an automatic transmission. (In neutral, no fluid is being pumped through the transmission, and the engine does not shift easily in and out of drive when the car is moving.)

4. It increases the load on the brakes and makes them more likely to overheat and fail on a steep hill. (Neutral removes the force of engine braking, which helps slow the car.)

YOUR DRIVING ENVIRONMENT
The 12-Second Rule

Knowing what's going to happen before it does is an asset in any business and likewise with driving. The sooner you know what's ahead, the quicker you can prepare for it in order to use less fuel along the way. Don't just think about where your car is right now. Consider the conditions you'll be facing in a few feet, in fifty yeards, or maybe even a couple of miles. By anticipating upcoming conditions, you can react immediately with gas-saving actions that will enable you to maintain your momentum, accelerate more slowly, drive more steadily, or avoid a wasteful sudden stop.

The U.S. Department of Energy has recommended that you look *at least* 12 seconds ahead of your present position in order to anticipate and adjust for circumstances which might influence your strategies for fuel efficient driving. If you get into the habit of anticipating where you'll be in twelve seconds and adjust immediately for this future position, you will have made a great deal of progress toward becoming the most fuel efficient driver you can be. In the city, this 12 seconds may mean a distance of a half block or less, while on the highway the same 12 seconds may cover as much as a quarter of a mile. The 12-second rule is excellent advice to keep in mind when you drive. But it is *general* advice. Some of the "messages" your driving environment delivers may provide much more than 12 seconds time in which to adjust, while others may give you only a few seconds or less.

Buffer to Relieve Gas Pains

As we've discussed, driving smoothly and moderately is an important component of fuel efficient driving. However, in order to achieve the smoothness and gradual changes of speed that efficiency requires, you need to have "space" in which to operate. Try to keep at least two seconds worth of space between you and the vehicles to your front and rear. As with the 12-second rule, the exact distance will depend on how fast and under what conditions you're traveling.

To check on the front section of your "buffer zone," watch the vehicle in front of you as it passes any stationary object or marking, such as an expansion

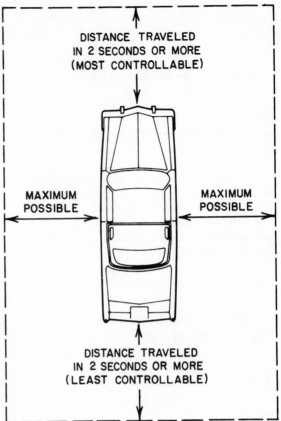

Fig. 4–12. By keeping a buffer zone around your vehicle, you'll have time to adjust safely and efficiently to changing conditions ahead and beside you. Try to stay at least two seconds worth of distance behind the driver in front. If a tailgater squeezes the rear of your zone, you should react by increasing your front buffer zone even further. After receiving a visual stimulus, it can take half a second for a typical driver to make the transition from gas pedal to brake, so the buffer zone is essential to safety and fuel efficiency.

DISTANCE TRAVELED
IN 2 SECONDS OR MORE
(MOST CONTROLLABLE)

MAXIMUM
POSSIBLE

MAXIMUM
POSSIBLE

DISTANCE TRAVELED
IN 2 SECONDS OR MORE
(LEAST CONTROLLABLE)

joint, then count to yourself to determine if at least two seconds pass until you get to the same point. If you get there before two seconds, you're too close and should back off a bit for both safety and fuel efficiency. The same technique may be applied to the vehicle behind, although you have less control over his speed than you do your own. In driving in multi-lane traffic, try to maintain a suitable buffer zone on *all* sides of your car. By doing so, you'll have more time and space in which to adjust in a fuel-efficient manner to the conditions around you.

In some cases, you may wish to retain more than a two-second buffer space between you and the vehicle ahead—for example, if you find yourself following a very inefficient driver, you should consider extending your front buffer zone beyond the two seconds distance. Likewise, if you are being followed too closely, you may have to enlarge your front buffer zone in order to compensate for the shrinkage at the rear. In case of a panic stop, you will then have enough room for both yourself and your tailgater to react without incident.

Read the Signs

"Stop sign ahead" should automatically tell you to get off the gas pedal and gradually slow down. Ignore this advance notice and you'll be just another magician who turns gasoline into brake lining dust. Other such warnings are "traffic signals ahead" and "toll booth ahead." Whenever a sign tells you that *anything* is ahead, it's bound to affect what you should do if you're driving for economy.

"Hill next two miles, trucks gear down" practically screams that any fuel you

Fig. 4–13. When you see a sign like this one, your car has valuable potential energy, so don't use any more gas than necessary in getting from here to the down-hill slope.

Fig. 4–14. If you were thinking about passing that driver up ahead, relax for a few curves and enjoy the scenery.

Fig. 4–15. Sign at right tips off the fact that this hill is going to start down very abruptly once you get to the top.

use between here and the steep hill is going to be wasted on the way down. Another hint that you should lighten up on the gas is the presence of a mountain elevation or summit marker.

"Curves ahead" describes a driving condition where you can save fuel by flowing slowly and smoothly, instead of rushing from one curve to the next. If you happen to be following someone you'd like to pass, back off and forget about it as soon as you see this sign.

"Merge ahead" tells you that you're going to have to interact with cars going in the same direction, and that you'd better check your speed, traffic spacing, and length of acceleration lane if you're going to get through the experience while using the least possible amount of fuel.

"No passing zone," "school zone," and "narrow bridge ahead" are all signs which can increase your fuel efficiency. By anticipating stops, slow-downs, and other special conditions, you can take your foot off the gas pedal earlier and slow down more gradually. Whether a sign warns of a rough road, falling rocks, or a troll under the bridge, chances are it's something for which you'll have to slow up. After all, there aren't many signs urging you to drive faster.

Reading the Red Lights

On frequently-traveled roads, learn to "read" the red lights ahead. If the lights are synchronized to encourage a certain speed, try to maintain that speed. If you see that a light is going to turn red before you reach it, ease up on the gas and approach the light as slowly as you can. If the light turns green, you've maintained your momentum and can accelerate more economically. If it's still red when you arrive, you've saved some fuel during your gradual approach. Hurry-up-and-wait isn't good for your fuel mileage. If you know that a certain stop light stays red for a long time, don't ruin your efficiency by rushing to it from far away when it's green. Even if you do have to stop for a seemingly perpetual red light, you can save fuel by turning off the motor while you're waiting.

Use Your Share of the Road

By anticipating successive curves and determining how you can utilize your lane to get through them in the shortest distance, you can shorten the length of a trip, better maintain you car's momentum, reduce your tires' rolling resistance, and get better fuel mileage. Not much better, but remember that all these little things add up. In general, by keeping to the inside of curves, you'll minimize the length of any trip, but be sure to stay in your own lane while you're doing it.

Use the Most Efficient Part of Your Lane

On many roads, gradual wear and tear has produced grooves in the roadway where most of the traffic has been traveling. Such grooves may also be the result of motorists using studded snow tires. In any case, the grooves are about the width of the distance between your wheels, are often more coarse than the remaining sections of the lane, and can collect appreciable amounts of water or snow. Figure 4-16 shows the grooves that can form in a road or lane. The rest of the lane is appreciably smoother (and requires less energy to roll the tires) than the grooves themselves. Whenever possible, it is a good idea to avoid driving in these grooves—not only does their rougher surface increase rolling resistance, but on rainy days your tires may tend to "hydroplane" on the water they have collected. If you live in a state where the roads are smooth and the grooves nearly non-existent, congratulations. If not, you can gain another increment of fuel efficiency by driving to either side of them.

The same type of advice applies whenever a section of a lane has been

450 Ways to Stretch Your Fuel Dollar

Following are 450 fuel-saving tips that summarize the information in this book. They are arranged according to the four principal strategies suggested—buying, driving, maintaining, and planning for fuel efficiency. In some cases a short explanation is provided to show why the tip works or its approximate potential for saving fuel. Not all of the tips will apply to your particular situation and some will have minimal effect, considered alone, but when you add them all up the savings can be considerable. If, using the tips in this book, you can't increase your mpg by 10%, you're just not trying.

BUYING

1. Buy a vehicle with the smallest frontal area that meets your needs. The result will be less air resistance for a given amount of carrying capacity.

2. Buy a vehicle with a streamlined shape rather than a more boxy design. More streamlining means a lower drag coefficient and more miles per gallon. Use either judgment or drag coefficient data, and remember that some shapes may be more streamlined than they look.

3. Select your next car with *typical*, not once-a-year uses, in mind. If you need a large station wagon only twice a year, buy a smaller car and rent or borrow the big wagon on those occasions when it's really necessary.

4. Use the EPA *Gas Mileage Guide* when comparison-shopping for a new car. It's available at new car dealers, or by writing to *Gas Mileage Guide*, Pueblo, Colorado 81009.

5. If practical, don't buy a car at all—consider more efficient substitutes for your transportation needs.

6. Don't buy any vehicle on impulse. Decisions made in haste are often regretted (and costly) over a long period of time. Avoid showroom fever and think about your decision at least overnight.

7. Buy the smallest, lightest car which will meet your transportation needs. Think "small is sensible" instead of "bigger is better."

8. If you've already read Chapter 3, read it again before making your decision. Think "efficiency" during the purchase process.

9. Buy for fuel efficiency instead of self image. Buy more expensive clothes or find other ways to express yourself.

10. For best efficiency and versatility, buy a compact or subcompact wagon. With the same frontal area, carrying capacity will be considerably greater than for the comparable sedan.

11. Sit in the car in the showroom for at least five minutes to see if it will be

1

comfortable during long periods behind the wheel. Note the presence or absence of arm rests, awkward positioning of arms, legs, or back. It's better to feel a little foolish for five minutes than to be very uncomfortable (and inefficient) for thousands of miles.

12. If your driving will include many long trips, buy more comfortable seats if they are available. Being uncomfortable will make you less patient and reduce fuel efficiency.

13. Before buying, look under the hood and check the accessibility of important service points. Whether or not you do your own tune-ups, the work is more likely to be done right if the job is easier.

14. Buy the standard gasoline engine instead of opting for a bigger-displacement alternative, which will be heavier and thirstier.

15. Buy a stratified-charge gasoline engine if it is available.

16. Buy a diesel engine if it is available. Fuel efficiency is likely to be about 50% greater than that of a comparable gasoline engine.

17. Select a diesel or gasoline engine which is turbocharged. The result will be the efficiency of a small engine with the power (upon demand) of a larger engine.

18. Buy an engine with a fuel-injection system. It allows better control of the engine's fuel requirements and emissions under a wide range of conditions, resulting in several extra miles per gallon.

19. With other factors equal, select a car with a higher voltage or electronic ignition system for better efficiency between tune-ups.

20. Don't buy automatic transmission unless convenience is more important than efficiency or you regularly pull a trailer. The penalty can be as much as 15%.

21. If you buy a car with automatic transmission, get one with a locking torque converter or an automatic overdrive function.

22. Buy a five-speed or overdrive manual transmission if you are even moderately proficient with your hands and feet.

23. Select an economy rear axle ratio (one that is numerically lower, e.g., 2.56 instead of 3.00) if available. The result will be fewer engine revolutions and better efficiency at highway speeds. A 10% reduction in the axle ratio can improve fuel efficiency by 2% to 5%.

24. Buy a limited slip differential if you live in a marginal snow area. You may be able to reduce your dependence on snow tires, which have high rolling resistance, without losing traction on hills.

25. Buy cruise control to maintain efficient and legal speeds during highway travel.

26. Drum brakes are better for fuel efficiency (normal disc brake drag can amount to a .5 mpg penalty), but the disc type is superior for all-around use.

27. Buy a car with front wheel drive and you'll have better traction, less drivetrain power loss, and more interior room for a given vehicle size.

28. Don't buy power steering or brakes unless you are physically impaired or you must purchase a vehicle which needs their assistance. Power steering can cost 1 mpg under some driving conditions.

29. Don't buy power windows, seats, or door locks unless absolutely necessary. They add expensive weight and use energy.

30. Purchase intermittent windshield wipers to avoid the electrical drain of constantly using the wipers during periods of very light rain.

31. Buy an air-conditioner cut-out which shuts off the compressor during passing, hill-climbing and other situations in which its power drain can be inefficient or dangerous.

32. Consider not buying an optional rear window wiper and washer system. The extra weight of the wiper, drive motor and fluid reservoir will add up with other accessories to less fuel efficiency.

33. Buy a high-quality set of the new generation of high-pressure radial tires designed to provide less rolling resistance without sacrificing riding comfort.

34. Buy slightly oversize radial tires for fewer engine revolutions per mile and (if you haven't gone overboard on tread width) less rolling resistance.

35. If you think you can't afford radial tires, do some calculations and think again. They are between 3% and 10% more efficient than belted bias tires, and fuel savings in this range can be considerable over the long run.

36. If you really can't afford radial tires, at least make the switch to bias ply tires which have tread belts for less rolling resistance.

37. Avoid selecting jumbo or oversize tires with a very wide tread. They may look nice, but they'll cost you money every mile you drive. The main reason is rolling resistance, but they also weigh more and require larger, heavier wheels.

38. Buy standard-size aluminum or alloy wheels for lightness.

39. Buy a space-saver spare tire. Besides being lighter, it will make more trunk space available to help you avoid carrying items on the roof.

40. Don't purchase a vinyl top. The rough surface increases air resistance.

41. If you live in a warm climate, buy a light-colored car to reduce the need to lower windows or use the air conditioner.

42. If you live in a cold climate, buy a dark-colored car to reduce the need to operate the heater and its fan.

43. Buy tinted windows if you live in a warm, sunny climate. They help reduce the buildup of interior heat and the need to use the air conditioner.

44. *Don't* buy tinted windows if you live in a cold climate. Clear windows will allow solar power to help heat your car.

45. Buy a set of halogen headlights. They produce light more efficiently and can save a fraction of an mpg.

46. Avoid the added weight of undercoating. Rustproofing adds some weight, but it is worthwhile to protect your car. No rustproofing at all is likely to provide a slightly more efficient car which won't last as long.

47. Don't buy bumper guards. They add extra weight and can reduce the aerodynamic "cleanness" of the body.

48. Don't buy extra seat covers. They add weight and just make the car look a little better for the next owner. For resale, add the covers just *before* you decide to trade.

49. Don't purchase side view mirrors which aren't really going to be used. They will add to air resistance and reduce fuel efficiency.

50. Don't install extra lighting (e.g., fog lights) which will add weight, increase air resistance, and use electrical power.

51. Don't modify the front hood to resemble a Rolls Royce, include fake air scoops, or otherwise make your car more cosmetic but less aerodynamic.

52. Don't install ornamental hood fixtures (flying bullfrogs or other "radiator cap" centerpieces).

53. Don't buy an air-resistant front "license" plate to tell the world what kind of car you drive, who your girl friend is, or to make some other point.

54. Don't buy mud flaps unless cleanliness is more important than aerodynamics and efficiency.

55. Install a front spoiler to reduce wind resistance at highway speeds. The result can be an mpg improvement in the 2% to 4% range.

56. Unless you're a very poor parker, don't burden your car with the extra weight and air resistance of curb feelers on the side of the vehicle.

57. Extra soundproofing packages will add weight in addition to absorbing noises from the engine and drivetrain. For better efficiency, accept a car that has less weight and a little more noise.

58. Don't purchase or use additional floor covering materials if you don't really need them. Rubber floor mats can add five pounds or more to vehicle weight.

59. Use cardboard instead of heavy rubber floor mats. If cardboard doesn't suit your fancy, compromise by selecting plastic mats which are as thin as possible.

60. Don't purchase after-market suspension additions like anti-sway bars unless performance is more important than economy. Add-on items mean extra weight to be hauled around.

61. Don't buy the trailer towing package unless you really need it. It is likely to include a less-efficient rear axle ratio along with other fuel consumers.

62. Don't buy or install a permanent roof rack. It will increase aerodynamic drag and reduce efficiency even when it's not carrying anything.

63. With other factors equal, select a vehicle with a large trunk. This will help avoid using a roof-top carrier or rack to haul luggage or bulky items.

64. Select a car with a large-capacity fuel tank. With a less-frequent need to fill up, you'll be able to avoid going to a higher-priced station simply because you don't have the range to reach one which is less expensive. This is also an advantage during rationing periods when odd-even plates or weekend closings may be a factor in determining whether you get to where you're going.

65. Buy a locking gas cap to help you keep the expensive fuel you've already purchased.

66. With other factors equal, select a vehicle with water temperature and electrical system instrumentation to help you detect fuel-efficiency malfunctions as early as possible. An alternative is to buy the gauges and install them yourself.

67. Consider buying and using a vacuum gauge to help you practice driving efficiently.

68. If your car has a tachometer, consider it as a fuel-efficiency device rather than as a high-performance instrument. If you don't have a tachometer, consider buying one and using it to keep your engine operating at efficient rpm's.

69. For the best possible instrument to measure and improve fuel efficiency, buy a fuel consumption meter which registers increments of .01 gallon or .01 liter of fuel used since resetting. With this accuracy, you can evaluate fuel-saving strategies for driving even very short distances.

70. Don't install a tachometer or other instrumentation on your hood. Likewise, avoid the kind of vehicle which has this non-aerodynamic feature.

71. Select a good-quality radio and speakers to help you maintain a patient, efficient state of mind on the highway.

72. Buy a CB radio to help keep you alert to possible problems, and their solutions, during both long and short trips. CB can help in finding open gas stations, food and lodging, and in keeping you informed and entertained.

73. Buy an under-dash mounting bracket for your CB radio so that the radio can be removed and its weight will not be a factor during everyday driving.

74. Buy a gutter-clamp or magnetic-mount CB antenna instead of a more permanent unit. Benefits include reduced air resistance when the CB isn't used and less likelihood of theft.

75. Buy a combination AM/FM/CB radio antenna so that only one mast will be necessary. This helps reduce air resistance and disguises the fact that you have a CB that's available for theft.

76. Buy a radio antenna which can be retracted for less air resistance.

77. Use a windshield antenna for even less air resistance, especially if you live in an urban area with good radio reception.

78. Don't buy and use a radar detector. If you're driving efficiently, you shouldn't need radar warnings.

79. When buying a second vehicle, choose one that complements your present car so that you'll be able to use the most fuel-efficient vehicle for every travel requirement. If you already have a large station wagon for all-around use, get a subcompact for the majority of trips when all that room isn't really needed.

80. Don't buy a pickup truck or van if you're just going to use it as a car.

81. If you do need a pickup truck or van, get diesel power if it's available.

82. If you do need a pickup truck or van, buy a mini-truck which fits your needs.

83. If you buy a van, use it for vanpooling if possible.

84. Buy a small utility trailer to bridge the gap between the small car you would like to have and the big gas-guzzler which is needed once in a while to haul bulky goods. These trailers are inexpensive, efficient, and versatile.

85. When pulling a high-profile trailer on a highway trip, consider purchasing a roof-top wind deflector to decrease air resistance.

86. If you trailer-camp, buy a low profile trailer which doesn't require over-size fender mirrors for rear visibility.

87. Buy a camper or trailer which folds down for more efficient highway travel.

88. Buy a wind deflector for your motorcycle.

89. Don't buy a trail bike for use on the highway. Gear ratios and tire types will be less efficient.

90. Don't buy knobby tires for use on a street motorcycle.

91. Before buying a used car, have it checked at a diagnostic center. The low cost of the check can help avoid buying an inefficient or worn-out lemon.

92. If you're buying (or have bought) a used car, call the NHTSA (National Highway Traffic Safety Administration) hotline to find out what, if any, safety recalls have been undertaken since the car was manufactured. Some of these problems may have an important bearing on fuel efficiency and can be corrected. The number is 800-424-9393.

93. Be suspicious of any "miracle" mpg improvement device. Chances are that it will be a miracle if it really works. When claims are extraordinary, there's usually a good reason for skepticism.

94. If available, buy an electric car for short trips. It won't use any gas at all.

DRIVING

95. Approach fuel efficient driving as a skill to be improved, a personal challenge instead of a belt-tightening chore. Take an interest in efficiency and try to be good at what you do.

96. Accelerate at a moderate pace rather than too fast or too slow. Fast acceleration wastes fuel by spending more distance in the lower, less efficient gears; slow acceleration wastes fuel because the engine will not be producing power efficiently.

97. Maintain your car's momentum whenever possible by avoiding full stops which are not required by legal or safety considerations. Accelerating from even 2 mph is easier than accelerating from 0 mph.

98. Don't accelerate more frequently than is absolutely necessary.

99. When accelerating with a manual transmission, get into high gear as quickly as possible.

100. When accelerating with an automatic transmission, ease up on the throttle in order to encourage the transmission to change into high gear as soon as possible.

101. With a multiple-barrel carburetion system, don't accelerate more rapidly than the point at which the secondary barrels open. This stage can be recognized by practice.

102. Keep the transmission in high gear whenever possible, but don't lug the engine.

103. Slow down before reaching the speed bumps installed in some residential and other streets. By slowing down in advance, application of the brakes will not be necessary.

104. Take your foot off the gas as soon as you see the traffic light turn red. Don't rush to the red light only to screech to a stop.

105. When approaching an intersection, be aware of "bunching up" and "spreading out" of cross traffic. If the light is red your way, and cross traffic is spread out and not accelerating, chances are the light will soon turn green and you can avoid a complete stop. If, on the other hand, the light is red your way and cross traffic is still bunched up and accelerating, chances are that you'll have to stop, so take your foot off the gas very early.

106. Every time you lift your foot from the gas pedal, ask yourself: "Could I have done this sooner?" If the answer is "yes," you've just wasted some fuel.

107. Don't downshift to slow the car during normal driving. Apply the brakes gently.

108. Don't use panic braking to avoid potholes and road irregularities. Take your foot off the gas and use engine resistance to slow down early.

109. Don't tap the brakes at every possible occasion, such as rounding slight curves at low speeds. You're wasting fuel if you do.

110. Whenever you apply the brakes, think "Did I really have to use the brakes?" or "By planning ahead, could I have avoided having to slow down?" The best sign of an inefficient driver is frequent and severe application of the brakes, which wastes fuel.

111. If you find yourself making frequent panic stops, chances are you're driving very inefficiently.

112. If you've just filled the tank, try especially hard to avoid rapid stops, starts or corners which may result in fuel spillage.

113. Don't tailgate. You'll be jumping back and forth between the brake and accelerator, a situation which is dangerous as well as inefficient.

114. When following a "brake-tapper" or other inefficient driver in a no-passing situation, either stop for a coffee break or give the car ahead a lot of space so that you won't have to react to his every action.

115. Don't allow yourself to be tailgated into driving inefficiently. Use emergency flashers to alert the tailgater that he's too close. If this doesn't work, find a convenient stop to pull over and let the individual pass.

116. If you become stuck on snow or ice, don't waste fuel and tire wear by spinning the wheels at a high rate of speed. Be gradual in the application of power and you'll have a better chance of getting going.

117. Ease off the gas pedal before entering a curve. Don't charge into a curve only to hit the brakes upon finding you're going too fast.

118. Don't pump the gas pedal or move it unnecessarily, since this actuates the accelerator pump and wastes fuel. Apply pressure slowly and steadily instead of just flooring it. Abrupt movements are wasteful of fuel.

119. Try to position your right foot in a steady position with the ball of the foot making contact with the gas pedal. The result will be better sensitivity and control and better mileage.

120. Don't rest your left foot on the clutch or brake pedals. Find a more comfortable and fuel-efficient location.

121. Don't wear heavy shoes or fashion boots when driving. They will encourage heavier pressure on the accelerator and will reduce your sensitivity to gas pedal manipulations.

122. Drive as if you have a fresh egg between your right foot and the gas pedal.

123. Drive as if fuel costs $5 a gallon.

124. If fuel already costs $5 a gallon, plan on using a moped for your next family vacation.

125. If your car has a lot of electrically operated accessories, don't use them unnecessarily. They use fuel indirectly by means of the alternator, which is engine-powered. This includes heater fan operation, shaving on the way to work, and unnecessary manipulations of the electrically operated windows which you shouldn't have purchased in the first place.

126. Turn off the air conditioner or heater a mile or two before your destination. Residual cool or warm air will keep you comfortable while you save fuel over the last section of your trip.

127. Turn off the air conditioner before parking. This will reduce the load on the electrical system whenever the car is restarted. The same advice applies to windshield wipers, heater fan, and other electrical accessories which indirectly consume fuel.

128. "Lights on for safety" is good policy when necessary, but the practice will use extra fuel during daytime driving.

129. Don't use high beam if you don't really need it. Besides blinding other motorists, you'll be using more electricity, which means more fuel consumption.

130. Remember to turn your lights off after leaving a tunnel during daytime travel.

131. Don't depend on the rear window defroster to clear ice and snow from the rear window. It consumes a great deal of electricity which the engine must supply. Constant use of this device will cost a fraction of an mpg and make it less likely that your car will start after a cold winter trip. Use a scraper instead—it is faster and uses no electricity.

132. Disconnect the electric seat warmer if your car has one. Wear thicker pants or carry a blanket out to the car with you. Like electric rear window defrosters, electric seat warmers use a lot of electricity and power.

133. For less air resistance and better efficiency, drive with the windows closed, especially at highway speeds.

134. If necessary for comfort, minimize the air resistance penalty by just cracking the windows open slightly.

135. If your car is equipped with flip-open rear windows, open them slightly and use the flow-through ventilation for interior comfort without sacrificing fuel efficiency.

136. In warm weather, make the best use of dashboard and other fresh air vents to avoid the necessity of lowering windows and reducing gas mileage.

137. Be familiar with your car's heating and ventilation controls so that you won't have to over-use the heater fan in order to keep the windshield clear.

138. During cold weather, you can make it easier for the heater to bring warm air into the passenger compartment if you crack open a vent window. This is especially useful on older cars which may be more air-tight and lack flow-through ventilation design.

139. During cold weather driving on the highway, don't waste energy by using the heater fan at speeds over 35 mph. Normal air resistance will force air into the car in sufficient quantities for most vehicles.

140. When driving through a cross wind during warm weather, it can be more efficient to crack open a window on the side of the car opposite the direction from which the wind is blowing. This assists the flow-through ventilation and reduces the amount of air buffeting.

141. If you must use the air conditioner, set it on the lowest possible setting which gets you close to being comfortable. By doing so, you can at least minimize the 1 to 2 mpg penalty the air conditioner demands.

142. When beginning a trip in hot weather, lower the windows for a few blocks so that built-up heat can be partially dispersed in order to reduce the load when the air conditioner is turned on.

143. Watch roadside flags, clotheslines, and trees for cues to cross winds and headwinds, and adjust your speed and ventilation accordingly.

144. If you're driving into a headwind, don't try to make up time. Remember that air resistance is a function of your car's speed relative to the air around it, so 55 mph into a 10-mph headwind will result in about the same fuel efficiency as traveling 65 mph through still air.

145. To lower air resistance, keep the sun roof closed or install an air deflector in front of it.

146. When driving a convertible, keep the top up for lower air resistance and better fuel efficiency.

147. Don't try to make up time when driving through cold, dense air or precipitation. Air resistance is proportional to the density of the air, and fuel efficiency will suffer.

148. Drive at speeds in the 35 to 40 mph range whenever possible. For most cars, this is the pace at which the maximum miles per gallon is obtained.

149. If driving 35 to 40 mph is not feasible, drive smoothly with the flow of traffic, or at the lowest highway speed which is safe.

150. Observe all speed limits. At 65 mph, your fuel consumption will be at least 12% greater than at 55 mph. Generally, the slower and smoother you go, the better.

151. For traffic signals on frequently traveled routes, learn the timing and synchronization patterns used for various times of the day, then drive at the speeds which the traffic planners had in mind.

152. Be your own automatic speed control by keeping a close watch on your speedometer and being aware of the noise level of the engine.

153. If you have an automatic speed control, use it whenever conditions permit.

154. Check the accuracy of your speedometer, especially after you've installed a new set of tires on your driving wheels.

155. Use simple mathematics and the techniques described in the book to construct your own "tachometer."

156. Use a vacuum gauge to practice efficient driving techniques.

157. Use a fuel consumption meter to monitor the success of your efficiency efforts and to evaluate alternate routes to the same destination.

158. Use a tachometer to keep your engine operating in the most efficient portion of its speed range.

159. As a convenient reminder, put a card on the sun visor or dashboard to indicate efficient shift points and speed ranges for your car.

160. Be sure to read the owner's manual for the right way to start your car under various conditions. Using improper starting procedures can waste fuel.

161. Don't use the "breakfast-table idle" to warm up your car while you finish your coffee. Idling cars get zero miles per gallon.

162. Don't carry coffee with you when you leave for work in the morning. You'll increase the likelihood of inefficient driving habits, especially with a manual transmission car.

163. Drive gently during the first few miles until tires and lubricants have a chance to warm up a bit.

164. During a start in the downhill direction, use gravity to assist your increase in momentum for the first few feet.

165. During a downhill start with a manual transmission, you can probably save some fuel by skipping a gear. This reduces engine revolutions and throttle manipulations, both of which tend to increase fuel consumption. Take advantage of gravity whenever the opportunity arises.

166. During an uphill start, use the brake, not the clutch or transmission, to keep the car from drifting backward.

167. Anticipate passing maneuvers so that you won't have to shift down or use passing gear in order to safely overtake the car ahead.

168. If you drive an automatic transmission, don't activate "passing gear" except in emergency situations. Making "passing gear" a normal part of the driving routine increases both fuel consumption and engine wear.

169. Anticipate "merge" situations so that you can fit into the traffic opening at the same time it arrives at the merging area. This helps eliminate unnecessary acceleration or braking so you can blend efficiently into the traffic flow.

170. Don't be a "lane-jumper" in rush-hour traffic. The small amount of time saved will be offset by heavy safety and efficiency costs.

171. Change lanes smoothly without excessive acceleration and without having to apply the brakes. This requires successfully anticipating the opening before it arrives.

172. Use highway signs as clues to fuel-efficient strategies. For example, "Hill ahead, trucks gear down" tells you that any extra fuel you use to reach the hill will be turned into brake lining dust on the way down.

173. When approaching a hill, try to build up speed before climbing—acceleration on the way up can be very wasteful. This is especially important for small cars which have low-power engines.

174. When climbing a hill, don't rush over the top. By backing off slightly before the peak, there will be less need to use the brakes on the way down the other side.

175. If you've shifted down in order to climb a hill, shift to a higher gear just *before* you reach the peak. The result will be fewer engine revolutions and better efficiency, and gravity will help you to pick up speed on the way down.

176. Don't be tempted to save fuel by coasting down hills. Brakes may overheat and fail, speed may become too great for safe control, and (if the ignition key is inadvertently removed) the steering wheel could lock and cause an accident. However, it is not necessary to apply the gas pedal when moving down a hill.

177. Drive on efficient road surfaces whenever possible. A gravel road will reduce fuel efficiency by about 35%, a patched-up asphalt road by about 15%.

178. When other factors are equal, select roads which have already been cleared of snow. A snow-covered road can cost 1 mpg or more.

179. During winter driving on snow-covered roads, follow in the tracks of those who have gone before you. It's fun to make fresh tracks, but the rolling resistance is considerably higher.

180. On any road, use the most efficient part of your lane whenever possible. On some roads, patched sections, rain-filled grooves, and potholes will reduce gas mileage by increasing rolling resistance. On concrete surfaces, studded snow tires or heavy truck traffic may cause some portions of the lane surface to be more coarse (and less efficient to travel) than others.

181. If you're stopping at a traffic signal where there is a bump or pothole, try to stop with your wheels on the forward side of the obstacle. Otherwise, you will have more resistance to overcome when you start out.

182. When approaching a railroad crossing, slow down in advance to avoid the brake, then select the smoothest section to travel so that you needn't slow down more than necessary.

183. Where it is legal, remember to turn right after a stop at a red light instead of waiting for the light to change. The less fuel you use idling at an intersection, the better your mileage.

184. At weight-activated traffic signals, know where the contact patch is and go over it slowly. By moving slowly, there will be a greater chance of the light changing before you are forced to come to a stop.

185. When stopped at a red light, place the transmission in neutral to reduce the load on the engine. With a manual transmission, don't hold the clutch pedal down, since this will tend to cause increased wear of the throwout bearing.

186. Don't rev the engine when stopped at a traffic signal. Besides wasting your own fuel, you'll encourage other drivers to do the same and waste theirs as well.

187. Shut off the engine if you are going to be stopped for more than one minute. Less fuel will be required for restarting than for idling for this time period.

188. If you're sitting in a gas station line, shut off the engine between moves. If there are no line-jumpers, move two spaces on each engine start for even less waste.

189. When possible, time your left turns to coincide with the arrival of an opening in oncoming traffic. This helps to avoid having to slow down unnecessarily or stop altogether, both of which waste fuel.

190. If you find it unsafe or nearly impossible to turn left across a busy highway, turn right, go with the flow, then turn left into a parking lot or other area and head in the direction you originally intended to travel.

191. Upon approaching an intersection where time delays can be lengthy, consider taking the easiest route through the intersection, then changing direction to end up in the direction originally desired.

192. When alternative routes are of comparable distance, avoid traveling the ones that have traffic signals or construction zones.

193. Keep a steady steering wheel position to minimize side-to-side movement that increases both distance traveled and rolling resistance.

194. On winding roads, minimize trip distance by driving on the inside of curves, but be sure to stay in your own lane.

195. If you're in a carpool, be sure to use express or carpool-only lanes when they are available.

196. During adverse weather conditions, don't be the "front door" in a convoy of vehicles. You can drive much more safely, smoothly, and steadily if you follow someone else through the snow and sleet, leaving a comfortable distance between you and the car ahead.

197. Although some have done it and lived, don't try to save fuel by "drafting" in the wake of a large truck—not even in an emergency. Commercial vehicles have enough decorations on the back without your car becoming one of them.

198. Consider the driving environment at least 12 seconds ahead of your present position, then act accordingly for best fuel efficiency. If you're always reacting to immediate events only, your mpg will be a disaster.

199. To help avoid fuel-wasting interactions with other motorists, keep a two-second "buffer zone" between you and the vehicle ahead of you and behind you.

200. Time your arrival at a stop sign to coincide with the departure of the last car to leave. Otherwise, you'll have to make stop-and-start position changes until it's your turn.

201. Use your rear view mirrors to help anticipate traffic openings so that passing and lane changing can be accomplished as smoothly as possible. This strategy also helps you to avoid getting boxed in behind a slower motorist on a multiple-lane highway.

202. In heavy commuter traffic involving frequent stops and starts, look at least two cars ahead to get early cues for acceleration and braking in order to better moderate your speed and improve mpg.

203. When driving any low-powered car, remember that planning maneuvers far ahead of time is even more important than for an average vehicle.

204. When you're in stop-and-go traffic at night, in the rain, or in a tunnel, you can anticipate stops and starts by noticing the reflections of brake lights of the vehicles ahead. Then moderate your speed to avoid complete stops and sudden starts.

205. Remember that pulling a trailer involves more weight to be accelerated and stopped, so try even harder to anticipate conditions ahead so that you can conserve the momentum of your car-trailer combination.

206. Don't wear earphones or play the radio too loudly when you drive. Such isolation from your driving environment will take your mind away from driving efficiently and can involve you in very dangerous situations.

207. Be aware of unusual mechanical noises which may be symptoms of future fuel inefficiency or other problems. Especially noteworthy here are squeaking air conditioner compressor, water pump, air pump or power steering bearings, which waste fuel when they become worn and more difficult to turn.

208. Know your car's dimensions so that you can drive smoothly on narrow streets or in tight quarters.

209. Practice running over paper cups or between two rows of cups so that you're better aware of the position of your car's wheels. This will be advantageous when you wish to avoid potholes, fallen mufflers from other vehicles, and inefficient coarse or patched sections of your lane.

210. Practice your parking techniques so that you won't waste fuel while making a large number of back and forth motions to get into a space.

211. In order to reduce fuel-wasting maneuvering and possible body damage, select a parking space with plenty of room in front and back. The beginning or end of a block is generally a good choice.

212. Backing with a trailer is not really very difficult, but you should practice at least briefly in a vacant parking lot before you tackle the tighter confines of a campground. Practice with the trailer empty and on a level area.

213. After a stretch of very hard driving, run the engine at a fast idle for a minute or so in order to dissipate cylinder head heat. This is especially important for a diesel-powered car. Follow the manufacturer's recommendations regarding shut-off idling instructions.

214. Use a key chain which permits easy removal of the garage door key without removal of the ignition key. Otherwise, you'll have to restart the car after opening the garage door, which will waste fuel in addition to causing needless wear and tear on the starting motor.

215. If you have an automatic garage door opener, send the "open" message far enough in advance so that you don't have to interrupt your momentum any more than necessary on your way into the garage.

216. Don't rev up the engine before shutting if off. This is a popular habit which can lessen fuel efficiency and increase engine wear. Raw gasoline will remove oil from pistons and cylinder walls, then run down into the crankcase and dilute the engine oil.

217. If your car continues running ("dieseling") after you've turned off the key, have the engine tuned or do it yourself.

218. Change lanes and return to retract disc brake pads slightly when driving on a highway where braking is infrequent.

219. To help ensure minimum drag, make sure that your handbrake is in the "off" position. Even though the warning light has gone off, the brake might still be slightly applied.

220. Lower the radio antenna to the minimum level necessary for good reception. Extra extension causes extra air resistance.

221. Relax behind the wheel. Drive by the fuel gauge, not by the clock, and don't worry about maximizing your average speed. Patience permits you to drive smoothly and steadily, increasing your miles per gallon. Urgency and haste will only increase your inefficiency.

222. Be especially patient when you're driving an un-turbocharged diesel. Even with your foot on the floor, you won't break any necks with acceleration, so forget about being in a hurry.

223. Recognize "pipeline" situations where you are stuck in a line of traffic and have no alternative but to poke along with the crowd ahead. These circumstances are frustrating but offer a good test of the fuel-efficient driver. Loss of temper means an automatic "flunk."

224. Be courteous behind the wheel. Like excessive braking, discourtesy and the use of expletives are sure signs of driving inefficiency.

225. Don't drive when you're tired or angry. If your passengers are tired or angry, try not to become upset.

226. When traveling with others on a long trip, change drivers frequently— and do it at your normal rest or refreshment stops. You'll increase fuel *and* driver efficiency.

227. If you pull off the road to switch drivers or whatever, try to select a downhill stretch of road. This will reduce the amount of fuel required to get back up to speed after resuming your trip.

228. Have someone who has read this book ride with you to provide an objective evaluation of how well you're following the advice contained here.

229. Test your skill by entering an economy run.

MAINTAINING

230. Don't waste fuel dollars by using a gasoline of a higher octane than your car really needs.

231. Different batches of gasoline can vary in density (energy content per gallon), and an unexpectedly high mph performance may be partially due to this variation. If so, go back to the same source next time.

232. Buy gasohol if it is approved by the vehicle manufacturer. Cleaner running, higher octane, and fuel savings are among the benefits being claimed for this alcohol-gasoline mixture.

233. Know how to translate your "E . . . F" fuel gauge reading into the number of gallons which will be required to fill the tank. If a "minimum purchase" restriction is being applied, be sure that your tank will hold the minimum amount without spillage.

234. To avoid expansion spillage and the tendency of some attendants to put the last quarter's worth on the side of your car, don't ask for a complete fill up unless necessary. Carry change to discourage topping off to the nearest half dollar.

235. Save money and spilled fuel by pumping your own gas at a self-service station.

236. Diesel fuel tends to "foam" during a fillup, so don't rush the process if you'd like to get a complete tankfull.

237. Turn off the engine when refueling. Besides wasting fuel, an idling engine can be dangerous and illegal in this circumstance.

238. When buying fuel, be sure that the pump has been reset to zero. Otherwise, you may be paying for the preceding customer's fuel as well as your own.

239. On older gas pumps which can't "handle" dollar-a-gallon prices, fuel may be sold according to the price per each half gallon. In these instances, you (or the station attendant) must multiply the price shown by two in order to arrive at the correct amount. Double-check to be sure your calculation matches that of the attendant.

240. At a self-service station where you've purchased a number of dollars' worth, the pump will shut off when the limit has been reached. If you keep the nozzle in the filler neck and lift the pump hose, you'll be able to get even more fuel for your money.

241. Some fuel stations have plastic guards which seal the gap between the filler nozzle and tank opening to reduce fumes during refueling. Since you can't use fuel which escapes into the air, try to frequent stations which are equipped with such devices.

242. When buying fuel, note the slope of the filling area and position your car accordingly in order to get a complete fill.

243. If you can't position your car properly to take advantage of the station slope, use a block of wood to raise the appropriate corner of your car. Being eccentric can help ensure a complete fillup—a benefit well worth the embarrassment during shortage and crisis periods.

244. After filling up on a hot day, don't park your car in the sun, especially with the filler neck at the downhill side of the car.

245. Don't be ashamed to drive out of a station if you arrive at the pump and the price is not competitive with other nearby sources.

246. Carry a diesel fuel directory if you drive a car requiring this kind of fuel. Mercedes-Benz and others publish listings of the more than 15,000 diesel stations across the U.S. Such a directory can help you locate several alternative stations so you can get the best price.

247. Be sure that your fuel cap is the proper one for the car. An improper fit can increase spillage or evaporation of gasoline.

248. After filing up make sure that your fuel filler cap has been replaced and tightened down.

249. Check the sealing gasket on the fuel cap for cracks and deterioration which can lead to evaporation or spillage.

250. Wash your car frequently to remove dirt and mud, which adds weight and air resistance. Don't forget the underside of the car and the wheel wells, especially if you live in an area where road salt is applied.

251. Wash your car with plain water to avoid removing the wax coating which is already present. That coating helps reduce friction and air resistance.

252. If you're making body repairs, sand all surfaces until they're smooth, even if it's an older car that doesn't seem worth the effort. Smooth surfaces will have less air resistance.

253. For top performance, use a high-quality, SE-rated oil in your gasoline engine.

254. Use a high-quality, CC-rated oil in your diesel engine unless the vehicle manufacturer recommends a different grade.

255. Use an oil which has been formulated for fuel efficiency—they really do work. Mileage improvements of 2% to 5% are not unusual.

256. For even greater gains in mpg, add a friction modifier (such as molybdenum disulfide) to make your engine oil even more slippery. Check with your dealer for recommendations and warranty requirements.

257. Use a multiple-viscosity engine oil whenever it is among those recommended for your usage conditions. The result will be much better efficiency and less engine wear, especially during short trips in cold weather.

258. Whether or not you use multiple-viscosity oil (which is generally best for fuel efficiency), use the lightest viscosity oil for the driving conditions you will be encountering. Again, follow manufacturer's recommendations for specific viscosity applications.

259. Change engine oil and filter at the recommended intervals. Just topping up isn't good enough, because combustion byproducts eventually contaminate the oil, and anti-wear additives become depleted.

260. Check engine oil only after the engine has been stopped for several minutes. This will give circulating oil a chance to settle into the crankcase and reflect a more accurate reading of oil level. Overfilling the crankcase will increase engine resistance as the crankshaft and connecting rods dip into the oil and slow down slightly on each rotation.

261. Clean or replace the fuel filter at the recommended intervals. This is especially critical on fuel-injection models where the filter may separate water from the incoming fuel in order to protect the injectors from corrosion.

262. On some models with a diesel engine, the fuel filter will have a water drain valve to allow periodic removal of water which has been trapped inside. If this item is ignored, an expensive injection system may be damaged.

263. Check fuel lines for cracks and leakage. Aside from being dangerous, fuel which never reaches the engine won't produce any power.

264. Clean or change the engine air filter at the recommended intervals or sooner. Every gallon of gas requires about 9,000 gallons of air, and a clogged air filter can easily cost 1 mpg or more.

265. Purchase good-quality oil filters and other replacement parts when they are on sale. Buy in multiple quantities and save even more. If you do your own maintenance, this saves fuel and money.

266. Use rear axle oil and manual transmission lubricants of multiple viscosity, if approved by the manufacturer, and use lubricants with the lowest possible viscosity range for your driving conditions.

267. For greater efficiency, add a suitable extreme-pressure friction modifier (e.g., molybdenum disulfide) to the rear axle and manual transmission lubricants. Remember that manufacturer recommendations should be heeded, especially where warranty questions may arise.

268. Maintain automatic transmission fluid at the proper level. If it is overfilled, the result can be excessive slippage which will waste fuel.

269. Wheel bearings and suspension fittings require grease at very infrequent intervals for most cars, so use only the best-quality lubricants for these jobs. Don't hesitate to spend a bit more to get a brand which is specifically formulated for extra-low friction.

270. Install magnetic drain plugs in the engine, transmission, and rear axle. These collect a surprising amount of metal particles which would otherwise be mixed with the lubricant. Some vehicles may have these plugs as standard equipment.

271. Check weather sealing for flexibility and tightness. Whether it's the air conditioner in summer or the heater in winter, you don't want to waste fuel while making the inside temperature more comfortable.

272. Apply rubber lubricant to keep weather sealing in good condition. Besides helping fuel efficiency, this will help the resale value of your car.

273. Be sure that your battery is sound, will hold a charge, and has clean terminals and connectors which don't create unnecessary resistance for the alternator to overcome or excessive periods of cranking before the engine starts.

274. A defective battery or voltage regulator may force the alternator to keep the battery at a higher voltage than it is capable of holding. In this case, the energy used to produce this electricity has been wasted.

275. If you have a weak battery that you're forced to nurse along during cold weather, use a battery charger to lightly charge the battery. In this way, you'll be using house current instead of the vehicle current which costs fuel dollars.

276. Don't waste fuel by charging the battery by idling the engine in the driveway. Use a home battery charger or buy a new battery.

277. Batteries are heavy. When replacing yours, purchase the smallest one which meets your needs.

278. A defective or clogged PCV valve will allow an improper combustion mixture to enter the combustion chamber and reduce fuel mileage. The valve costs only a few dollars and is well worth the periodic investment.

279. Check the condition and tightness of accessory drive belts. If they're too tight, worn bearings, greater engine resistance, and less fuel mileage will be likely results.

280. Tune up the engine when it's necessary. The 10% to 15% mpg improvement will be well worth the effort.

281. Have cylinder compression checked to ensure that the engine will really benefit from a tune-up and is capable of producing good fuel efficiency.

282. If fuel efficiency has been low, even after a tune-up, excessive fuel pump pressure may be forcing more fuel than is needed into the carburetor or injection system.

283. If your engine has mechanical valve lifters, have the clearances checked at the recommended intervals. Improper clearance will cause excess wear or valve damage and adversely affect gas mileage.

284. Have engine idle set at the lowest point within the recommended range specified by the manufacturer.

285. Some cars have an idle-speed step-up system for increasing idle speed when the air conditioner is in operation. On other vehicles, you may be able to save some fuel by reducing idle speed slightly when colder weather arrives and the air conditioner will not be used.

286. Adjust carburetor idle mixture to the most efficient setting allowed by the limiting cap or other mechanical constraint. A rich setting will waste fuel both at idle and at low engine speeds.

287. Check the carburetor mounting flange and intake manifold for looseness which can allow unwanted air to enter and disrupt the air-fuel mixture that is so critical for efficient engine operation.

288. Check the carburetor accelerator pump to ensure that it is not squirting more fuel than is really needed during the transitional stage of switching from steady speed to acceleration.

289. Don't try to save fuel by disconnecting the carburetor accelerator pump. You'll lose the ability to accelerate quickly in an emergency, a loss which the small amount of fuel savings can't justify.

290. Have your carburetor rejetted if you move from a low altitude area to one of higher altitude. At higher altitudes, sea-level carburetion will tend to produce a mixture which is too rich and fuel-expensive.

291. If your engine has a viscous-type cooling fan which "slips" on its hub according to the temperature of the air around it, check to be sure that the fan does not wobble on its hub. If it is too loose, vibrational forces will increase engine resistance and may eventually persuade the fan to fly into the radiator, causing no small amount of damage.

292. If your engine has a conventional cooling fan, consider replacing it with a viscous-type fan or a thermostatically operated electric fan, either of which will provide better efficiency under highway conditions when the cooling fan isn't really needed.

293. Consider replacing the steel bladed fan with a flex-fan.

294. If the temperature gauge runs unusually cold, or the heater doesn't produce much heat, the thermostat may be stuck in the open position, causing the engine to operate at a temperature which is too cool for maximum fuel efficiency. The result can be a mpg penalty of 3% or more.

295. If the temperature gauge runs unusually hot, or the heater seems like a blast furnace, the thermostat may be too hot for your driving conditions. Possible engine damage could result, leading to efficiency problems in the long run.

296. If recommended by the manufacturer for use in cold climates, install a higher-temperature thermostat for winter operation.

297. Don't remove the thermostat for better fuel efficiency—it won't work. Although coolant pumping losses will be reduced, the car will take much longer to warm up and will run at temperatures too cool for best economy.

298. Check the exhaust system for dents and restrictions. A clogged exhaust system will increase engine resistance and lower your fuel mileage.

299. When replacing a muffler or exhaust pipes, be sure of a proper fit. A system that drags, or hangs too low, can lead to exhaust system damage as well as greater air resistance because of increased air turbulence beneath the vehicle.

300. If legal and available, install a dual or low-restriction exhaust for less engine resistance.

301. Periodically inspect and lubricate the exhaust manifold heat control valve. If it's stuck in either the open or closed positions, reduced fuel efficiency and increased engine wear are likely.

302. Watch for black exhaust smoke. It indicates a mixture which is too rich for best efficiency. This could be caused by a number of problems, including a clogged air cleaner or a stuck carburetor choke.

303. Don't tamper with the emission control system in an attempt to improve fuel efficiency. Chances are that you'll only make matters worse. Besides that, such tampering is likely to be illegal.

304. Lubricate the accelerator pedal and linkage for smoother operation. This helps to avoid abrupt movements which tend to actuate the accelerator pump.

305. Install a stronger accelerator return spring to make the pedal progressively harder to depress. This is a good physical and psychological reminder that you may be using too much power too often.

306. Don't allow the clutch pedal to have an improper amount of free play. If free play is insufficient, the resulting slippage will lower clutch facing life as well as fuel mileage.

307. If your speedometer needle jumps around, your speedometer cable may need to be lubricated or replaced. While this is not a major source of engine resistance, it does give an inaccurate speed reading, which may account for wasted fuel.

308. If your car has dashboard lights which are adjustable for brightness, adjust to the dimmest setting which allows good visibility. Brighter lights use more electricity, which requires the engine to reproduce more power to turn the alternator.

309. Keep all tires (including the spare) inflated to the recommended pressures. Some recommend inflating to even higher pressures, but for safety, handling characteristics, and tire life, it's advisable to stay within the manufacturer's recommendations.

310. Check tire pressures when the tires are cold. Bleeding air from a hot tire will result in underinflation, since recommended pressures assume that the tire is cold.

311. Gas station pressure gauges are notoriously inaccurate. Buy a good tire gauge and use it weekly.

312. Don't sacrifice safety for efficiency by driving on bald tires. Although rolling resistance will be minimized, so will resistance to punctures and other damage.

313. Use a screwdriver to remove small stones from your tire treads. This will help reduce imbalance and rolling resistance, and increase the chances of identifying potential tire problems before they leave you stuck with a flat.

314. Check the automatic choke for free operation and proper adjustment position. If it's stuck, mpg can drop by three miles per gallon.

315. During the summer months, consider adjusting the automatic choke to a leaner setting for better efficiency during short trips.

316. If it doesn't interfere with starting in your climate, adjust the automatic choke for faster opening.

317. Check the cooling system for kinked or collapsed hoses. They will increase the workload on the water pump, requiring extra fuel to pump coolant through the system.

318. Clean and flush the cooling system at the recommended intervals and use a generous amount of top-quality antifreeze in both summer and winter. Besides making the coolant more slippery and easier to pump, this will help prevent the formation of sludge and corrosion which can lead to mechanical and efficiency problems.

319. Check the gasket on the radiator cap to be sure that it will not allow pressure leakage from the radiator. Coolant is pumped more easily when it's under pressure. Do this check only when the engine is cold.

320. Periodically clean the radiator of accumulated bugs, leaves, and other obstructions which reduce its cooling efficiency. By keeping the radiator clear, the possibility of overheating will be reduced, as will the operating requirement time of the electric fan which many cars have.

321. Check the heater control linkage adjustment to be sure that the heater is really off when the temperature control is in the "off" position. It requires extra fuel to pump coolant through the heater core when the heat isn't really necessary for passenger comfort. In addition, this maladjustment can increase the percentage of time that the air conditioner must operate to maintain a given temperature during summer driving.

322. Regular maintenance of your air conditoner will keep it running at top efficiency and can reduce the amount of time it is on and the energy it uses when engaged.

323. With the engine idling and the air conditioning operating at its coolest setting, inspect the sight glass for foam or bubbles in the passing refrigerant. If they are present, the system's efficiency will be improved by having the refrigerant recharged.

324. Keep all four wheels balanced. At 55 miles per hour, a 3-ounce imbalance can make your car's wheels react as if a 22-pound force were bouncing them up and down. The result will be higher rolling resistance, greater fuel consumption, and prematurely worn-out tires.

325. Notice the position of the steering wheel when you are driving on a straight road. If the position required to travel in a straight line changes noticeably, there is a good chance that the front end needs to be aligned.

326. Have toe-in checked periodically. Have toe-in set as close to zero as the allowable range permits, especially when using radial tires. Incorrect toe-in can cost .3 miles per gallon.

327. Proper camber of the front wheels is important. An improper setting will increase rolling resistance and waste fuel.

328. Proper caster of the front wheels ensures good directional stability so that the identification of frequent steering wheel corrections can be minimized.

329. Tight front wheel bearings will reduce mileage. Be sure they are adjusted properly when they are repacked with grease or when the brake drums are removed for safety inspections.

330. Spin the wheels by hand to help detect dragging brakes which hold back the car and reduce gas mileage.

331. Periodically check the universal joints or constant-velocity joints to avoid excessive drive train resistance which can result when these components are worn or loose.

332. Keep disc brake rotors clean and rust free to help reduce drag. If the caliper is also rusty, the pads may not retract at all, causing even greater mpg reductions.

333. Check and replace shock absorbers as necessary. Weak shocks will increase air and rolling resistance and lead to variations in weight distribution and decreased driving efficiency.

334. Replace spark plugs at the recommended intervals. Just replacing the spark plugs alone can increase mpg by 3.4%.

335. Examine old spark plugs to check on the condition of the engine. They'll give you an insider's view of why your car may not be delivering the kind of gas mileage you'd like.

336. Periodically check ignition wires for cracks and deterioration.

337. Adjacent ignition wires may exchange sparks instead of delivering electricity to the spark plugs, where it belongs. Don't tape adjacent wires together or such spark-jumping will only increase.

338. Keep spark plug wires from contacting engine compartment parts which could serve as electrical grounds which can temporarily short out a cylinder.

339. If you've replaced your spark plug wiring, be sure that the wires are no longer than necessary. Each inch of length adds resistance which will weaken the spark.

340. Use a wire-type gauge to measure the gap of spark plugs and ignition points. A leaf-type gauge will not provide an accurate measurement when the components are slightly worn.

341. If your car is equipped with a conventional ignition system, change the ignition points and condenser at the proper intervals. Remember to adjust the timing whenever points have been replaced or filed.

342. Periodically squirt engine oil into the lower part of the distributor to keep the centrifugal advance weights moving freely. If they stick, timing will not be advanced properly at higher engine speeds, and fuel efficiency will suffer.

343. With the distributor cap removed, check the freeom of the mechanical ignition advance by lightly turning the rotor against the spring action. If it's stuck, you may be losing several miles per gallon because of improper timing.

344. Periodically check ignition timing. A spark that is just 5 degrees too late can cost 1 miles per gallon.

345. You'll be a more fuel-efficient driver if you understand the technical workings of automobiles in general. Excellent sources of such information are the *Bosch Automotive Handbook*, available from the Society of Automotive Engineers, 400 Commonwealth Drive, Warrendale, PA 15096 and Chilton's *Easy Car Care*.

346. For more detail on your own vehicle and its repair and maintenance, buy a repair and tune-up guide for your personal library.

PLANNING

347. Sit down and analyze how you use your vehicle and how you might change your habits and drive fewer miles or get more miles per gallon.

348. Sit down and analyze the vehicle usage patterns of your friends and neighbors; then cooperate in informal carpooling so that you can all save.

349. Carpool or rideshare to and from work.

350. Try especially hard to reduce the number of your short trips. The average driver makes approximately 1,000 trips each year that are less than 5 miles long, and these trips use about one-third of the gasoline purchased. Before every short trip, ask yourself: "Is this trip really necessary?"

351. Think about how you'd get from point A to point B if you didn't have a car and seriously consider using the alternatives.

352. Use.the telephone as a substitute for some short trips.

353. Use the mail as a substitute for short trips.

354. Use an alternate vehicle (bicycle, moped, etc.) to replace the car for short trips.

355. Walk or jog instead of using the car for short trips.

356. Use public transportation whenever convenient.

357. Call ahead to see if a shopping item is in stock before going to the store in person.

358. Use mail order purchasing whenever feasible.

359. Use home delivery services whenever possible.

360. Before undertaking a short trip to pick up a convenience food item, calculate the cost of the item in terms of total price, including gasoline. Driving a full-size car two miles to pick up a loaf of bread can easily double the price of the bread, especially at today's fuel prices.

361. Buy a large supply of groceries on each major shopping trip. The result will be fewer trips and less money spent on fuel. You may even be able to save significantly on your grocery bill by purchasing some items by the case.

362. Consider buying locally instead of traveling more than 10 miles for a "sale" item.

363. Calculate your fuel cost per mile, then determine the "price" you'll have to pay for each short trip. Remember that short trips are less than half as efficient as your overall average mpg.

364. Perhaps the most wasteful trip of all is the special trip to buy fuel. Combine fuel-purchase trips with other useful errands.

365. Combine short trips into one longer one whenever possible. Your car runs very inefficiently during those first few miles, and a single trip means only a single warm-up.

366. Arrange each trip so that the stops are made in the most efficient order, minimizing the number of miles necessary to cover them.

367. Schedule social events and recreational activities so that several members of the family can go on the same trip. This applies to swimming at the YMCA, evening classes and other potential family activities.

368. Arrange club and committee meetings to minimize travel for the participants. (Or have the meetings at your own house so you won't have to travel at all.)

369. Schedule dentist or doctor visits so that more than one family member is able to go along at the same time.

370. Try to cluster separate trips into the same part of the day—this means a warmer engine for each errand.

371. If you have more than one car, try to carry out a short trip in the vehicle that's already warmed up.

372. If you have more than one vehicle, use the most efficient one for each trip.

373. Keep your car in the garage between trips. If you don't have a garage, park in the sun so that the car will be as warm as possible for the next trip.

374. Use an engine block heater for better efficiency during short trips in winter. This can be advantageous even if you keep your car in the garage.

375. Before starting the car, make sure that you've already adjusted the seat and mirrors, fastened your safety belt, and so on. Otherwise, you'll be doing these things while the car is idling at zero miles per gallon.

376. After starting your car, drive away as soon as the engine runs without stalling. This shouldn't take more than 30 seconds, even during frigid weather.

377. For trips which are made frequently, plan possible shortcuts in the event of accidents, construction, or other obstructions along the way.

378. During highway travel, don't haul luggage and other items on the roof unless there is no alternative. A rooftop carrier can make your economy car into a gas guzzler.

379. If you can't pack trip items inside the car, leave some of them at home.

380. If you're forced to haul items on the roof, try to arrange them in a wedged-shaped configuration, with smaller items in front, larger in rear.

381. If possible, remove your luggage rack when it's not in use.

382. For less wind resistance, distribute passenger and luggage loads as evenly as possible during highway travel.

383. Use a map and a "cheat-sheet" to help you stay on the correct route when traveling through unfamiliar territory, especially in urban areas. A small index card with descriptions of important decision points can be invaluable, especially when you are alone or your navigator is asleep.

384. If you have a CB radio, use it as a road map supplement, since some routes may be under construction and others may be newly available for use since your map was published.

385. On any trip, measure distance in gallons, not miles. Longer distances may involve more efficient routes and be less expensive than shorter alternatives.

386. If you're in a hurry and are tempted to speed up, reconsider the urgency of your arrival time. By rushing, you may be able to save only a few minutes of time at a high cost of fuel and personal risk.

387. Before starting a trip, calculate exactly how much time you would save by driving 60 mph instead of 55 mph. The few minutes saved will be insignificant compared to the fuel you'll use, especially if you leave home exactly that much earlier than originally planned.

388. Time your travel through dense urban areas so that periodic daytime congestion can be avoided.

389. Try to arrange your work schedule to avoid rush hour traffic.

390. Select an appropriate location on the dashboard or console for placing or taping small amounts of change so that you can avoid delays at toll booths and take advantage of "correct change only" lanes.

391. Don't use electrical accessories which plug into the car cigarette lighter and use up both electricity and gasoline. These include vacuum cleaners, air pumps, spotlights and other devices which are not really part of the transportation process.

392. Dress cool in summer to reduce the need for air conditioning or to lower the vehicle windows.

393. Dress warm in winter to reduce use of the heater and its electrical fan.

394. On a hot day, begin traveling early in the day to reduce the load on the air conditioner or air resistance from lowered windows.

395. On a cool day, begin traveling later in the day to minimize use of the heater and its fan.

396. On a Sunday drive, if you don't really care which direction you go first, go with the wind to greatly reduce air resistance. Chances are that it will be calmer later in the day.

397. Clean out the car periodically to remove extra weight in the form of tennis shoes, bowling balls, vacation leftovers, snow chains and other items which are not likely to be needed.

398. Don't drive around with a full tank of fuel. Gasoline weighs about six pounds per gallon—it takes fuel to haul fuel.

399. To reduce weight and gain miles per gallon, remove anything from the car that is not needed for safety, emission control, or other useful purposes. This includes ash trays if you don't smoke, soundproofing and insulation.

400. If possible, remove the trailer hitch during seasons when it will not be used.

401. Remove oversize fender mirrors which may be necessary for some trailering, but are simply a waste of fuel under other conditions.

402. If you car has been parked overnight in a snowstorm, be sure to brush off accumulated snow from the roof, trunk, hood, and fender wells. Wet snow can easily add 100 pounds to the weight of your car, not to mention its effect on air resistance. Brush the snow off *before* starting the car.

403. If you carry extra windshield washer fluid, carry it in concentrate form instead of premixed. You can find water to mix with it practically anywhere.

404. Use a cardboard box for tools. A metal toolbox is heavier, and usually larger, encouraging you to take along more tools than you need for most roadside emergencies.

405. Have your snow tires installed on their own wheels. This will make it easier to take them off during periods when they aren't really needed.

406. Don't install studded snow tires unless your car really needs the extra traction. They have even greater rolling resistance than conventional snow tires.

407. Aim the windshield wiper nozzles where the spray will do the most good. This reduces use of the windshield wiper motor and makes your washer fluid last longer.

408. Don't carry spare fuel in your car. Gasoline is highly explosive and should only be carried in the car's fuel tank.

409. Don't carry ski racks or bike carriers except when they are being used to carry skis or bikes. Besides adding extra weight, they increase air resistance and lower fuel efficiency.

410. Don't mount your spare tire on the front of your van or pickup truck.

411. If possible, move a side-mounted spare tire to a rear location on the vehicle in order to get it out of the air stream.

412. Reduce pleasure driving by finding other sources to satisfy your recreational and relaxation needs. Bicycling and walking are fun.

413. Don't use or carry snow chains except in severe snow or ice emergencies. If installed, they increase rolling resistance. If carried, they add extra weight to the vehicle.

414. During winter months, a full tank can help prevent evaporation of the more volatile winter gasoline grades as well as reduce the formation of water condensation in the tank.

415. If you have added some extra weight to help traction during winter driving, be sure to remove it when the traction advantage is not necessary.

416. If you have a tape player in your car, keep the tape library at home instead of carrying it along. Besides increasing the likelihood of theft, extra tapes take up space and are a source of added weight.

417. Put together checklists for items required on vacations and frequent family-visit trips. This reduces not only the number of "go-backs" to pick up items left at home, but helps eliminate wasted time and fuel dollars to run shopping errands for items you could have brought with you.

418. Vacation with another family. Look at it as an extended carpool.

419. Vacation by train, plane, or bus, then rent a car if you need one at your destination.

420. Combine vacations with visits to family or friends in other geographic areas. This saves on motel bills as well as fuel.

421. When planning a driving vacation, go to a popular area during the off-season.

422. When planning a driving vacation, go to an unpopular area anytime.

423. Vacation in the summer instead of winter for better fuel efficiency on the highway. Colder temperatures mean lower mpg.

424. Anticipate and plan for the gas rationing requirements in states through which you'll be traveling.

425. Use CB radio inquiries to find out about local traffic, fuel prices and availability.

426. Phone ahead for motel reservations instead of searching for a place to stay after you've arrived at your destination. Phoning ahead will also make it unnecessary to rush to beat the crowd.

427. Avoid the time and fuel waste of long stops by eating during off-peak hours when traveling. (Those cold starts cost fuel.)

428. For camping vacations, buy or rent a fold-down camping trailer for a lot of room at the campground with a minimum of air resistance on the highway.

429. If vacationing with a motor home, consider towing a subcompact or hauling a motorcycle for side journeys or short trips at the campground.

430. Use a boat trailer instead of "cartopping". The boat trailer will follow in the wake of the car's path through the air, resulting in very little additional fuel being consumed.

431. If you do cartop your boat, try to position it with the bow forward and on a downward tilt in order to minimize the air resistance penalty.

432. Remove the camper section of a pickup truck when you aren't going to be camping—the result will be less air resistance and more mpg.

433. When you're forced to wait in a gas line, minimize the penalty by waiting in the most efficient (e.g., downhill) line. Before committing yourself, drive by once to see which line would be best.

434. If you have a large car and a smaller model which uses the same type of fuel, use the larger car for fuel storage during periods of extreme shortage.

435. Carry a hand-operated siphon hose so that you'll be able to borrow some fuel from a friend to make it through an emergency shortage.

436. Get to know your local service station owner—he can be a real friend during shortage periods. Be sure to develop the friendship during a nonshortage period.

437. If you live near a turnpike, consider hopping on for a short two-way fuel trip if other stations are closed during a shortage.

438. On round trips, use the first leg of the trip to check fuel prices, then fill up at the cheapest place on the way back.

439. Avoid filling up on a Friday, especially during summer months. When prices increase, this seems to be the day when the jump occurs.

440. Park and walk instead of cruising and looking. Besides saving fuel, the exercise will do you good.

441. When parking at events where drivers will all be leaving at about the same time, back into your parking space (if legal). This makes it easier to get into the flow when the rush begins.

442. If you've parked indoors for a movie or shopping, either leave early or wait until the line dwindles. Your lungs and your fuel bill will thank you.

443. Park in the front of a block in order to avoid getting blocked in and having to maneuver to get back out.

444. Park your car with the engine positioned in the warmest part of the garage, especially during the winter months.

445. During summer weather, reduce interior temperatures (and air conditioner use) by parking in the shade.

446. During winter weather, increase interior temperature (and reduce the work required of the heater) by parking in the sun.

447. Keep this book in your glove compartment as a constant reminder to drive efficiently.

448. Visualize your odometer as representing the meter on a taxicab, since every new digit means more money out of your pocket. At today's prices, each mile will probably cost a nickle or more for fuel alone, with the future likely to mean even higher costs. Dime-a-mile rates are not far away.

449. Join an organization like the American Automobile Association for trip planning, fuel information, and other useful services.

450. Read this book at least one more time, then pass it on to other family members who use up fuel from the same budget.

Fig. 4–16. On this road, wear and tear has led to the formation of grooves in the pavement which can increase rolling resistance because of their rough surface. In addition, they tend to collect water which can cause hydroplaning.

patched or expanded, with some portions tending to be more coarse than others. If you have a choice between traveling entirely on a rough section versus having two wheels on the coarse section and two on a smoother section, rolling resistance will be reduced if you do the latter. However, this means that on wet roads or during quick stops, your tires will have different amounts of traction.

Change Lanes Efficiently

Try to "read" the flow of the various lanes available to you in congested driving situations. Observations of the traffic patterns in your everyday driving can help you pinpoint exactly where lane one begins to slow down and lane two begins to speed up. It's not efficient to zig-zag down the road, jumping into every open spot that arises; on the other hand, you should not limit yourself to one lane and ignore the others. Race drivers practice on courses until they know exactly where they must hit the gas when coming out of each turn. While driving to work in the morning is a little less thrilling, you can still practice different strategies until you find the one that works best for you in the lane patterns you're up against.

When traveling in traffic, always watch the red lights and traffic flow ahead so that you can maintain your car's momentum by moving into the lane with the least congestion. Through awareness of the cars around you and allowing acceleration room between you and the car ahead, you can make a smooth changeover without the need to stand on the gas pedal.

Temporarily switching to a slower lane can sometimes be advantageous. For example, if a heavy truck is stopped at the red light near the bottom of a hill, the natural tendency is to choose the passing lane so that you won't have to creep up the hill behind him. However, since other drivers will share this tendency, they may have the passing lane backed up a long way. Under these circumstances, you're better off behind the truck—at least he and you will be through the intersection by the time the light turns red again, while the backed-up drivers may end up waiting for the same red light twice.

Don't Tailgate

Whether driving in traffic or on the freeway, tailgating wastes fuel. In addition to its safety hazards, tailgating ruins the tempo of your driving and leads to jerky, momentum-wasting changes in order to avoid rear-ending the car ahead. When driving for efficiency, you can't afford to change speeds every time the brake-tapper in front decides to accelerate, decelerate, or swerve. If possible, pass the slower driver; if not, drop back and try to find a relaxing song on the radio. Don't let the driving behavior of others anger you or lead you to lose sight of your fuel efficiency goal.

Use the Rear View Mirrors

Proper use of the mirrors will enhance the smoothness of your driving by keeping you aware of the changing conditions around you. Your ability to respond efficiently to traffic situations ahead of you depends upon knowing what vehicles behind you are doing.

Many a middle-distance runner has been "boxed in" by other runners while

Fig. 4–17. Proper use of the rear view mirrors can help you anticipate conditions ahead in terms of your position relative to other vehicles. A big part of looking ahead is being aware of what's behind.

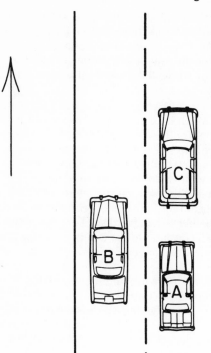

Fig. 4–18. An example of how *not* to change lanes smoothly. With vehicles A and B both overtaking slower vehicle C, the driver of vehicle A finds himself boxed in, and he'll have to disrupt his car's momentum in order to pass C. He should have anticipated the pass before creeping up so close to the vehicle in front. Proper use of the rear view mirrors would have helped driver A to avoid this situation.

running on the inside lane of a tiny indoor track. There's no way he can improve his position, and he's forced to follow the pace of the man in front, which may not be the best pace for him. The same situation can come up in driving on any multiple-lane highway, as shown in Figure 4-18. If you're approaching a slower driver at the same time that a faster driver is approaching you, be sure to pace your pass so that you aren't boxed in behind the driver ahead and forced to slow down. Anticipation of who-is-going-to-be-where-and-when is a key to efficient driving, and frequent glances at your rear-view mirrors are indispensable.

Don't Watch the Wrong Car

Everybody knows that, in traffic, the most important car is the one directly in front of you. After all, if you make a mistake, he's the one you're going to hit. That's a fine rule of thumb for safe driving, but when driving for efficiency we should try to go one step further. In this case, it's really one car (or more) farther ahead. Instead of concentrating entirely on the car directly ahead, look also at the car ahead of that one, as shown in Figure 4-19.

If you were to watch commuter or other heavy traffic from the air, it would look like a giant screen-door spring expanding and contracting as it wiggles down the highway. Cars spread out as each takes its turn to accelerate, then bunch

Fig. 4–19. In heavy traffic, the driver of car A can reduce the abruptness of acceleration and deceleration by watching cars B and C in addition to the one directly in front.

together as they take turns slowing down. The normal reaction is to accelerate as soon as the person in front of you begins to accelerate and to slow down as soon as he begins to slow down. This alternate hurry-up-and-wait and wait-and-hurry-up activity detracts from the smoothness which driving for efficiency demands. However, unless you're driving a bulldozer, it will be impossible for you to maintain a steady speed.

The next best thing is to reduce the amount of speeding-up and slowing-down you have to do, and the secret is to watch cars that are further ahead than the one in front. Whenever the second car ahead begins to accelerate, anticipate your own movement by taking your foot off the brake and starting to accelerate very slightly—by the time your turn comes, you'll already be moving and won't have to accelerate as quickly to keep up with the flow. Likewise, as the cars ahead start slowing down, begin to reduce your own speed before you really have to. By looking further ahead and beginning your speed changes earlier, you'll be able to enjoy the economy of smoother driving and smaller momentum changes. As you practice this strategy, you'll continue to get a better feel for the traffic clues that can give you fuel-saving advance notice of necessary changes in your speed.

Even better advance notice is possible when driving in traffic through a tunnel or on a wet road. The shiny walls and roof of the tunnel or the wet pavement will reflect the brake lights of cars further ahead, giving you a slow-down cue even when you can't see the cars themselves. Likewise, the successive switching off of brake lights gives you advance notice that you need to accelerate sooner and more slowly.

If you are directly behind a truck or other large vehicle, it will be impossible to implement your looking-ahead strategy. In this case, it's appropriate to do a courteous turn for your fellow drivers—back off and let a few of them in front of you.

Bend with the Wind

With today's engines, wind doesn't have much effect on how fast you can go. However, it can be a factor in deciding how fast you *should* go. By watching flags, factory smoke, bushes, trees, and skinny telephone poles, you can determine if the wind is for you or against you. Drive a little more slowly when the wind is against you—air resistance depends on the relative speed between you and the air, not just on your speedometer reading. With the wind at your back, higher speeds will be much less expensive. Recall once again that the increase in air resistance is far out of proportion to the increase in your speed, and that a 10% increase in speed means a 33% increase in the horsepower your car needs to overcome air resistance.

In one mileage study, a standard size car was driven at high speed with and against a stiff wind. Going 70 mph into the 18 mph wind, the car was able to achieve only 11.6 miles per gallon. However, when driven 70 mph with the wind at its back, the car's mileage increased to 16.6 miles per gallon.[10]

DRIVING BY THE INSTRUMENTS

There are several gauges available to help you react to minute-to-minute driving situations in a fuel-efficient manner. They were discussed briefly in Chapter 3—here we will be concerned with using them as guides for efficient driving.

The Vacuum Gauge

Long used in helping mechanics tune automobiles, the vacuum gauge measures the amount of vacuum in the intake manifold and can be effective in train-

Fig. 4–20. Flags, smokestacks, and other wind-affected objects can help you determine whether or not the wind is with you. Making up lost time into a headwind can be very expensive, since your car's air resistance depends on the *relative* speed of the vehicle through the air around it.

ing individuals to drive efficiently. In essence, the vacuum gauge will have a higher reading whenever you are obtaining better fuel efficiency, and will read lower when your gas pedal habits are using more fuel than necessary. Normal gauge readings will vary considerably from one vehicle to another and from one engine to the next, but the same principle applies in every case: while you drive, try to keep the needle reading as high as possible. As a general rule, below 7 in./Hg means poor fuel economy; 7 to 15 in./Hg means fair fuel economy; 15 to 22 in./Hg means good fuel economy; and over 22 in./Hg means slow down. Naturally, though, these numbers will vary with individual cars.

As a practical matter, you may set a lower limit and try not to go below that reading during any of the driving modes in which you operate. The "feel" that the vacuum gauge provides, combined with your knowledge of fuel-efficient driving, should help you to use your right foot in a way that saves fuel. Since diesel engines have no vacuum in the intake manifold, the vacuum gauge is only applicable to conventionally powered gasoline vehicles. If you drive a gas-powered car, you will probably find that, dollar for dollar, the vacuum gauge is one of the most valuable instruments you can purchase as a training and driving aid.

The Fuel Consumption Meter

These gauges were discussed in Chapter 3 (see page 61). On the miles per gallon gauge, higher needle readings or digital readouts reflect better fuel mileage, based directly on miles per gallon. The fuel totalizer, which measures the number of one-hundredths of a gallon of fuel that have entered your carburetor since the instrument was reset, provides the opportunity to measure the fuel efficiency of different trip routes and other strategies with your own vehicle. It is like owning your own fuel efficiency experimental laboratory. The so-called "trip

Fig. 4–21. If you have a tachometer, such as the model shown here, you may wish to adjust the movable pointer to the rpm at which peak torque is produced by your engine. For most engines, the economy range of operation is generally a bit lower than this point. Keeping rpm's below the "redline" may be fine for racing, but for efficient driving, the maximum torque point should be of more interest.

computer" is a somewhat exotic combination of these two instruments, and provides an awesome amount of additional information, most of which is more entertaining than helpful.

The Tachometer

A tachometer is an instrument that measures engine speed in terms of revolutions per minute (rpm). While most engines operate anywhere between 500 to 5,000 rpm, they are not equally efficient at all rpm's. In terms of fuel consumption, most engines operate most efficiently at the rpm corresponding to peak engine torque.

Torque, usually expressed in foot-pounds, is the twisting effort the engine is able to exert on the crankshaft and ultimately on the tires and road. Torque drops off at very high and very low rpm's, and most engines reach their maximum torque somewhere between 2,000 and 4,000 rpm. (Horsepower is a measure of the rate at which the engine can exert that twisting force. Unlike torque, horsepower keeps going up as engine rpm increases, and usually peaks in the 4,000 to 5,000 rpm range.)

As mentioned above, your engine's efficiency at converting fuel to energy (it's volumetric efficiency) is highest at the rpm corresponding to maximum torque. Your owner's manual, your dealer, or some automotive repair manuals can tell you the maximum torque and horsepower of your engine and the rpm values at which they are reached.

To be most fuel efficient, you want to drive so your tachometer registers in an rpm "economy range" which is, for most engines, slightly lower than the rpm at which the maximum torque is produced. Figure 4-22 shows an example of the horsepower, torque, and fuel consumption curves for a typical engine. Maximum torque is obtained in this engine at about 3,000 rpm. The economy range, shown between 2,000 and 3,000 rpm, is the lowest part of the fuel consumption curve. This is the range in which the engine consumes fuel at the lowest rate for the amount of power it is producing.

Staying in the economy range of rpm's will be most important—and most

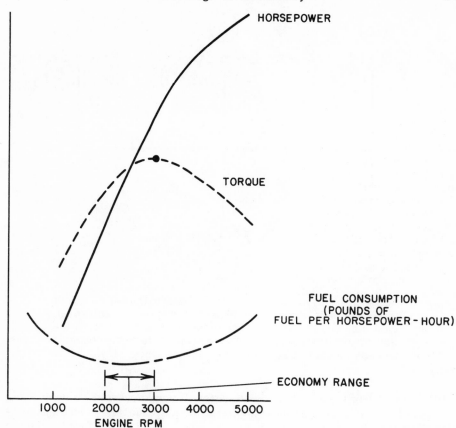

Fig. 4–22. In the economy range, an engine will require the least amount of fuel for the amount of work it is producing. For most engines, this range will be slightly lower than the rpm at which the engine achieves its peak torque. The engine shown here reaches its peak torque at about 3,000 rpm and has its minimum fuel consumption rate between 2,000 and 3,000 rpm. This curve is just an example, and your own engine may have a economy range different from that shown here.

fuel conserving—when you shift gears in a manual transmission car. If you're accelerating and shift into a higher gear too soon, your engine's rpm will drop well below the optimum range for peak torque, and the engine will be unable to generate enough torque to efficiently do the job. On the other hand, waiting too long before shifting up wastes fuel because of the unnecessary use of the lower gear. Experience will tell you at what speed you can optimally shift in order to maintain optimum rpm.

If you don't wish to keep eyeing the tachometer, you may wish to attach a small diagram, such as the one shown in Figure 4-23, to the dashboard or sunvisor. In the figure, the vehicle speeds which correspond to 2,000 and 3,000 rpm are shown at the approximate location of each of the five transmission speeds. For example, in fourth gear, the economy range of 2,000 to 3,000 rpm corresponds to vehicle speeds between 32 and 48 miles per hour, and in fifth gear to speeds between 41 and 62 miles per hour.

If your vehicle has an automatic transmission, a heavy foot can cause your transmission to shift too late for best fuel efficiency because the vehicle will stay

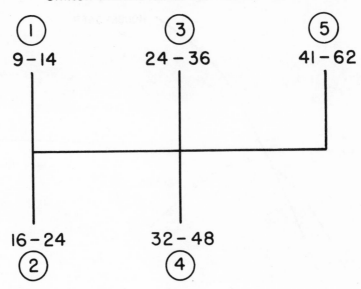

Fig. 4–23. After you've used the tachometer to translate efficient engine speeds (rpm's) into efficient road speeds in each gear, you may wish to attach a reminder such as this one to the dashboard or sun visor in order to keep aware of the desirable speeds for each gear.

in the lower gear in order to acclerate faster. If you know your economy range, you can lift your foot slightly near the top of the range and allow the transmission to select the higher gear.

DRIVING A DIESEL

The first thing different about driving a diesel-powered automobile is immediately apparent: after inserting the key, you will not be able to start it immediately from cold. The diesel engine, which has no spark plugs and uses high compression to squeeze and ignite the air-fuel mixture, relies on preheated glow plugs to help start the engine at lower temperatures. Depending on the outside temperature, the engine temperature, and the kind of diesel car you are driving, you may have to wait anywhere from 0 to 60 seconds until the dashboard indicator light tells you that it's time to operate the starter. For most cars, the waiting time is not very long at moderate temperatures, and no waiting time at all is required if the engine is already warmed up. General Motors has developed a new type of glow plug that allows the car to be started within about 6½ seconds after glow plug warm-up has begun, and has incorporated the design into its corporate diesel output. Other manufacturers may be following suit, which would make the passenger car diesel engine as convenient to start as its gasoline counterpart.

The second thing you'll notice about the diesel engine is a bit more vibration at idle and somewhat more noise from the engine compartment. When idling or running at low speeds and light loads, diesel engines tend to emit a rattling noise known as "cold knock," a pleasant mechanical sound to some, but an annoyance to others. The sound is especially noticeable after a cold start, but it may persist at lower levels after the engine has warmed up. While some

Fig. 4–24. Modern passenger car diesels, such as the Volkswagen Rabbit Diesel shown here, are a far cry from the accelerates-like-a-glacier stereotype which some mistakenly associate with diesel-powered automobiles. This one drives like any other car and better than most, cruises easily with traffic, and can get 60 miles per gallon without your trying too hard.

diesels may sound like someone's under the hood shaking a can of marbles, don't worry about the noise—think of it as the sound of efficiency, which it certainly is.

After you have the diesel on the road, you'll notice that it may not have quite as much power as the gasoline-powered vehicle you're used to driving. However, because the engine design does not require a multitude of under-hood emission control pipes, hoses, wiring, and switches, you are likely to find that the engine runs a lot more smoothly than you expected, that there is less hesitation and jerking, and that it is not really as slow as you may have anticipated. The acceleration capability of a diesel automobile is enough to keep up with most traffic, to pass in reasonable situations, and generally to get you from point A to point B with a minimum of fuss and a maximum of fuel efficiency. The Volkswagen Rabbit Diesel, shown in Figure 4-24, is capable of accelerating to 50 miles per hour in 11.5 seconds and had an EPA highway rating of 55 miles per gallon for the 1979 five-speed model.

When driving the diesel, you will be rewarded by planning ahead and anticipating moves you'll be making further down the road. Because of the relatively low output of the engine for its size, proper application of the other suggestions in this chapter will be even more beneficial if you are driving a diesel. While truck diesels are large, slow-turning engines, the passenger car diesel is not unhappy at higher revolutions, and you will probably find yourself (or your automatic) shifting much more frequently than in the past. However, you will be well repaid in terms of fuel efficiency. A surprising but true example of what can be done with a diesel-powered automobile is presented as part of the discussion in Chapter 8.

DRIVING AN AUTOMATIC

If you're driving a car with an automatic transmission, don't despair. Look at the bright side—by increasing your miles per gallon by 10% to 20%, you'll save more money than the stick driver who makes the same improvement. There are several reasons why.

For one thing, most cars with an automatic transmission are provided with a lower, more economical rear axle ratio to help compensate for efficiency lost through torque converter slippage. In addition, since the torque converter dampens the uneven running that often occurs with lean air-fuel mixtures, an engine with an automatic transmission can use a slightly leaner carburetor mixture than the same engine with a manual transmission. Another compensating factor is that high speeds tend to lessen the disadvantage of an automatic transmission because the torque converter becomes more efficient at higher speeds.

In addition, an increasing number of models have automatic transmissions with either low-slip torque converters or converters that lock up altogether to eliminate any slippage at all in high gear. The combination of these design improvements with the lower rear axle ratios and more efficiently tuned ignition and carburetion systems causes the new automatics to provide driving convenience without as much fuel efficiency penalty as in the past.

Besides applying the general techniques discussed so far, you can get more miles per gallon from your automatic by following these hints. Keep the car in high gear whenever possible. This may sometimes require a very light foot in order to avoid the selection of a lower gear. In some situations, it may be advantageous to use your left foot for braking. When you're trying to maintain your momentum by avoiding the brake, yet feel that a sudden stop or slow-down may become necessary, having your left foot in position near the brake will reduce your reaction time. Any time you are traveling downhill or decelerating, it's a good idea to keep your braking foot poised near the pedal. However, be sure not to ride the brake. Since your automatic transmission locks up and is more efficient at higher speeds, make a strong charge at the hills which lie ahead. Maintain or gradually build up speed as you approach the hill, then gradually press the gas pedal to maintain it on the way up.

ATTITUDE IS IMPORTANT

Driving for efficiency requires a certain state of mind. You should be relaxed enough that you aren't in a hurry and are free of the temptations to tailgate, lane-jump, or attempt race-driver passing techniques. On the other hand, you must be alert to your driving environment and possible changes in it that may affect your speed, acceleration, and braking decisions. In short, driving for efficiency requires that you think efficiency. Every time you move the gas pedal, brake pedal, steering wheel, or shift lever, one of the main thoughts in your mind should be—how is this going to affect my fuel mileage?

Relax in the "Pipeline"

You'll encounter some situations where your speed is sharply reduced and in which you may become totally frustrated. It's morning rush hour and there are 5,000 cars in front of yours; or you're following a cement mixer on a one-lane road; or you're stuck in the crowd that's taking a 14-mile detour. In these circumstances, it's sometimes hard to think sanity, let alone economy. But try. Whether you curse the mayor, sing Christmas carols, or play tic-tac-toe on the windshield, it isn't going to make one minute of difference in the time at which you'll arrive at your destination. When in these "pipeline" situations where you're trapped and can't do anything about it, try to relax and let the pipeline

Fig. 4–25. Slow, crowded traffic conditions such as this put you in a "pipeline" situation. Relax, go with the flow, and don't be tempted to fight it with inefficient driving techniques.

Fig. 4–26. Driving for efficiency is more fun if you compete with others or with yourself. In this photo, a contestant in the National Fuel Economy Challenge, sponsored by the U.S. Department of Energy, the Champion Spark Plug Company, and the Sports Car Club of America, prepares her car prior to beginning the contest. Winners are determined by actual fuel mileage divided by the combined EPA mpg estimate for their cars. (Courtesy of the U.S. Department of Energy.)

carry you at its own rate. Along the way, though, get the best fuel mileage you can by anticipating the movement of the cars in front of you and by applying various other tips presented here. Listening to the radio or tape deck can calm you down and help you drive more economically. However, don't pump the gas pedal in tune with the music.

Enjoy the Trip

Though sometimes more boring than frustrating, long trips can benefit from the same philosophy that is useful in the "pipeline." Radio equipment and gauges can help fight fatigue and impatience, as can keeping track of your average speed or competing with yourself to improve your mileage from one fill-up to the next.

HOW FAST ARE YOU REALLY GOING?

When you're driving for efficiency, it helps to know how fast you're going. Your speedometer may not be as accurate as you think, especially if you have oversize or snow tires on your car. Because of their larger diameter, snow tires can fool your speedometer into reporting that you're going as much as five miles per hour slower than you really are. Thinking that you're going 55 when you're really going 60 may not seem like much, but it can be important to air resistance as well as to the radar cop down the road. At 60 mph, you'll require almost 30% more horsepower to overcome air resistance than you would at 55.

You can easily give your speedometer a lie detector test while driving on any highway equipped with mile markers. In addition, some roads have special mile-marked sections for the specific purpose of testing your speed. Drive at a constant, comfortable speed that you can easily maintain over a distance of either one or two miles. Have a passenger time how long it takes to complete the course, then refer to the following table to determine your actual speed:

Two-Mile Time		Actual Speed	One-Mile Time	Two-Mile Time		Actual Speed	One-Mile Time
min.	sec.	mph	sec.	min.	sec.	mph	sec.
2	0	60	60	2	24	50	72
2	4	58	62	2	28	48.5	74
2	8	56	64	2	32	47.5	76
2	12	54.5	66	2	36	46	78
2	16	53	68	2	40	45	80
2	20	51.5	70				

For example, if you maintain a constant speed over the one-mile course, a time of 68 seconds would indicate that your average speed was a very economical 53 mph. Be sure to check your speedometer accuracy from time to time, especially after you have switched to a new set of tires.

If you're mathematically inclined and have access to a chronograph or stop watch, you can compute your exact speed by using this formula:

$$\text{Miles per hour} = \frac{3600}{\text{seconds to cover 1 mile}}$$

POOR MAN'S TACHOMETER

You can buy a tachometer to tell you when your engine is operating in the area of its maximum torque or horsepower rpm. However, if you're not interested in that kind of expense or accuracy and simply want some idea of how fast your engine is turning at various road speeds in different gears, you can use a tape measure and some simple arithmetic to tell you your rpm. Here are the steps involved in making your "poor man's tachometer":

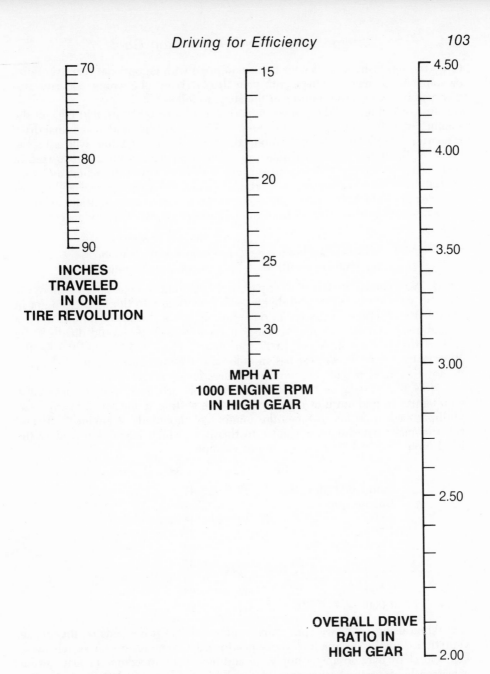

Fig. 4-27. This plus a pencil and paper will enable you to make a "poor man's tachometer."

    1. First you need to find out how far your tires will carry you in one rolling revolution. Lightly dab some white shoe polish or other marking liquid near the center of the tread of one of your rear tires. (Use a front tire if you have front-wheel drive.) Next, drive the car straight forward or backward until the tires have made at least two complete turns. Now measure the distance between any two white spots on the ground.

    2. Look in your owner's manual for your car's overall drive ratio in high gear. For most cars, this will be the same as the rear axle ratio. In case your car has an indirect-drive top gear (i.e., not 1.00:1), just multiply the rear axle ratio

times the top gear ratio. If your car is equipped with an optional rear axle ratio, or you think it may be, check with your dealer. Using the wrong axle ratio will give you inaccurate rpm figures in the steps to follow.

3. Using Figure 4-27, place one end of a ruler or other straight edge at the number of inches you measured in Step 1. Place the other end at the final drive ratio you looked up in Step 2. Along the way, the straight line will cross the center scale at the number of miles per hour your car travels at 1,000 rpm in high gear. For example, if the measurement in Step 1 was 80 inches, and your overall drive ratio in high gear is 3.00, this means that your top gear will deliver 25 miles per hour from each 1,000 engine rpm. If you're arithmetically inclined, you can calculate this yourself from the following formula. For any gear:

$$\frac{\text{Miles per hour}}{\text{per 1000 engine RPM}} = .944 \times \frac{\text{inches covered in one tire revolution}}{\text{overall drive ratio}}$$

4. Now comes the tachometer part of the operation. Look up the other gear ratios in your transmission and divide each gear ratio into the figure you got in Step 3. For example, if the car in our example had a third-gear ratio of 1.40, a second-gear ratio of 1.95, and a first-gear ratio of 2.70, we would divide 25 by each of these to get mph per 1,000 rpm figures of 17.9, 12.8, and 9.3 for the other gears. (Note: If your car has an indirect-drive high gear, you'll need to use the formula in Step 3 to get your mph figures for each gear.)

Now that you know the long-leggedness of each gear, you can use these mph figures to find out how many rpm's you're getting at any speed in any gear. Multiply each mph figure times the number of thousands of engine RPM and you can make a tachometer similar to this one, which happens to reflect the RPM-mph relationship of the car in our example:

	1st	2nd	3rd	4th
mph/1,000 rpm	9.3	12.8	17.9	25
Engine rpm:				
1,000	9 mph	13 mph	18 mph	25 mph
1,500	14	19	27	38
2,000	19	26	36	50
2,500	23	32	45	63
3,000	28	38	54	75
3,500	33	45	63	88
4,000	37	51	72	100

When using your own rpm chart, remember that it depends on the size of your tires and the accuracy of your speedometer. Whenever you switch tires, your old chart may no longer apply. In addition, your speedometer may not be consistently accurate at all speeds, especially in the lower end of the scale. For this reason, don't rely on a tachometer chart for an upper limit of speed in each gear. If you're looking for maximum acceleration, you'll have to get a real tachometer in order to have the rpm accuracy that a speedometer-based chart can't provide.

The normal expansion of tires (especially the nonbelted variety) at higher speeds will tend to make the actual mph figures slightly higher than the ones you've calculated. In order to make your chart a little more operational, you may want to place thin tape strips on your speedometer to indicate the miles per hour at which maximum torque is available in the various gears.

Chapter 5
Fuels and Oils for Efficiency

A little attention to your car's dietary needs will help you get the most from every fuel dollar you spend. Selecting the proper fuel and lubricants can make a significant contribution to your more-miles-per-gallon savings and it will extend the life of your engine as well.

GASOLINE CHARACTERISTICS
Octane

The octane rating of a gasoline is its ability to resist engine knock, a sharp metallic noise resulting from detonation or uncontrolled combustion within the cylinder. Among the least harmful effects of engine knock is an increase in fuel consumption. Other, less innocuous consequences may include cracked cylinder heads and damaged pistons. Octane measurements made under laboratory conditions result in "Research" or "Motor" octane numbers for the same gasoline. In general, the Research octane number tends to be about six to ten points higher than the Motor octane.[1]

In addition, there is a "Road" octane which is determined by automobile road testing under standardized conditions. The Road octane rating is generally lower than the Research octane number and higher than the Motor octane. One commonly used anti-knock index is really the average of the Research and Motor octane numbers.

Your owner's manual will probably indicate the type and octane of gasoline recommended for use in your car. Since the 1971 model year, most cars have been designed to operate satisfactorily on 91 Research octane gasoline. However, octane requirements can vary according to the vehicle and the conditions under which it is operating. If you encounter sustained engine knock, wait until your tank is nearly empty, then try a gasoline with a higher octane rating. Don't overbuy—it's a waste of money to buy gasoline of a higher octane than your engine requires in order to satisfy its anti-knock need.

As a new car is driven, combustion deposits build up and the octane requirement increases until an equilibrium level, normally between four and six octane numbers higher than the new-car requirement, is reached.[2] Other factors which can increase the octane an engine requires are higher air or engine temperatures, lower altitudes, lower humidity, a more advanced ignition spark timing, a leaner carburetor setting, sudden acceleration, and frequent stop-and-go driving which increases the build-up of combustion chamber deposits.

Lead

Since 1975, most cars have been equipped with catalytic converters which require the use of unleaded fuel. If you own a car equipped with a catalytic con-

105

verter, you've probably been well aware of this fact, since all such vehicles have a restricted filler neck opening that will only permit the use of the smaller nozzles on unleaded gasoline pumps. If you pump leaded gasoline into a car equipped with a catalytic converter, you may not harm the engine, but you risk breaking the law, destroying the effectiveness of the converter in reducing emissions, and voiding your new-car warranty.

Older, higher-compression engines usually require a gasoline with a relatively high octane rating. The most efficient way of increasing the octane rating of a gasoline is to add a compound called tetraethyl lead. Therefore, if your owner's manual specifies the use of premium gasoline, you may have to use leaded fuels in order to avoid having your engine knock. However, should circumstances force you to use a low-lead or no-lead gasoline with a lower octane than the car manufacturer specifies, you should temporarily retard the ignition timing very slightly in order to lessen the possibility of knocking.

Some cars, though designed to operate on leaded gasoline, may be able to use the new low-lead and no-lead fuels. Again, experimentation is helpful in determining the gasoline octane which your car and your driving require. Don't automatically rule out a low-lead gasoline—if you haven't tried it, don't (sorry) knock it.

Volatility and Density

The volatility of any liquid is its ability to vaporize, and gasoline must vaporize in order to burn. A highly volatile gasoline will help a cold engine start easily and run smoothly while it is warming up. However, the use of a highly volatile gasoline in warm weather tends to cause vapor lock, a condition in which the gasoline actually vaporizes before it arrives at the carburetor jet where vaporization is supposed to take place. This premature vaporization may occur in the fuel line, fuel pump, or in a section of the carburetor. The engine becomes starved for fuel and will either lose power or stall. Although refiners vary the percentage of volatile fuel in their gasoline according to season and locality, vapor lock is more likely to occur in the early spring when some stations may not have received supplies of less volatile gasoline.

Density is another property of gasoline that can affect your fuel economy. It indicates how much chemical energy the gasoline contains. Density is generally measured in BTUs per gallon (the BTU, or British Thermal Unit, is a standard unit of energy), and usually varies less than 2% among most gasolines in the market. However, one study showed that 6% of commercially available gasolines varied by 4% to 8% in their BTU per gallon content.[3] This finding indicates that gas mileage could vary by as much as 4% to 8%, depending on the density of the gasoline you happen to choose.

Additives

Practically as important as octane rating and volatility are the additives that refiners put into their gasolines. Carburetor detergent additives help clean the tiny passages in the carburetor, thus assuring the consistent fuel-air mixtures necessary for smooth running and good gas mileage. Winter additives include fuel line de-icers to reduce carburetor icing at the throttle plate. Carburetor icing, if it doesn't stall the engine, will at least restrict the carburetor opening and cause a richer fuel-air mixture which will lower gas mileage appreciably. Other additives are used to help control combustion chamber deposits, gum formation, rust, and wear.

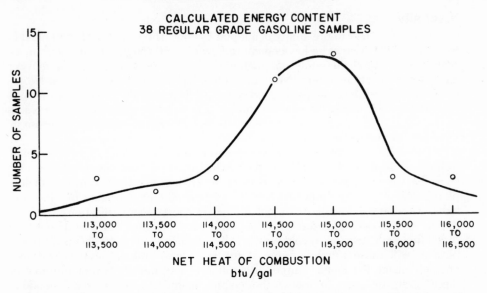

Fig. 5–1. The amount of energy contained in the gasoline you buy will tend to vary from one tank to the next, as shown in the range measured in these samples. If you happen to purchase a tank of fuel on the high side of the range, you may notice a slight increase in your fuel mileage. (*Source:* D. E. Foringer, *Gasoline Factors Affecting Fuel Economy,* SAE Paper No. 650427, 1965.)

DIESEL FUEL CHARACTERISTICS

Because of its different combustion process, the diesel engine requires fuel oil instead of gasoline.

In the not-too-distant past, the only place you could find diesel fuel was at a truck stop. Today, in response to the growing number of diesel-powered automobiles on the road, more and more service stations are carrying diesel fuel as well as gasoline. Estimates place the number of diesel stations at over 12,000, and most diesel automobile manufacturers publish diesel fuel directories which are quite complete. However, because diesel automobiles combine superior fuel efficiency with the same size fuel tank as their gasoline counterparts, fill-ups tend to be few and far between.

Diesel fuel used in automotive applications is available in two grades, No. 1 diesel fuel and No. 2 diesel fuel. No. 1 is the more volatile of the two. The two grades of fuel will mix and burn in the engine, but the engine manufacturer will undoubtedly recommend one or the other for use in your diesel-powered vehicle. Be sure to follow the manufacturer's recommendations very closely.

Cetane Number

The cetane number of a diesel fuel refers to how easily it will ignite, and it is not be be confused with the octane rating of a gasoline. High cetane numbers mean that the fuel will ignite relatively easily or that it will ignite well at low temperatures. Naturally, the lower the cetane number, the higher the temperature must be to ignite the fuel. Most commercially available fuels have a cetane rating between 35 and 65. Most diesel engine manufacturers recommend fuel with a minimum cetane rating of about 45.

Viscosity

Viscosity refers to the ability of a liquid to flow. The viscosity of diesel fuel is important since it must be low enough to flow easily through the filter and injection system, and at the same time high enough to properly lubricate the moving parts of the injection system. No. 2 diesel fuel has a higher viscosity than No. 1, which means it lubricates better, but does not flow as well. Because of this and its lower cetane rating, No. 2 diesel fuel is generally not as satisfactory as No. 1 in extremely cold weather. Some manufacturers also recommend No. 1 for use in high altitude operation.

Two further suggestions regarding diesel fuel: First, don't substitute home heating oil in place of No. 2 diesel fuel. While the fuel itself may be less expensive, the sulphur content will tend to be much higher, which can lead to sulphuric acid residue accumulating in the engine oil and damaging bearing surfaces. In addition, heating oil is not refined to the same specifications as No. 2 diesel. As a second suggestion, it is generally recommended that you do not thin diesel fuel with gasoline in cold weather. The lighter gasoline, which is more explosive, will cause rough running at the very least and may cause extensive engine damage if enough is used. If gasoline is specified for winter thinning of diesel fuel, be sure to follow the engine manufacturer's recommendations regarding the amount to be added.

GASOHOL AND OTHER FUELS

In the 1980s, automotive fuels might be very much different from those of the past. For example, one potential source of fuel is a vast renewable resource called "biomass," which consists of vegatation and organic wastes that can be turned into ethyl alcohol. Currently, this resource, those who advocate its use, and the price of oil have combined to make feasible the production and sale of "gasohol," a mixture of gasoline with about 10% ethyl alcohol. Gasohol containing such small proportions of alcohol is generally usable in conventional gasoline-powered vehicles without any need for engine modifications, and it is said to provide benefits in terms of both fuel savings and engine emissions. Iowa motorists bought nearly 2 million gallons of gasohol in 1978, although nationwide, the sale of gasohol accounts for less than 1% of the total motor fuel sales. The best advice is to follow the recommendation of the manufacturer when deciding whether or not to use a given fuel in your vehicle.

There are two problems with producing gasohol. First, is the cost. It currently costs about $1.00–1.30 to distill a gallon of gasohol, roughly four to five times the cost to distill a gallon of gasoline. Gasohol is currently exempt from the Federal excise tax on motor fuel and some states offer other tax breaks to make the price more attractive. The second problem is one of supply. Distilleries now produce almost 100 million gallons of ethyl alcohol a year. Increasing the output so that every car could run on gasohol would require a plant investment of roughly $10 billion in addition to the grain or organic matter to distill enough alcohol.

Other possible fuels of the 1980s include those processed from our plentiful supply of oil-containing shale rocks, and from coal, which is an abundant national resource. However, it seems that environmental and economic problems may provide at least temporary obstacles for these sources to overcome. Some have experimented with blending diesel fuel with used engine oil, others with using hydrogen as a source of power, while continuing efforts are being made to improve battery technology to allow electric vehicles to travel greater distances between charges.

FILLING 'ER UP
Know Your Fuel Gauge

Learning to read your fuel gauge is more than just knowing that "F" means full and "E" means walk. By noting the gauge needle position whenever you fill up, you'll soon become good at estimating how many gallons it will take to fill the tank. This can be helpful when you're in a hurry and just want to get X dollars' worth instead of fussing with change and credit cards. In addition, knowing how to convert the needle position into gallons needed or gallons remaining will reduce the anxiety of wondering if you can make it from here to there on what you've got left. Remember that the gauge readings may change slightly if the car is going uphill, downhill, accelerating, braking, or traveling a sweeping curve.

If the Price Isn't Right

One of the best practices in filling up is knowing when *not* to fill up. If you're on a trip and drive into a strange gas station only to find that the price on the pump is beyond reason, don't be afraid to ask for a dollar's worth (if you're shy) or for the directions to Punxatawney (if you're not). Driving out of an overpriced station may not be proper etiquette but, as a wise man once said, better them mad than you.

If a station appears to be overcharging, providing fuel only to certain preferred customers, or requires the purchase of nonfuel goods and services with any fuel purchase, it may be violating federal pricing regulations. In this case, the U.S. Department of Energy's Economic Regulatory Administration may wish to know about it and may be able to provide some relief. If a station turns you away only to sell fuel to a more familiar customer who comes along immediately afterward, consider calling the E.E.R.A. hotline toll-free at 800-424-9246 (in Washington, D.C., 254-5474). Chances are your problem won't be solved right away, but you'll probably feel better for having made your voice heard.

Adding Gas and Oil

When filling your tank, watch for spillage—it can reduce your miles per gallon purchased. The most obvious source of spillage is the careless station attendant who thinks he's doing you a favor by topping up your tank to the very limit and beyond. Another is a loose filler cap which has not been fully tightened. The third source of spillage occurs when you fill up and allow your car to sit in the hot sun during a warm day—expanding fuel may seep out of your filler neck and be wasted.

Either instruct the attendant not to squeeze more fuel into the tank after it appears in the filler neck, or buy according to the number of dollars' worth you estimate will be needed. Don't trust the attendant to have tightened (or even to have replaced your filler cap—it's unbelievable how many times a spot check will reveal a loose cap. Avoid warm-weather expansion spillage by not filling the tank completely when the car will be sitting shortly afterward.

While at the station, especially if you're traveling, check your oil level and add a can from your trunk if a top-up is necessary. In case you never noticed, service station prices for oil, anti-freeze, and windshield washer solvent are generally much higher than you'll find at your local discount or auto supply store. Naturally, you shouldn't expect the attendant to be cheerful about checking your oil when you're going to add a quart of your own. In addition to the obvious reason of courtesy, do-it-yourself checking and adding will ensure that you weren't "short-sticked," a practice in which a few unethical attendants push the dipstick only partially into its tube, then announce that you need oil when in fact you don't.

Pumping Your Own

With many service stations providing less and less "service" at higher and higher prices, the incentive becomes greater to save a few cents per gallon by frequenting a self-service pump. By pumping your own fuel, you may be able to save as much as a dollar on every fill-up. It takes very little additional effort to pump your own fuel and pocket the savings. In addition, by doing your own fill-up, you can ensure that fuel is not spilled all over your car or on the ground, that the filler cap really has been replaced, and that paint and body hardware is not scratched through careless handling of the pump nozzle. Be careful with the nozzle restrictor (see Figure 5-2) in the filler neck of a car requiring unleaded fuel—some are relatively fragile and can be bent or broken. Do not introduce leaded fuel into a car requiring unleaded—this is prohibited not only by federal regulations, but also by laws in a number of states.

In the case of diesel fuel, if self-service is available, you can top the tank at a slower rate in order to reduce foaming of the fuel and ensure that your tank really is full when you're finished. Whether diesel or gasoline, Figure 5-3 describes the typical procedure involved in pumping your own fuel—it's not very difficult and is still another fuel "discount" you can provide yourself.

ENGINE OIL SELECTION

Three ways you can improve your car's fuel mileage and ensure that it will continue to deliver good efficiency for a longer time are to: (1) understand the important function of oil in your engine, (2) choose a high-fuel-efficiency oil of the proper type for the operating conditions you encounter, and (3) have the oil and filter changed at the recommended intervals.

The Functions of Engine Oil

What does oil do in your car's engine? If you answered "lubricate," you're only partially right. While oil is primarily a lubricant, it also performs a number of other functions vital to the life and performance of your engine.

In addition to its role as a lubricant, oil also dissipates heat and makes parts run cooler; it helps reduce engine noise; it combats rust and corrosion of metal surfaces; it acts as a seal for the pistons, rings, and cylinder walls; and it combines with the oil filter to remove foreign substances from the engine. In return for the performance of all these tasks, oil requires a modest wage—about a tenth of a penny for every mile you drive.

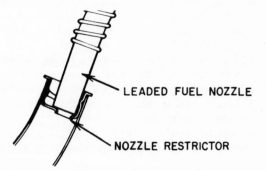

Fig. 5–2. On cars with catalytic converters, there is a restrictor in the fuel filler neck to prevent the use of larger nozzles used on the leaded fuel pumps.

LEADED FUEL NOZZLE

NOZZLE RESTRICTOR

Fig. 5–3. Pumping your own gasoline is not difficult and can provide savings of up to $1 per tank for your effort.

Types of Engine Oil

Engine oils have been classified by the American Petroleum Institute into "S" (normal gasoline engine use) and "C" (commercial and fleet) applications. The listing in Figure 5-4 describes the latest API classifications along with those previously in use.

As a rule, only oils identified as suitable for API service SE should be used in your engine, "C" classifications, which might appear in addition to the SE code, refer primarily to oils for use in diesel engines, with CA, CB, and CD corresponding to light, moderate, and severe duty respectively. Oil classified as CC is designed for diesel engines used in moderate duty and for certain heavy-duty gasoline engines. Follow the engine manufacturer's recommendations for the right oil classification to use.

In addition to meeting the SE classification of the American Petroleum Institute, your oil should be of a viscosity suitable for the outside temperature in which you'll be driving. Viscosity is defined as a resistance to flow—maple syrup has a high viscosity, sewing machine oil has a low viscosity. Proper oil viscosity is important for both maximum gas mileage and maximum engine life.

MOTOR OIL GUIDE

The American Petroleum Institute (API) has classified and identified oil according to its use. The API service recommendations are listed on the top of the oil can and all car manufacturers use API letters to indicate recommended oils.

Almost all oils meet or exceed the highest service rating (SE), but viscosity should be selected to match the highest anticipated temperature before the next oil change. **(S = Gasoline   C = Diesel)**

API Symbol	Use and Definition
SF	This is a new (in 1980) improved version of SE gasoline engine oil with improved oxidation stability and anti-wear performance. It will probably replace SE oil in the future.
SE	SE represents the most severe service. It is recommended for use in all 4-cycle gasoline engines, and cars used for stop and start or high speed, long distance driving. It has increased detergency and can withstand higher temperatures, while providing maximum protection against corrosion, rust and oxidation. Meets all service requirements for classifications SD, SC, SB and SA.
SD (formerly MS 1968)	These oils provide more protection against rust, corrosion and oxidation than oils classified SC. Meet minimum gasoline engine warranties in effect from 1968–70.
SC (formerly MS 1964)	These oils control rust and corrosion and retard the formation of high and low temperature deposits and meet minimum warranty requirements in effect for 1964–67 gasoline engines.
SB (formerly MM)	These oils have anti-scuff properties and will slow down oxidation and corrosion. Oils designed for this service afford minimum protection under moderate operating conditions.
SA (formerly ML)	These oils have no protective properties and have no performance requirements.
CD (formerly DS)	These oils provide protection from high temperature deposits and bearing corrosion in diesel engines used in severe service.
CC (formerly DM)	These oils provide protection from rust, corrosion and high temperature deposits in diesel engines used in moderate to severe service.
CB (formerly DM)	These oils are designed to provide protection from bearing corrosion and deposits from diesel engines using high sulphur fuel. Service is meant for engines used in mild to moderate service with lower quality fuels.
CA (formerly DG)	This is a general diesel service classification. These oils should not be used when sulphur content of fuel exceeds 0.4%. Oils will provide protection from bearing corrosion when high quality fuels are used.

Fig. 5–4. A breakdown of the American Petroleum Institute (API) classifications for engine oil, including designations used in previous years. "S" indicates gasoline engine, "C" is applicable to diesel. (*Source:* American Petroleum Institute.)

This is the oil's SAE viscosity grade. The numbers followed by a 'W' indicate an oil with low temperature performance characteristics and the 'non-W' numbers describe an oil with high temperature characteristics. If there is one number, it is a single grade. Two or more numbers indicate a 'multi-viscosity' oil which has both low and high temperature characteristics.

This is the manufacturer's brand name.

This means that the oil will protect expensive engine components. Even if your car is no longer under warranty, it indicates that the oil is of good quality.

These letters generally mean that the oil meets or exceeds established standards for use in gasoline (indicated by 'S' and a following letter) and diesel and commercial engines (indicated by 'C' and a following letter). These designations replace the older classifications which may be called for in some owners' manuals. The SE rating is the highest standard for gasoline automobiles.

Fig. 5–5. The top of the oil container can tell you all you need to know about the oil inside. Note that this is an SE-rated oil.

Oil must be thin enough to get between the close-tolerance moving parts it must lubricate. Once there, it must be thick enough to separate them with a slippery oil film. If the oil is too thin, it won't separate the parts; if it's too thick, it can't squeeze between them in the first place. Either way, excess friction and wear take place. To complicate matters, cold-morning starts require a thin oil to reduce engine resistance, while high-speed driving requires a thick oil that can lubricate vital engine parts at temperatures up to 250° F.

The answer to this problem is multiple-viscosity oils. According to the Society of Automotive Engineers' viscosity classification system, an oil with a high viscosity number (e.g., 40) will be thicker than one with a lower number (e.g., 10W). (The "W" in 10W indicates that the oil is desirable for use in winter driving.) Through the use of special additives, multiple-viscosity oils are available to combine easy starting at cold temperatures with engine protection at turnpike speeds. For example, a 10W-40 oil will have the viscosity of a 10W oil when the engine is cold and that of a 40 oil when the engine is warm. Using such an oil will decrease engine resistance and improve your miles per gallon during short trips in which the oil doesn't have a chance to warm up.

Some of the more popular multiple-viscosity oils are 5W-20, 5W-30, 10W-30, 10W-40, 20W-40, 20W-50, and 10W-50. In general, a 5W-20 or 5W-30 oil is suitable for temperatures below 0° F, 10W-30 or 10W-40 whenever the lowest temperature expected is 0° F, and 20W-40 whenever the lowest temperature expected is 32° F. However, consult your owner's manual or a reputable oil dealer for the recommended viscosity range for your car and the outside temperatures in which it operates.

Additives

A high-quality engine oil will include a number of chemical compounds known as additives. These are blended in at the refinery and fall into the following categories:

Pour point depressants help cold starting by making the oil flow more easily at low temperatures. Otherwise, the oil would tend to be a waxy substance just when you need it the most.

Oxidation and bearing corrosion inhibitors help to prevent the formation of gummy deposits that can occur when engine oil oxidizes under high temperatures. In addition, these inhibitors place a protective coating on sensitive bearing metals which would otherwise be attacked by the chemicals formed by oil oxidation.

Rust and corrosion inhibitors protect against water and acids formed by the combustion process. Water is physically separated from the metal parts vulnerable to rust, and corrosive orrosive acids are neutralized by alkaline chemicals. The neutralization of combustion acids is an important key to long engine life.

Detergents and dispersants work together. Detergents clean up the products of normal combustion and oxidation while dispersants keep them suspended until they can be removed by means of the filter or an oil change.

Foam inhibitors prevent the tiny air bubbles which can be caused by fast-moving engine parts whipping air into the oil. Foam can also occur when the oil level falls too low and the oil pump begins sucking up air instead of oil (like when the kids finish a milkshake). Without foam inhibitors, these tiny air bubbles would cause hydraulic valve lifters to collapse and reduce engine performance and economy significantly. Bubbles are OK in champagne, but not in engine oil.

Viscosity index improvers reduce the rate at which an oil thins out when the temperature climbs. These additives are what makes multiple-viscosity oils possible. Without them, a single-weight oil that permitted easy starting on a cold morning might thin out and cause you to lose your engine on a hot afternoon. If you use a multiple-viscosity oil, it's this additive that helps your gas mileage during those short trips in cold weather.

Friction modifiers and extreme pressure additives are valuable in so-called boundary lubrication, where there is metal-to-metal contact due to the absence or breaking down of the oil film between moving parts. Friction modifiers, or anti-wear agents, deposit protective surface films which reduce the friction and heat of metal-to-metal contact. Extreme pressure additives work by reacting chemically with metal surfaces involved in high pressure contact.

If you use good-quality fuel and oil, make reasonable efforts to maintain proper mechanical tune and adjustments, and change your oil and filters at the recommended intervals, the benefits from using additional additives yourself will be minimal. Under certain conditions, though, it may be desirable to thicken your oil with a well-known viscosity index improver—for example, during high-speed, hot-weather driving when the oil in your crankcase is of a lower viscosity than would be called for under these circumstances. However, if you're already using a high-mpg type oil (see next section) of the proper rating and viscosity, use of this additive becomes harder to justify.

When it comes to possible additives for increasing fuel mileage, my personal choice would be the molybdenum disulfide (MoS$_2$) concentrate, a very effective lubricant recommended by its marketers for the engine, manual transmission, and rear axle, but not for use in an automatic transmission. In tests using the EPA simulated driving cycle, adding molybdenum disulfide to the engine oil and the rear axle lubricant improved the EPA combined (city/highway) fuel economy by approximately 5%.[4] However, not all car manufacturers are excited about the use of additives in their vehicles, and some have specified in their owner's manuals a blanket directive that additives are neither necessary nor desirable. But it's your car, your warranty, your money, and your choice.

The New Fuel-Efficient Oils

Some of the newer oils are designed specifically to improve fuel efficiency by reducing still further the amount of friction within the engine. While the specific additives and approaches may differ, the intent is still the same: less friction and more miles per gallon. Tests of fuel-efficient oils suggest that mileage improvements of 2% to 5% or more may be possible. In one controlled fuel economy test involving a fleet of nineteen automobiles, the average improvement was 4.6% over a 10W-40 reference oil of the SE classification.[5] As with most fuel-efficient oils, this improvement was achieved gradually over a period of engine conditioning, in this case after about 1,500 miles. The improvement curve is shown in Figure 5-6.

In tests of a high-mpg oil that uses graphite as a friction modifier, it was found that fuel economy improvements ranged from 6% to 7.1% (cold engine) to 3.5% to 4.2% (warm engine), suggesting that greater benefits are realized during cyclical conditions, such as occur during short-trip operation.[6]

Don't automatically dismiss the fuel efficiency claims being made by well-

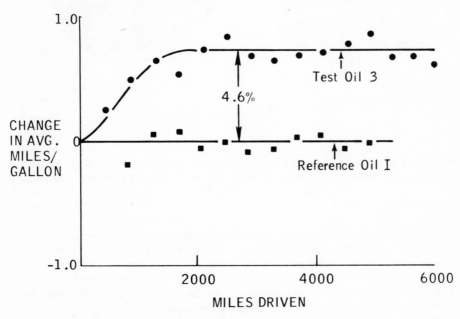

Fig. 5–6. Some fuel-efficient engine oils will require a period of engine conditioning before delivering maximum benefit. In this test, the full efficiency advantage was achieved after about 1,500 miles. (*Source:* W. E. Waddey, H. Shaub, and J. Pecoraro, *Improved Fuel Economy Via Engine Oils,* SAE Paper No. 780599, 1978.)

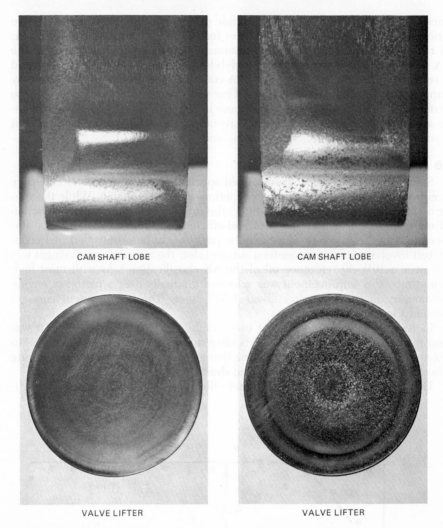

CAM SHAFT LOBE   CAM SHAFT LOBE

VALVE LIFTER   VALVE LIFTER

Fig. 5–7. As these comparisons indicate, a fuel-efficient engine oil can also mean less wear on mechanical parts. The camshaft lobe and valve lifter on the left were lubricated by Arcographite, a 10W-40 high-mpg oil with graphite as a friction modifier, while those at right were lubricated by a conventional 10W-40 oil. Engines were in police cruisers which covered 34,000 miles. (*Source:* Atlantic Richfield Company.)

known companies for the mileage improvements their oils can deliver. While the specific amount of improvement may vary, depending on your car and the type of driving you do, the purchase of a top-quality brand of fuel-efficient engine oil is likely to be a good investment. However, since the cost is immediate (when you buy the oil) and the benefit accrues gradually (as you accumulate miles and purchase less fuel), such an investment may not come naturally.

Makers of fuel-efficiency oils claim that an oil that reduces engine friction will also reduce engine wear, and they're right. From the discussion in Chapter 2, you will recall that engine resistance is only one of many forces which must be overcome in order to travel down the highway; thus, a slight improvement in fuel mileage must be accompanied by a disproportionate reduction in engine friction. As an example of the wear-reduction possibilities that may result from lower engine friction, consider the photographs in Figure 5-7 in which wear comparisons were made after two police cruisers with 460-cubic-inch engines covered 34,000 miles. One engine used a well-known oil of fuel-efficiency formulation, while the other used a high quality conventional 10W-40 engine oil.

While some approaches to high-mpg oils involve modifying the frictional characteristics of the oil, other strategies may involve both viscosity reduction and friction modification. Still others involve the separate addition by the owner of friction modifiers, such as a concentrated dispersion of molybdenum disulfide (MoS_2) to enhance the frictional properties of the oil already in the crankcase.

Note: Before switching to one of the fuel-efficient oils, be sure that it is satisfactory for use in your vehicle and driving conditions, and that it does not invalidate your warranty or otherwise lack the approval of your car's manufacturer.

That's the oil story. For best fuel mileage, use a top quality, multiple-viscosity, SE- or SF-rated engine oil that has been formulated for high fuel efficiency.

Chapter 6
Maintaining for Efficiency

Whether you're a do-it-yourselfer or a fugitive from the customer's lounge, attending to your car's mechanical needs is one of the most important ways to save your fuel dollars and break your previous miles-per-gallon records. As a matter of fact, you can save 11% on one item alone—by having your engine tuned up if it has gotten out of tune. According to the Car Car Council, driving with an untuned engine has the same effect as hauling 750 pounds around in your trunk.

Improper maintenance adds up, and this chapter discusses a great many areas that can save or waste fuel, depending on whether or not they are attended to. When your car has even a few things left unattended, the extra fuel consumed can be quite considerable. The following table is based on Car Care Council estimates, and assumes a large automobile getting 15 miles per gallon, driven 1,000 miles per month, and requiring $1.10 per gallon of fuel. With just four important components not doing their job properly, the owner is incurring the equivalent of a 25% surcharge on the price of fuel, and is spending an extra $18.34 per month:

	Fuel Consumption Penalty	Monthly Cost of Inefficiency
Car needs a tune-up:	11%	$ 8.07
Tires are underinflated by 8 pounds:	5	3.67
Front wheels are ¼ inch out of alignment:	2	1.47
Thermostat is stuck in the open position:	7	5.13
	25% extra fuel	$18.34 per month

Naturally, if a few more of the car's many mechanical systems were to be operating inefficiently at the same time, this monthly penalty would reach much higher levels, both in percentage and in all-important expenditures for the extra fuel that is wasted.

As an example of how many things are likely to be functioning inefficiently in the typical automobile, consider the results of a two-year test conducted by the Champion Spark Plug Company to determine engine condition and consumer maintenance habits. The test covered 5,666 cars in twenty-seven cities throughout the United States and Canada and uncovered some surprising results:[1]

> Cars judged to be in need of a tune-up recorded an 11.36% improvement in fuel economy when tuned to manufacturer's specifications.

New spark plugs alone accounted for an average 3.44% improvement in fuel economy.

More than 27% of all cars tested were more than a quart low on oil.

34% of all cars tested had dirty air filters.

More than 40% of the cars tested experienced hesitation during acceleration.

Nearly 80% of the cars tested had one or more maintenance deficiencies which would adversely affect fuel efficiency and engine emissions.

In addition to the fuel efficiency advantages of a tune-up, the environment benefits as well. In Champion's test program, average carbon monoxide (CO) emissions at idle were lowered by more than 45% and hydrocarbon (HC) emissions were decreased by more than 55% as the result of tune-ups on the vehicles tested. Another survey by Champion revealed that a tune-up is twice as effective against winter starting trouble as is battery service by itself.[2] If you've ever been stuck in a nonstarting car during a snow storm, you can appreciate the dependable starting as well as the clean and efficient operation a tune-up can help provide.

Your engine will operate much more efficiently if it is serviced at the proper intervals and if you keep alert for indications that a malfunction or gradual deterioration may be reducing your fuel mileage. Although you should follow your owner's manual or other reliable service guide, the services and intervals presented here are typical for most engines. If the engine is hard to start, idles poorly or stalls, misses at various speeds, lacks power, pings or hesitates during acceleration, or burns an excessive amount of oil, a tune-up or repairs may be in order.

The mechanical checks and adjustments described in this chapter are all-important in determining your car's fuel efficiency performance. While other maintenance operations should not be ignored, they will not have as great an effect on fuel efficiency in the short run. To accommodate the increasing popularity of do-it-yourself work, some of the tune-up and maintenance steps are described in greater detail than others. Since it is impossible to give specific procedures for each individual make/model of car, one of the best investments for do-it-yourself work is a repair and tune-up guide for your car. Chilton Book Company publishes a complete line of guides for individual makes/models of cars and light trucks. These guides contain specific maintenance, tune-up and repair procedures, maintenance intervals and required equipment and tools to perform various tasks. In general, you should find that investments in do-it-yourself equipment will be quickly repaid through lower maintenance and fuel costs.

MECHANICAL CHECKS
Compression

Before tuning the engine, it's a good idea to check cylinder compression in order to get an idea of how successful you're likely to be. If the engine has one or more weak cylinders, smoothness and top efficiency will be impossible to achieve through normal tuning, and mechanical repairs may be necessary. An accurate compression gauge will cost about $10.

CAUTION: Do not try to check compression on diesel or rotary engines. A normal compression gauge cannot handle the extreme pressure of a diesel engine, and special equipment is necessary to check compression on a rotary engine.

To test the compression, first warm up the engine to its normal operating temperature, then turn it off. Stick numbered pieces of tape onto the spark plug

wires so that you'll be able to put them back where they belong. Carefully disconnect the wires from the spark plugs. Don't pull on the wires themselves,
because you might separate them from their insulating boots. Using a a spark
plug wrench (costs about $2), and being careful not to drop any dirt or particles
into the cylinder, remove each spark plug.

At this point, you'll need an assistant to floor the gas pedal and switch on
the starter. With the compression gauge held firmly in the spark plug opening,
crank the engine until the needle reaches its highest reading. This will generally
take less than four seconds.

CAUTION: When working under the hood, be sure to avoid the fan, drive
belts, and other moving parts. Neckties, loose clothing, jewelry, and long hair
are all hazardous when you're working around a moving engine. Make sure that
the handbrake is firmly applied.

After recording the readings in all cylinders, compare the lowest with the
highest. If the compression of any cylinder is less than 75% of that recorded by
the highest, the low cylinder is likely to have either burned valves or worn piston rings. Check your compression readings with those specified as acceptable
from various manuals or from dealer service departments.

It's a good idea to check and record cylinder compression readings at periodic intervals. Although readings will vary with temperature, oil viscosity, altitude, and other factors, knowing how readings tend to vary between cylinders
can give you early notice of advancing ring and valve wear. Since compression
testing involves the flow of gasoline into an engine that isn't running normally, it
can cause dilution of the engine oil. For this reason, it's advisable to schedule
your compression test just before an oil change.

Valve Clearance

Since most cars are equipped with hydraulic valve lifters, you probably
won't need to bother with routine valve clearance checks. Hydraulic lifters do
the same job as a mechanical lifter, but they are self-adjusting, operate with no
lifter-to-valve-stem clearance, and use normal engine oil pressure for their
operation. However, with the increasing popularity of smaller vehicles with
engines that have an adjustable valve mechanism, there is a good chance that a
high-economy car will have valves that must be adjusted periodically for proper
clearance.

Drive Belts

Inspect the drive belts for wear, cracks, and tension. A belt that is too tight
will reduce gas mileage and lead to rapid wear in the bearings of the device it's
operating. In general, a belt will have correct tension if you can use firm thumb
pressure to depress it one-half inch in the middle of its longest travel between
pulleys. A preferable method of checking is to use a special tension gauge recommended by some manufacturers. Be sure to check with your owner's manual for
the proper tension specifications for your car. To adjust a drive belt, loosen the
bracket nuts of the accessory involved and rotate the bracket slightly.

If, as in Figure 6-1, two drive belts are used to operate an accessory and
there is a difference in the tension of the two belts or one belt is worn, it is a
good idea to replace *both* belts in order to maintain proper tension on the
pulleys.

Exhaust Manifold Heat-Control Valve

The often-neglected manifold heat-control valve controls the flow of gas
through the exhaust manifold and normally aids fuel economy by helping the
engine to warm up more quickly. When the engine is cold, the valve directs hot

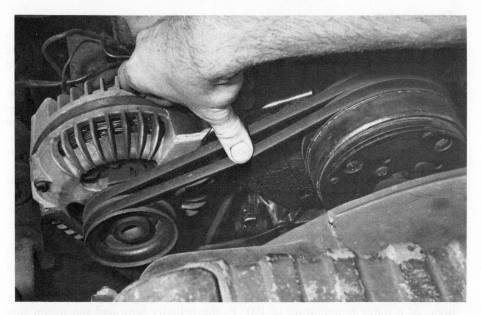

Fig. 6–1. If one belt is loose, tight, or in need of replacement when an accessory is driven by two belts, replace both belts in order to maintain proper tension on the pulleys.

exhaust gas through a passage in the intake manifold to heat the incoming air-fuel mixture, helping it to vaporize more easily. As the engine warms up, the valve rotates and allows exhaust gas to follow its normal route through the exhaust system. The presence of this valve in your car is indicated by a shaft and counterweight below the exhaust manifold.

A valve stuck in the "cold" position will cause hot exhaust gas to circulate even when the engine is warm, leading to overheating of the engine and spark plugs, knocking, and loss of power and fuel economy. It will also reduce gas mileage by extending engine warm-up time and fouling spark plugs. Check its freedom of movement when the engine is cold—the counterweight should move easily. Should it be sticking, tap it lightly and apply a special penetrating oil to the ends of the shaft. To help prevent future problems, it's best to use a penetrating oil that won't leave high-temperature deposits that can cause further sticking.

COOLING SYSTEM

Burning gases within the cylinders can reach a temperature of 4,500° F. Because of this intense heat, an effective cooling system is a must for engine reliability and efficiency. About one-third of the engine's heat is carried away by the cooling system. If it carries away too much or too little, efficiency and reliability will suffer.

Hoses and Clamps

A collapsed or leaking radiator hose will, at best, reduce your gas mileage. If you're less fortunate, the resultant overheating could ruin your engine. Check all heater and cooling system hoses for cracks, and their clamps for tightness. Use a water pump lubricant and rust inhibitor to lower water pump friction and reduce the formation of rust scales, which could lower cooling efficiency.

Thermostat

If your engine never warms up completely, or warms up very slowly, you may be losing miles per gallon because of a faulty thermostat. Besides helping the engine to warm up quickly, the thermostat helps ensure that economical running temperatures are maintained.

The heat range of a thermostat is usually described by two temperatures—the one where it starts to open, permitting water to circulate through the cooling system, and the one at which it is fully opened. A 180°–200° thermostat will begin to open at 180° F and be fully open at 200° F. With increased emphasis on engine emission control, thermostats in recent models begin to open near 190° F and open fully at about 210° to 215° F.

Until the lower temperature of the thermostat range is reached, no water is circulating and the engine heats up quickly. Within reasonable limits, higher temperatures result in better fuel mileage. When a car is traveling at 30 mph, for instance, increasing the water temperature from 120° F to 190° F can improve gas mileage by 3%.[3]

A bad thermostat can lower your miles per gallon, lengthen your engine's warm-up time, accelerate engine wear, and cause dilution of oil and formation of sludge in your engine.

Wear of the cylinder bore and piston rings at lower temperatures is very high. At a water temperature of 100° F, the cylinder bore and top piston ring will wear out at the rate of about .001 and .002 inch, respectively, each thousand miles.[4] However, at temperatures over 170° F, their rate of wear is practically zero.

Never remove the thermostat permanently from your engine. Without it, your engine will stay in the low-temperature, high-wear zone and engine lifetime will suffer considerably.

If you suspect that your thermostat isn't providing the quick warm-ups and proper running temperature for maximum economy, you can easily check and replace it. To remove the thermostat, drain the cooling system until the water is below the level of the thermostat housing, then remove the housing and thermostat. With the thermostat and a high-temperature thermometer in a pot of water, heat the water to boiling and observe the expansion of the thermostat to determine the exact temperatures at which it begins to open and is fully open. (Note: If the thermostat is supposed to open fully at a temperature above 212° F, it may not reach this temperature in an open pot of boiling water.) When replacing the thermostat, be sure to use a new housing gasket.

Radiator Cap

The radiator cap is necessary to pressurize the cooling system in order to increase water pump efficiency and prevent boil-over at higher temperatures and elevations. For example, in the mile-high city of Denver, water will boil at only 200° F. A 4 psi (pounds per square inch) radiator cap will increase water's boiling point to about 215° F at this altitude. Visually check the radiator cap for cracks, damage, or a worn gasket. For safety, check the cap when the engine is cold. If the engine is hot, cover the cap with a thick rag before removing it.

A better test is to have your local service station or dealer pressure-test it to measure the pressure at which it allows air to escape. If the cap can't hold the pressure at which it's rated, replace it.

Cooling Fan

The radiator cooling fan uses a significant amount of power, especially at higher road speeds when it isn't really needed at all. Your car may be equipped with either a friction-controlled fan (which doesn't speed up as much when the engine speed increases) or an electric fan (which cools the radiator only when water temperature reaches a given level). On the friction-controlled fan, check for excessive wobble on the shaft. For the electrically powered fan, make sure that the motor turns easily and the electrical connections are sound.

CAUTION: On some models with electrical fans, the fan will operate to cool the engine after the motor has stopped, so examine the electrical fan only when the engine is cold or after you have disconnected the fan from the rest of the electrical system.

FUEL SYSTEM

The emissions system is discussed later in the chapter. At the carburetor itself, idle speed and idle mixture may also require adjustment. Naturally, if your vehicle is diesel-powered or equipped with fuel injection, your maintenance requirements will not only be different from those described here, but also are likely to be far beyond the capability of the tools and instruments in your garage.

Carburetor

The two most common carburetor adjustments are the idle speed and idle mixture. For either adjustment, a dwell-tachometer is desirable. It costs about $40, but it is useful in ignition tuning as well.

The idle speed is adjusted by turning the throttle valve stop screw, which should be set to the manufacturer's specifications. The engine must be warm for all cars, with manual transmission in neutral and automatic transmission in the gear specified. Other idle speed setting requirements might include operating the headlights and air conditioner while the speed is being adjusted. Refer to your owner's manual or read the label in the engine compartment for the correct rpm and setting conditions.

Many vehicles now have a throttle solenoid which controls the warm engine idle speed. To see if your engine has an idle speed solenoid, shut off the air conditioner, open the throttle by hand, and have someone turn the ignition key to "on" (but don't start the engine). If there's a solenoid, you will see its stem extending under these conditions. If the idle speed of an automatic transmission car is set too high, the car will waste gasoline by trying to "creep" when it is stopped.

The idle mixture adjustment is a matter of history for most recent models because the idle mixture screws on these cars have a locking cap that limits the range of adjustment. On earlier cars, turn the idle mixture screw in or out until the tachometer reading is at its peak, then check the idle speed and reset it if necessary. Owners of models with an adjustment limiter should follow the same advice and do the best they can within the range provided by the limiter cap. Tampering with or removing the limiter cap is against the law if done by a commercial service facility and, in some states, if done by anyone, including private owners.

Other carburetor adjustments that can affect gas mileage are the fast-idle speed, the stroke of the accelerator pump, and the float level. The fast-idle setting causes the engine to idle a little faster when it is warming up, while the accelerator pump stroke adjustment determines how much raw gas gets squirted into the engine when you push on the gas pedal. If the carburetor float is set too low, leaks, or is too heavy, the rich mixture that results will sharply lower your fuel economy.

An automatic choke that's not working right can cost you 3 miles per gallon.[5] With the engine cold, the choke plate should be completely closed. As the engine warms up, it should gradually approach the vertical position. If the choke sticks, use a degreasing solvent to remove deposits from the plate pivot points.

Using engine oil could cause future sticking by attracting dirt to these critical locations. Be sure that the choke is set to the leanest possible setting for proper starting and operation of the car. The best way to find out is to gradually adjust it in the lean direction until starting becomes difficult, then back off slightly for less choking and more miles per gallon.

Be sure that there are no leaks at the carburetor base or intake manifold. These leaks can be detected by applying engine oil to the edges of the surfaces involved. Clean and lubricate the carburetor linkage so that it will move smoothly and easily when your right foot is coaxing the pedal downward during a driving-for-economy start.

Fuel Lines

In addition to being dangerous, leakage in the fuel lines and connections can waste gas before it has a chance to get to your engine. Check the integrity of the fuel lines between the carburetor and fuel tank, and between the tank and filler cap. While you're at it inspect the tank, too—the seams of an older fuel tank might have weakened over the years. Carefully tighten the various carburetor and other bolts and screws along the way, but don't be heavy-handed or you could strip their threads.

Fuel Filter

There are various types of fuel filters in use and various locations in which they are installed. The important thing is that you clean or replace the fuel filter at the recommended intervals. A clogged fuel filter can allow dirt to enter the carburetor and narrow the passages that are critical for the proper air-fuel mixture.

Air Filter

If your car has a clogged air filter, it can cost you 1 mile per gallon.[6] Every gallon of gasoline you use requires up to 9,000 gallons of air to do the job. Whenever the air filter becomes even partly clogged with dirt, the result is the same as if the automatic choke were in operation. The passage of incoming air is restricted and the air-fuel mixture comes rich, resulting in lower gas mileage. Because this loss of economy is gradual, the air filter is easier to ignore than other gasoline robbers which are more obvious, but less important. For example, a clogged air filter may waste five times as much gas as a 200-pound set of weights carried in your trunk.

For most cars equipped with the paper-element type of air filter, replacement of the element involves removing the wing nut which secures the top of the air cleaner, taking out the old element, and replacing it with the new. The oil bath air cleaner used in some cars requires removing the entire filter body, rinsing the base in gasoline, then refilling the base with fresh oil. Always change or clean the air filter according to the manufacturer's recommendations, and more frequently if dusty driving conditions are encountered.

One air filter which often escapes attention is the small oil-wetted gauze filter in the oil filler cap of some cars. It cleans air that is drawn for crankcase ventilation. It should be removed, washed in gasoline, dried, and re-oiled at periodic intervals.

LUBRICATION SYSTEM
Engine Oil

In the miles you cover between oil changes, your engine oil gradually becomes contaminated with dirt, dust, metal particles, acids, soots, water, gaso-

Fig. 6–2. When replacing the old air filter (top), don't forget to check the small crankcase breather filter (bottom) and replace it if necessary.

line, oil oxidation products, and various other unfriendly substances. If the oil is used too long, additives become depleted and can no longer offer protection against these contaminants. In addition, a dirty or clogged oil filter can offer no assurance that dirt and metal particles will be removed from the oil. When a filter becomes clogged, oil will flow directly to your engine by way of a filter by-pass designed to protect against loss of lubrication when the filter is blocked or the oil is too thick to flow through it.

By ignoring periodic oil changes which remove contaminants that the old oil has collected, you'll only hasten your car's journey to that great highway in the sky. Your gas mileage will also suffer in both the long and short run—contaminated, worn-out oil increases engine resistance as well as wear, ensuring that neglect will haunt you both now and later.

Automobile manufacturers recommend oil changes at maximum time and mileage intervals, and these recommendations vary from year to year and from manufacturer to manufacturer. However, the recommendations presented in Figure 6-3 are typical. Short trip, stop-and-go, cold weather, heavy duty, and extended idling conditions all make it advisable to change oil more often than you may think necessary. Under ideal conditions, such as turnpike driving or other sustained operation, engine oil will last longer and be less contaminated by the acids, water vapor, and other substances that tend to form during cold-engine, low-speed operation.

By changing your own oil, you can save more than enough money to pay for the fuel-efficient oil you you should be using. The fuel-efficient oil, in turn, raises your fuel mileage and provides an excellent return on your investment of time and cash.

Oil Filter

Your oil filter will probably be of the disposable canister type, which screws on and can be removed either by hand (cost: $0) or by oil filter wrench (cost: about $3–$5). While a filter that has been in place for many miles may require the use of the wrench, the use of a clean rag or piece of inner tube for a better grip should enable you to remove it by hand. After removing the old filter, wipe the dirt from the area where the new filter will contact the engine. Spread a light layer of engine oil on the gasket surface of the new filter. Before installing the filter, read the tightening instructions on its side, then use hand pressure to screw it on tight. Don't use the wrench on a new filter.

Other filters may employ a replaceable cartridge. In this case, instead of replacing the entire filter, you need only buy a new cartirdge, but the cartridge housing should be removed and cleaned, too. Before removing this type of filter, check to see if a drain plug is provided to drain oil from the filter housing. If so, use it and thank the designing engineers. Remove the housing bolt or nut, take out the housing and cartridge, then clean the housing and other permanent parts with gasoline. Install the new cartridge into the housing, lubricate its gasket, and replace the housing to its base. Replace the drain plug, if any. Tighten down the center bolt or nut.

After installing an oil filter of either type, add the necessary quantity of oil, then start the engine and check closely for leaks. Figure 6-3 summarizes the operations involved in changing your oil and filter.

PCV Valve

The positive crankcase ventilation (PCV) system "freshens" the crankcase with a current of clean air and recirculates crankcase fumes back into the engine for more complete burning. In addition to preventing crankcase fumes from entering the atmosphere, the PCV system helps reduce oil contamination caused by combustion by-products. The heart of this system is the PCV valve, which prevents an unbalanced air-fuel mixture by metering the amount of crankcase fumes allowed to enter the intake manifold. If the PCV valve is clogged, there will be two major results. First, the unbalanced combustion mixture will provide

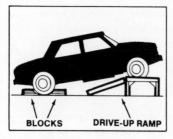

1. Warm the car up before changing the oil. Raise the front end and support it on drive-on ramps or jack-stands.

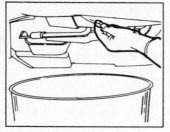

2. Locate the drain plug on the bottom of the oil pan and slide a low flat pan of sufficient capacity under the engine to catch the oil. Loosen the plug with a wrench and turn it out the last few turns by hand. Keep a steady inward pressure on the plug to avoid hot oil from running down your arm.

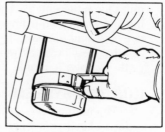

3. Remove the oil filter with a filter wrench. The filter can hold more than a quart of oil, which will be hot. Be sure the gasket comes off with the filter and clean the mounting base on the engine.

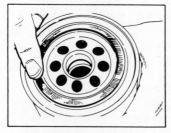

4. Lubricate the gasket on the new filter with clean engine oil. A dry gasket may not make a good seal and will allow the filter to leak.

5. Position a new filter on the mounting base and spin it on by hand. Do not use a wrench. When the gasket contacts the engine, tighten it another ½-1 turn by hand.

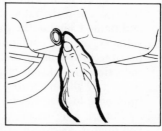

6. Using a rag, clean the drain plug and the area around the drain hole in the oil pan.

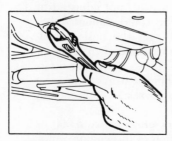

7. Install the drain plug and tighten it finger-tight. If you feel resistance, stop and be sure you are not cross-threading the plug. Finally, tighten the plug with a wrench.

8. Locate the oil cap on the valve cover. An oil spout is the easiest way to add oil, but a funnel will do just as well.

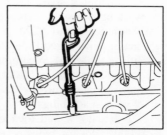

9. Start the engine and check for leaks. The oil pressure warning light will remain on for a few seconds; when it goes out, stop the engine and check the level on the dipstick.

Fig. 6-3. A summary of the operations involved in changing your oil.

poor engine performance and economy. Second, the lack of crankcase ventilation will lead to heavy sludge formation and possible engine damage.

Periodic changes of oil and filter will help keep the PCV valve clean and functioning properly. However, because of its low cost (about $2) and important function, it should be replaced at the intervals recommended by the manufacturer, typically every 12 months or 12,000 miles for checking and 24 months or 24,000 miles for replacement. You can check your PCV valve by pulling it from its housing and putting your finger over the end. With the engine idling, you should notice a strong suction. If not, the valve is defective and should be replaced. Another test involves removal of the PCV valve. If you shake it and it doesn't rattle sharply, it should be replaced.

IGNITION SYSTEM

The ignition system in all gasoline engines requires periodic maintenance in order to keep your engine working at its fuel efficient best. Maintenance intervals vary depending on ignition system type and car manufacturer. Proper ignition system service is essential to a good tune-up. As mentioned early in this chapter, an average fuel efficiency increase of 11.36% was achieved on the cars tested after they had been tuned, and a change to new spark plugs alone provided an increase of 3.44%.

Electrical Connections and Wiring

Before tuning the ignition system, you should check the electrical connections at the distributor, coil, and spark plugs. All connections should be clean and tight. Examine the high tension coil and spark plug wires for fraying, cracks, softness, and oil contamination. When the engine is running in the dark, it is possible to visually inspect for leakage from the spark plug and coil wires and for induction cross-firing of plugs served by adjacent spark plug wires. While the wires may all have a very slight glow, serious leaks from a wire to the car body or from wire to wire will be evidenced by lightning-like sparks.

Spark plug wires can be checked visually by bending them in a loop over you fingers, as shown in Figure 6-4. Any wire revealing cracks or burned insulation should be replaced, and, since all the wires are likely to be the same age, it's not a bad idea to replace all of them if a bad one is found.

Spark Plugs

A fouled spark plug can cost you 2 miles per gallon if it's not adjusted or working properly.[7] That may not seem like much, but this could amount to between $100 and $200 per year for a typical family. To get the best fuel efficiency, it's a good idea to make sure that the plugs are replaced at the time or mileage intervals recommended by the car manufacturer. If you want your do-it-yourself time to be spent as profitably as possible, it's difficult to recommend a more money- and fuel-saving project than the simple removal and replacement of your spark plugs.

It's not a bad idea to remove a couple of the spark plugs every 5,000 or 6,000 miles (or twice a year) just to check on the condition of the engine. After you've removed the plugs, refer to Figure 6-5 to read what they have to say about your engine, your driving, and your maintenance habits. The most talk-

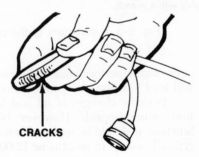

Fig. 6–4. Cracks in a spark plug wire can cause misfiring and reduced fuel efficiency. Cracked or broken insulation can often be determined by bending the wire in a loop, as shown.

CRACKS

NORMAL

Brown to grayish tan color and slight electrode wear. Correct heat range for engine and operating conditions.

RECOMMENDATION. Service and reinstall. Replace if over 10,000 miles of service.

MODIFIER DEPOSITS

Powdery white or yellow deposits that build up on shell, insulator and electrodes. This is a normal appearance with certain branded fuels. These materials are used to modify the chemical nature of the deposits to lessen misfire tendencies.

RECOMMENDATION. Plugs can be cleaned. If replaced, use same heat range.

OIL DEPOSITS

Oily coating.

RECOMMENDATION. Caused by poor oil control. Oil is leaking past worn valve guides or piston rings into the combustion chamber. Hotter spark plug may temporarily relieve problem, but positive cure is to correct the condition with necessary engine repairs.

CARBON DEPOSITS

Dry soot.

RECOMMENDATION. Dry deposits indicate rich mixture or weak ignition. Check for clogged air cleaner, high float level, sticky choke or worn breaker contacts. Hotter plugs will temporarily provide additional fouling protection.

PREIGNITION

Melted electrodes. Center electrode generally melts first and ground electrode follows. Normally, insulators are white, but may be dirty due to misfiring or flying debris in combustion chamber.

RECOMMENDATION. Check for correct plug heat range, overadvanced ignition timing, lean fuel mixtures, clogged cooling system, leaking intake manifold, and lack of lubrication.

TOO HOT

Blistered, white insulator, eroded electrodes and absence of deposits.

RECOMMENDATION. Check for correct plug heat range, overadvanced ignition timing, cooling system level and/or stoppages, lean fuel/air mixtures, leaking intake manifold, sticking valves, and if car is driven at high speeds most of the time.

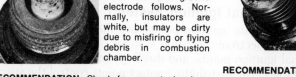

HIGH SPEED GLAZING

Insulator has yellowish, varnish-like color. Indicates combustion chamber temperatures have risen suddenly during hard, fast acceleration. Normal deposits do not get a chance to blow off, instead they melt to form a conductive coating.

RECOMMENDATION. If condition recurs, use plug type one step colder.

SPLASHED DEPOSITS

Spotted deposits. Occurs shortly after long delayed tune-up. After a long period of misfiring, deposits may be loosened when normal combustion temperatures are restored by tune-up. During a high-speed run, these materials shed off the piston and head and are thrown against the hot insulator.

RECOMMENDATION. Clean and service the plugs properly and reinstall.

Fig. 6–5. The condition of your car's spark plugs can tell you quite a bit about your gas mileage. (Photos courtesy of Champion Spark Plug Co.)

ative parts of an engine, the spark plugs can give you an insider's view of why your car may not be giving you the gas mileage you'd like.

Depending on the results of your spark plug inspection, you may want to check with your dealer about the advisability of installing either hotter or colder spark plugs to better suit your engine and your type of driving. Remember that while a hotter plug will tend to rise fuel economy and carbon up less, it will also be more prone to pre-ignition and overheating.

If you intend to re-use the spark plugs you've just examined, scrape all deposits from the electrodes, body, and insulator, then use an ignition file (cost: about $1) to clean up the electrodes. Whether installing new or used plugs, check the gap with a round feeler (or wire-type) gauge (cost: about $1). Don't use a flat leaf gauge on used plugs—you'll get an inaccurate measurement. With the gap tool portion of the gauge, bend the outer (ground) electrode until the proper gap is obtained. Never try to adjust the gap by bending the center electrode.

If the manufacturer specifies a range for the spark plug gap, try to stay near the center of the range, since normal wear will increase the gap by about .001 inch every 1,000 miles. Don't make it too narrow to compensate for the expanding gap that occurs over the miles, as a too-small gap won't be able to supply a strong spark. If you're interested in maximum economy at the cost of some of your time, gap the plugs as wide as specifications allow, then re-gap at this setting every 2,000 miles.

After you've adjusted the gap, clean the spark plug hole and apply a drop of oil to the plug threads. Being careful to avoid cross-threading the plugs, screw them in firmly with hand pressure, then tighten with a wrench. Don't twist too hard on the wrench, as this could damage the threads in the cylinder head. If possible, use a torque wrench and tighten the plugs to the manufacturer's specifications.

Ignition Points (Conventional Ignition System)

The distributor contact points (ignition points) are the heart of all conventional and some solid state (electronic) ignition systems. (Many electronic systems have no conventional ignition points, and dwell (point gap) is electronically controlled and nonadjustable). The distributor contact points control the spark to each cylinder, and in doing so they may have to open and close as often as 300 times each second. (If you tried to clap your hands that fast, your elbows would disintegrate.) When the points are closed, they conduct an electrical current that allows the coil to build up an intense magnetic field. Then, as the points open, the interruption in current causes a rapid drop in magnetism which creates the 20,000 volts available to spark your plugs.

The length of time that the points are closed is called the dwell angle. If the points are not closed long enough (too little dwell), the coil won't have time to build up a strong magnetic field and the resulting spark will be weak. If they are closed too long (too much dwell), electrical current will heat up the coil, increase its resistance, and likewise result in a weak spark. In order to give the coil enough time to build up voltage, but not enough time in which to lose it, the dwell angle must be just right.

The time-honored way of measuring ignition point dwell has been the flat leaf feeler gauge. This technique relies on the fact that dwell decreases when the points are set far apart and increases when they are close together. The feeler gauge measurement is, at best, an approximation of the actual dwell angle specified by your car's manufacturer. Not only is it an indirect measure of the actual degrees of dwell, but it's often not even a good measure of the gap between the points. While not too bad for measuring the gap between brand new points, the

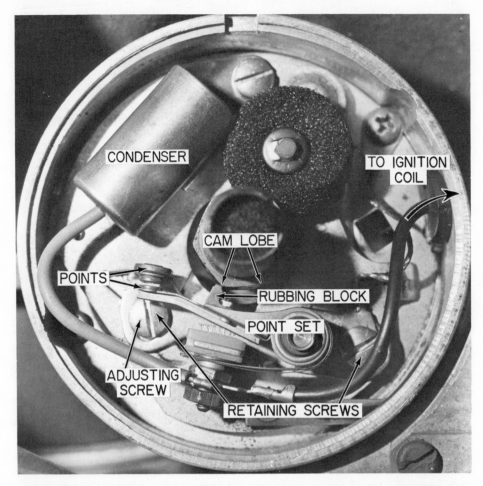

Fig. 6–6. Top-side view of a set of points in the correct position for setting the gap. Note that the rubbing block is exactly at the high point of a cam lobe. When you insert the feeler gauge to check the clearance, be sure that the gauge is not at an angle to the gap. After tightening the retaining screw, recheck the clearance to make sure that it hasn't changed.

feeler gauge will always underestimate the actual distance between used points. This is because pits and craters develop on even recently installed points.

Because of the inaccuracies of the feeler gauge, if you're going to do your own ignition point setting, it's recommended that you invest in a dwell meter (about $15) or combination dwell-tachometer (about $30). With the dwell meter hooked up, you'll know exactly what the dwell angle is and how it compares with the setting, specified by the manufacturer, that will give you the best spark and the most miles per gallon.

You can examine your ignition points by removing the distributor cap and rotor, then using a small screwdriver to spread the points apart. If they're excessively burned or pitted, replace them. If not, file them smooth and readjust them. The job of the condenser (see Figure 6-6) is to reduce the electrical arcing which causes transfer of metal from one point to the other. If one point has a large peak which matches the other's crater, the condenser should be replaced when new points are installed.

Before leaving the distributor, check the distributor cap for cracks, carbon tracking, terminal erosion, and excessive wear of the center contact button. Inspect the rotor for physical damage and erosion of the tip. Any of the preceding conditions can lower the voltage available to your spark plugs and hurt your gas mileage.

If you're thinking about buying a dwell-tachometer to help you in your pursuit of better gas mileage and lower maintenance bills, buy a unit that provides two rpm scales. For example, 0–1,000 rpm and 0–5,000 rpm scales have their own specialties, the former for idle accuracy, the latter for higher speed checks. Some meters try to squeeze all 5,000 rpm into a narrow band only a few inches wide, thus making small rpm changes difficult to see.

Whether you've used a feeler gauge, a dwell meter, a dwell-tachometer, or a surveyor's transit to set the point gap, you'll now need to adjust the ignition timing. Any change to the contact points automatically requires that the ignition timing be checked.

Ignition Points (Electronic Ignition Systems)

On solid-state ignition systems which have no conventional ignition points, dwell is electronically controlled and nonadjustable.

Ignition Timing

Now that you have a spark of the proper strength, you need to make sure it arrives at the proper time. A spark that gets to the cylinder just 5 degrees too late can cost you 1 mile per gallon.[8] Ignition timing is best done with a stroboscopic light (about $5–$25) and must be carried out after the dwell or point gap has been adjusted. While any stroboscopic light will do the job, the more expensive ones plug into a 115-volt wall socket and make it much easier to see the timing marks that you're supposed to be lining up.

CAUTION: In using the stroboscopic light to time the engine, you'll be working near the fan and fan belt. Loose clothes, jewelry, neckties, and long hair are hazardous under these conditions. Be sure to have adequate ventilation to prevent carbon monoxide poisoning.

Conditions and specifications for setting the timing are in your owner's manual or on a label under the hood. The timing marks are generally found on the vibration damper or crankshaft pulley, with a pointer located on the cover of the timing chain or belt.

Figure 6-7 shows a typical timing degree scale and pulley mark. In general, timing marks are usually difficult to locate and read. While this scale has the degrees clearly marked, many scales do not.

Put a chalk mark on the pointer and on the specified timing mark on the scale. Unless the manufacturer has specified otherwise, disconnect the hose from the vacuum advance unit on the side of the distributor and plug it with a blunt pencil. Hook up the timing light according to the instructions which accompany it, then aim the light at the timing pointer or scale, whichever is stationary. With the engine warmed up and idling slowly, the timing light will flash each time the spark plug in number one cylinder fires. The light should "freeze" the motion of the pulley or damper so that the chalk marks line up perfectly. If they don't line up, loosen the distributor clamping bolt and gradually rotate the distributor until they coincide. (If your first try moves the marks further apart, turn the distributor in the other direction.) After tightening down the distributor, recheck to ensure that the setting has not changed.

With the pencil removed and the vacuum advance hose connected, observe

Fig. 6–7. This is a typical timing mark arrangement, cast into the front of the engine. A stroboscopic timing light will make these marks "freeze."

the movement of the "frozen" mark as you increase the engine speed. It should advance the timing smoothly. If you alternately connect and disconnect the vacuum hose while the engine is running, the mark should move quickly back and forth. If it doesn't, the vacuum diaphragm has a leak and should be replaced. Never "power time" the engine on the road, especially if yours is one of the majority of engines with emission control devices.

EMISSION CONTROL SYSTEM

In some form or another, your car has a variety of emission control equipment which is required by law, helps make the air cleaner, and tends to reduce

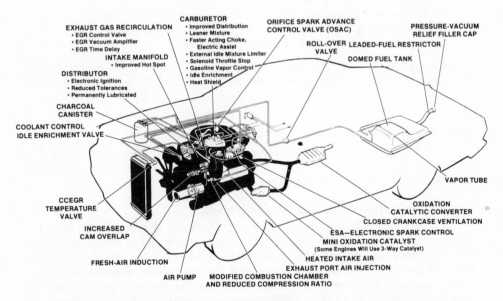

Fig. 6–8. This diagram illustrates most of the emission control systems in use today. The multitude of devices and mechanisms used by various manufacturers has not made do-it-yourself emission system troubleshooting a promising avenue for the average motorist.

your fuel mileage. These devices make it even more critical that you pay close attention to routine maintenance and adjustment—if even a tuned emission-controlled car can run a little poorly, one that is out of tune may be lucky to run at all. There is a wide variety of such devices, many of which are shown in Figure 6-8, and we can't hope to cover all of them here. However, we will examine four main systems and then discuss fuel-efficient strategies to deal with a few of the others. Four main systems are in use today for the control of engine emissions: the catalytic converter system, the positive crankcase ventilation (PCV) system, the air injection reactor (AIR) system, and the exhaust gas recirculation (EGR) system.

The Catalytic Converter

The catalytic converter, looks somewhat like a muffler. It is inserted in the exhaust system for the purpose of treating exhaust gases so that harmful carbon monoxide (CO) and hydracarbons (HC) are converted to harmless carbon dioxide (CO_2) and water vapor (H_2O). It contains a catalyst (generally beads of platinum) that chemically encourages the reactions required for the conversion of CO and hydrocarbons into harmless gases. The principal problem associated with the catalytic converter is the need to use unleaded gasoline; otherwise, the catalyst will become poisoned and the converter rendered useless. Because the catalytic converter operates at very extreme temperatures (well over 1,000°F), overheating of the converter may also become a problem. To maintain the converter and encourage optimum efficiency, practices or situations should be avoided:

1. Using fuel system additives or cleaning agents.
2. Operating the car with an inoperative choke.
3. Extended periods during which the engine "diesels" (runs on after being shut off).
4. Shutting off the ignition with the car in motion.
5. Failure of the ignition or charging system.
6. Misfiring of one or more plugs.
7. Disconnecting a spark plug wire while the engine is running.
8. Pushing or tow-starting the car when the engine is hot.
9. Pumping the gas pedal to start a hot engine.

Aside from the necessity of using unleaded gasoline, the catalytic converter does not require routine maintenance for the performance of its emission-related duties.

The Positive Crankcase Ventilation System

The PCV valve, as discussed in the Lubrication System section on page 126, should be checked at intervals of 12 months or 12,000 miles, whichever comes first, and replaced every 24,000 miles or two years.

The Air Injection Reactor (AIR) System

This system is based on a belt-driven air pump that injects air into the exhaust valve ports to help oxidize hydrocarbons and carbon monoxide before they can enter the atmosphere. As in the catalytic converter, the hydrocarbons and CO are converted to water vapor and carbon dioxide. Because of the extreme operating temperatures, stainless steel nozzles are used to direct the air into the vicinity of the exhaust valve port. In addition to the pump there is a check valve that prevents hot exhaust gases from flowing back into the pump and hoses, and a gulp or diverter valve that diverts air from the pump into the intake manifold during deceleration conditions when the throttle is closed. Without the gulp or diverter valve, the high vacuum under closed-throttle conditions could cause excess fuel entering the exhaust to explode upon contacting the fresh air being pumped into the same vicinity. The result could be a muffler which is no longer in one piece.

The vacuum sensing line is responsible for determining when closed-throttle, high-vacuum conditions dictate diversion of the air pump's output. Aside from checking that the air pump drive belt is not too tight, that the pump filter (if present) is clean, and that the pump turns freely, no other routine maintenance is required on the AIR system.

The Exhaust Gas Recirculation (EGR) System

If your car is equipped with an EGR system, part of the exhaust gas is sent back through the intake manifold to help lower the peak temperatures of combustion and decrease the emissions of nitrogen oxides. While emissions of nitrogen oxides at low combustion temperatures is not severe, as the combustion process exceeds 2,500°F, the production of this pollutant is drastically increased. While performing the social function of reducing the output of nitrogen oxides, the EGR's less potent air-fuel mixture also tends to decrease fuel mileage. EGR systems have a vacuum control, operated by the EGR valve, to determine under what conditions to recycle exhaust gases into the intake manifold. The vacuum control may also be supplemented by a temperature control. On some engines, the temperature control will eliminate exhaust gas recirculation until the engine has reached a specified operating temperature. Aside from checking for freedom of movement (if the EGR valve sticks open, the idle will be very rough), the EGR valve does not usually require periodic maintenance.

Other Emission Systems

Your car may also depend heavily on engine modifications to lower emissions. If so, its ignition timing is slightly retarded, the spark advance curve a little slow, the compression ratio lowered, and the carburetor adjusted about as lean as it will go. Don't be tempted to advance the timing arbitrarily. Besides putting your engine emissions beyond legal limits, you can end up with too much advance at high speed and damage your engine. Keep the engine adjusted as specified in your owner's manual or on the label beneath the hood.

To reduce emissions under certain operating conditions, your car may employ the automatic spark retard. On some models, distributor vacuum advance is totally eliminated whenever you're operating in the lower forward gears. This spark retard is controlled by a switch at the transmission and may include a cold-temperature and a hot-temperature override. With this set-up, distributor vacuum advance may be available only in top gear, or with a four-speed, in the top two gears. If you have a car with transmission-controlled spark retard, try extra hard to get into that economical high gear as soon as you can.

The drop in gas mileage due to the various emission control systems and devices is significant but hard to pinpoint, since cars have become heavier (partly due to crashability and safety requirements) at the same time that they've become emission-controlled. One study, using gas mileage data collected by the EPA, concluded that a 4,000-pound 1971–1973 model traveled 12% fewer miles per gallon than a pre-1968 model of the same weight.[9] In another study, in which engine adjustments on four 1977 models were optimized for best fuel efficiency regardless of engine emissions, the average city/highway gas mileage was improved by 4.1%.[10]

Tampering with Your Emission Control Systems

The safest advice regarding your tampering with the emission control systems on your car is "Don't." The federal Clean Air Act specifically prohibits auto makers, dealers, repair garages, and fleet operators from knowingly tampering with auto emission controls. Mechanics are subject to a $2,500 fine, while a maximum fine of $10,000 per vehicle can be levied against dealers and manufacturers. While an antitampering clause is included for these commercial individuals and institutions, no specific penalties for private owners are mentioned. However, this gap has been filled in about twenty states where residents are prevented by law from tampering with the emission control systems of their own private automibiles. It seems likely that the future will find more states jumping on the bandwagon.

EPA surveys have found that the majority of tampering has involved the catalytic converter, the EGR system, the vacuum advance and retard for spark timing, idle limiter caps, fuel filler pipes, and PCV valves. Before you tamper with any emission compomponent or system, keep in mine that (1) there is an equal chance you will gain or lose mileage; (2) you may be breaking the law in your state and be subject to a fine or other penalty; and (3) you may damage your engine. Emission systems are somewhat complicated and the components under your hood are very much interdependent on each other. Tampering with one can cause inadvertent mechanical problems in addition to contributing to pollution.

In addition to the antitampering laws at the state level, a growing number of states and localities are moving toward compulsory exhaust inspection programs (tailpipe sniffer tests) to monitor the emissions of private vehicles and enforce repairs or maintenance as needed to bring them into compliance with standards for pollutants such as carbon monoxide and hydrocarbons. In some states, private garages carry out the inspection, while others employ government-run inspection stations. In some states only a few counties subject their vehicles to periodic emission checks. The federal government and lucrative highway funds will no doubt accelerate the push towards compulsory emission inspectations and repairs. In 1977, amendments to the Clean Air Act dictated that, by 1983, states must either put the inspection programs into force or else take other steps to bring air quality up to federal standards. With the dependence of states on federal highway funding, your tailpipe will probably be sniffed within the next few years if it hasn't already been, so if you have the urge to tamper with anything under the hood that's not presently under legislative control, don't do anything irreversible—the tailpipe sniffers mean business, and chances are that, sooner or later, your car will have to give off a clean scent.

Since there may be little that you can do legally to avoid fuel mileage losses due to emission controls, try to keep these systems maintained as recommended by the manufacturer. If you do this, at least your mileage won't be reduced any further than authorities deem necessary for the clean air effort.

DIESEL ENGINE MAINTENANCE

Compared to their gasoline counterparts, diesel engines are relatively uncomplicated in terms of maintenance services that can be carried out by the mechanically inclined owner. Because the diesel has no carburetor, spark plugs, distributor, points, or condenser, and virtually no emission controls, the routine maintenance really is routine. Perhaps the most critical duty is to diligently change the oil and oil filter at the intervals recommended by your car's manufacturer. The products of the diesel combustion process tend to contaminate the oil, and it's even more important than with a gasoline engine that the oil and filter be kept as clean as possible.

In addition, the air and fuel filters may be a bit more demanding than they were on your previous automobile. Because the diesel engine is unthrottled, ingesting all the air it can on every intake stroke, the air filter must process a much greater volume of air. Thus it will either be a lot more expensive or require changing at more frequent intervals, depending on the particular manufacturer. Likewise, the fuel filter price may tend to shock you, since it incorporates very fine filtration along with the ability to separate water from the fuel in order to protect the high-precision fuel injectors from corrosion. Between fuel filter changes, it may be necessary to loosen a special drain tap on the filter in order to remove the small amount of water that has accumulated in the bottom.

The diesel engine is not likely to have any of the conventional emission controls. Because the engine allows great amounts of fresh air to mix with the fuel mist, it already burns very completely and produces only low levels of carbon monoxide and hydracarbons. By the mid-1980s, however, this relative ease in meeting emission constraints may change with tightened standards on allowable levels of substances such as particulates and nitrogen oxides. Particulates are not controlled by federal regulation at this writing, but control will probably be forthcoming as the diesel car population grows. In the case of nitrogen oxides, lower permissible emission levels are scheduled to take effect in a few years. In complying with the future regulations in both of these emission categories, it may prove difficult to retain the superior fuel efficiency of present diesel engines.

With the diesel engine, even more than with the conventional type, it is strongly suggested that you follow or exceed the maintenance schedule recommended by the manufacturer. With relatively long distances possible between fill-ups, you may have to remind yourself to check the engine oil level at more frequent intervals than a shorter cruising range would encourage.

As with a gasoline engine, valve clearance checks and adjustments are required periodically, but involve basically similar procedures. Unless you have special training and equipment, don't even think about checking the compression pressure on your diesel engine. The pressure is far too much for conventional gauges to handle, so entrust this duty to a service facility that is properly equipped for the job.

TRANSMISSION AND DRIVE LINE
Rear Axle

If your car is of conventional front-engine, rear-drive design, you can reduce rear axle friction by keeping the differential topped up with a high-quality lubricant of the type specified by the manufacturer. If a multiple-viscosity lubricant (e.g., SAE 80W-90) is among those specified, use it instead of a higher viscosity single grade (e.g., SAE 90). Be sure not to use a lubricant which will be too thin for your driving conditions—again, your owner's manual is the best guide. In general, an SAW 80W-90 grade will be more energy efficient than an SAE 80W-140 type. Because the rear axle requires very little oil, which is changed only each two years or 24,000 miles, it's very inexpensive to use the best. Oil should be added until the level reaches the bottom of the filler plug hole, or a quarter-inch below, depending on the manufacturer's recommendation. If you're using a suction gun for oil removal and refilling, be sure to let the excess flow out before you install the filler plug.

Limited-slip rear axles don't use the same oil as conventional designs, so be careful to use the proper lubricant. If you're using an ordinary oil can (the kind you pump with your thumb), make sure that you don't get it mixed up with a similar can containing ordinary engine oil.

Fuel efficiency improvements in the range of 1 or 2% are likely if you are able to use a multiple-viscosity lubricant and your driving consists mostly of short trips during which the lubricant does not have a chance to warm up. As an example of how long it can take for the rear axle to warm up, at ambient temperatures of 41° to 59°F, it can take 15 miles of commuter driving for the oil to reach a steady temperature, as illustrated by the test results of Figure 6-9. In European tests of lubricant characteristics in truck fleet fuel efficiency, one study found that there was a 1.86% reduction in fuel consumption for the vehicles using 80W-140 lubricant versus the thicker 85W-140 grade.[11] Again, remember that while lower viscosity grades tend to be better for fuel efficiency, you should stay within the grades recommended by your car manufacturer.

Improved rear axle lubricants that might improve your miles per gallon by 5% in short-trip winter driving and 1% overall at normal temperatures may become available in the next few years.[12] In the meantime, you may wish to try a dispersed solid lubricant additive, such as molybdenum disulfide (MoS_5) to help out your present lubricant. EPA combined mpg can be improved as much as 5% by adding MoS_2 to the engine oil and rear axle lubricant. "Moly" is a very slippery substance capable of withstanding extreme pressures. The makers of

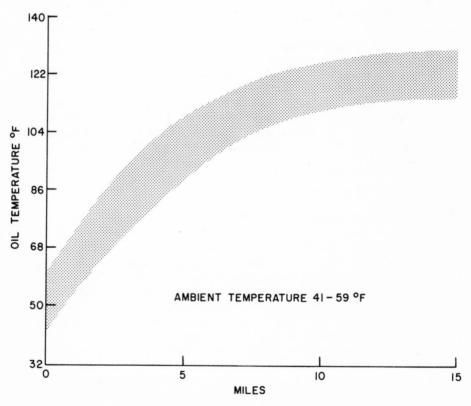

Fig. 6–9. Typical rear axle and transmission temperatures during short-trip commuter driving from a cold start. Lubricants took nearly 15 miles to warm. (*Source:* B. M. O'Connor, R. Graham and I. Glover, *European Experience with Fuel Efficient Gear Oils,* SAE Paper No. 790746, 1979.)

Molygard®, an MoS$_2$ concentrate, recommend that the product be added to engine oil, manual transmission lubricant, and rear axle oil for greater fuel efficiency. They stress, however, that it should not be added to automatic transmissions. If you decide to use an extreme-pressure additive such as molybdenum disulfide, remember that you might be on your own as far as your vehicle warranty is concerned, since some manufacturers do not recommend the use of lubricant additives in their products.

Automatic Transmission

To ensure fuel-efficient operation, the automatic transmission should be serviced at the recommended intervals, typically 6 months or 6,000 miles for checking fluid level and condition, and 24 months or 24,000 miles for changing transmission fluid, replacing filters, and cleaning screens.Incorrect fluid level can cause an automatic transmission to slip and waste fuel. Before checking the fluid level, warm up the car until the transmission is at its normal operating temperature. If the vehicle has just been used to haul a trailer or has just been returned from an extended trip, wait a short while before doing the check. With the car on a level surface, shift the transmission through all drive positions and return it to the park position. With the engine idling, locate the dipstick and clean all dirt and grease from the cap. Remove and wipe off the dipstick, then return it to the filer tube until it is fully seated. Withdraw the dipstick and observe the fluid level. Add enough fluid to raise the level to the "full" mark, but *don't overfill*. Use a good quality fluid of the type recommended by your car's manufacturer.

When checking the fluid level, it's a good idea to note the color and to rub a small amount of fluid between your fingers to check for grit. Normal fluid will be clear and red. If it is aerated or foamy, there may be an internal air leak or the level may be too high, causing the gears to churn up the fluid. If there is solid residue, defective bands or bearings are among several possible mechanical problems. If the fluid is very dark red or brownish, internal damage may be present as the result of overheating. A varnish coating on the dipstick indicates that the transmission fluid is overheating.

Manual Transmission and Clutch

For efficient operation of the gears, keep the transmission topped up to the level of the bottom of the filler hole, or slightly below. For the smooth shifting that efficient driving demands, lubricate the pivot points of the shifting arms (if present). Be sure that the car is on the level when you're checking the oil level and that you don't overfill. Excess oil could find its way to the clutch lining and reduce your fuel efficiency to zero. Before venturing beneath the car, have the transmission in gear and the handbrake firmly set.

As with other lubricants, be sure to use one that meets the specifications set forth by the auto manufacturer. In some instances, such as the front-wheel drive configuration, the transmission and differential (there is no rear axle in this case) will share the same lubricant. Again, lower viscosities will tend to deliver better fuel efficiency, and multiple-viscosity lubricants (if among those specified by the manufacturer for your driving conditions) will provide better fuel efficiency, especially during short trips in cold weather. As with the rear axle, the use of a molybdenum disulfide additive may be considered for reduced friction and better efficiency. Again, keep in mind that the owner's manual may contain a blanket disapproval of additives in general, so act accordingly, especially if your car is still under warranty. However, as the owner of the vehicle, the final decision is yours.

The transmission oil should be changed only after the lubricant has reached operating temperature, and the drain plug cleaned if it is of the magnetic type. When refilling, add oil until the level is at (or just below) the filler hole. (If your transmission doesn't have a magnetic drain plug, try to obtain one. With the magnet, small metal particles are held and kept from being held in suspension in the lubricant.)

When the clutch pedal is lightly depressed, it should move very easily for about an inch, then become more difficult to push. The distance traveled before resistance increases is the free play. If your clutch pedal doesn't have enough free play, the resulting slippage will lower clutch facing life as well as your fuel mileage. (There are several ways to adjust the clutch. If you want to do it yourself, your best bet is to buy a repair and tune-up manual for your vehicle.)

Wheel Bearings and Brakes

Faulty wheel bearings and dragging brakes can make your engine think it's pulling a horse trailer. With the car lifted on a jack, rotate the wheels to check resistance to turning. Because of their constant pressure against the rotor, disc brakes can be expected to drag slightly. Drum brakes should spin freely. Because of drive train resistance, the driving wheels will not spin as easily as the other two. Even so, you'll be able to detect the rumble of a bad bearing or the sound of a dragging brake, in which case your brakes need adjusting.

If the wheels have too much "wobble" or are difficult to turn, the problem may be with the wheel bearings instead of the brakes. Periodic inspections of drum brakes in some states require removal of one or both brake drums to examine the linings. After the drum is replaced, the front wheel bearing will have to be adjusted, which leads to the possibility of an improper adjustment or to dirt entering the wheel bearing area. The best time to check the ease with which your wheels turn is after the state inspection.

From the efficiency perspective, bearings and brake drag are the key points to be checked. However, proper brake system maintenance, will help ensure that the braking components do not detract any more than necessary from your fuel mileage. If the parking brake is adjusted properly, there will be little or no drag whenever the brake is released. You can help keep it that way if you follow a driving tip: keep your foot on the brake pedal when you engage the parking brake. This will make it easier for the parking brake cable to do its job, since the brake shoes will already be in the locked position. The result will be less tension on the cable, a longer lifetime for it, and a reduction in the chance that the cable will stick when it is called upon to release the parking brake.

You can inspect disc brake rotors by removing the wheels. If there are deep grooves worn in the disc brake rotors, it will be more difficult for the wheel to turn against the resistance of the brake pads, and fuel mileage will drop. Rotors with deep grooves should be resurfaced, along with the one on the other side of the car. If you drive as efficiently as possible, you will be amazed at how long your brake pads and linings last.

TIRES

Proper tire care is important for both safety and fuel efficiency, with advisable maintenance ranging from tire pressure checks every fuel stop or two weeks to rotation and a check of tread depth every 6 months or 6,000 miles. In addition, you should occasionally take a few minutes to clean stones, glass, and other debris from the tread.

Pressure

Underinflated tires, with their higher rolling resistance, can cost you 1 mile per gallon.[13] In addition, soft tires will wear out faster, run hotter, and have a

Fig. 6–10. Effects of inflation pressure on the shape of the tire and its footprint. Overinflation will improve fuel efficiency, but at the cost of tread wear (the center will wear out much more quickly) and, on some vehicles, adverse handling characteristics which reduce safety.

higher risk of failure. If your tires have been wearing on the outside edges of the tread, chances are that they've been underinflated—give them more air and you'll burn less fuel. Keep pressures on the high side of the manufacturer's recommendation, and be very cautious in going over the recommended range. While an overinflated tire will roll easily, it will also wear out more quickly than one carrying the correct pressure. Figure 6-10 shows the effects of over- and underinflation on the shape of the tire and its footprint on the pavement. Don't mistake the characteristic sidewall bulge of the radial tire for underinflation— radial tires always look that way, even when fully inflated.

Tire pressures should be checked when the tires are cold, never when warm or after driving. Setting a warm tire to the correct cold pressure will result in the tire being too soft. When driving at high speeds or hauling loads, check your owner's manual for the extra pressure needed for these conditions.

If you buy a good tire gauge and use it, it will save fuel dollars as long as you own a car with tires. It will also be more accurate than the gas station tower gauges you may otherwise use. A study by the National Bureau of Standards revealed that 45% of the station gauges tested were off by at least 3 psi.[14]

Tread Thickness

A bald tire will give better fuel mileage—at least until it goes flat. With less rubber on the tread to squirm, a worn-out tire will have less tread flexing and lower rolling resistance. However, bald tires are illegal, they are up to 44 times more likely to go flat, and if you drive them in the rain, you'll think your car's wearing water skis. Replace any tire that has less than $1/16$ inch of tread. You can use a Lincoln penny to check your tread depth—if you insert the top of Mr. Lincoln's head through two adjacent tread grooves, you should not be able to see the top of his head. If you can, you need new tires. Since 1968, tread wear indicators are built into new tires and will show up as bars across the tread whenever $1/16$ inch remains. If you want your tires to have low rolling resistance, don't rely on thin tread to help. Instead, go out and buy a good set of radials.

Rotation

For even wear and long tread life, tires should be rotated every 6,000 miles. (*Do not include the new "space-saver" spare tires in the rotation pattern. These are for temporary emergency use only.*) If you have a mixture of radial and belted bias tires, it's best to leave them where they are. While snow tires should not be rotated unless you're using four of them, you can equalize wear on your present tires by having the fronts and backs take turns sitting out consecutive winters.

(When removing radial or studded tires from the car, mark them so that they can be installed in a position where they will keep the same direction of rotation.) Since some manufacturers do not recommend periodic rotation for their tires, check with your dealer before rotating.

Balancing

When do 3 ounces weigh 22 pounds? When they're rotating on your car's wheel rim at a road speed of 55 miles per hour. A wheel that is out of balance by as little as three ounces can make your car's front wheels act as if they were being hopped on by a 22-pound kangaroo. While such imbalance might not have much effect on your economy today, it could lower gas mileage quite a bit in the future. With a worn-out front end controlling tires that don't know which way to roll, gas mileage won't be good. The faster you drive, the more important it is to have your front wheels balanced, both for safety and economy.

Wheel balancing takes two forms—static and dynamic. Static balance is obtained when the weight of the wheel and tire is evenly distributed around the axis of the wheel, and it is tested with a bubble balancer. Dynamic balancing checks the distribution of weight about the vertical centerline of the wheel, and it is often done with the wheel installed on the car. A small electric motor turns the wheel at high speed while a stroboscopic light winks each time the heaviest point is at the bottom. The result is a "freezing" of the wheel while the serviceman determines which part of the rim needs more weight. Sophisticated off-the-car equipment is also used for dynamic balancing.

While the rear wheels are less sensitive to imbalance problems, you should have the front ones balanced every 6,000 miles or so. Although static balancing is better than nothing, dynamic balancing is preferable if you do most of your driving at highway speeds.

WHEEL ALIGNMENT
Toe-In

The car in your driveway is pigeontoed, and the reason for this stance is to ensure that the front wheels end up running parallel when rolling resistance forces them outward at highway speeds. Toe-in is generally expressed as the amount by which the front wheels are closer together at the front than they are at the back. For example, if the toe-in were zero, the wheels would be parallel. Tires with little rolling resistance—those radials again—rquire almost no toe-in because they are not forced outward as readily as other tires. So if you've installed radial tires on your car, be sure to have the mechanic set the toe-in accordingly. The same advice goes for belted bias tires, except that their higher rolling resistance won't permit quite as much reduction in the amount of toe-in. Even if you have conventional bias tires, you should still have the toe-in set as close to zero as specifications allow. As with so many other adjustments, improper toe-in can lower your gas mileage. It has been estimated that, besides wearing out tires more rapidly, incorrect toe-in can cost you about .3 miles per gallon.[15]

Camber

Camber is the angle at which a wheel deviates from the vertical, being positive when the top of the wheel tilts outward, negative when it tilts inward. Proper camber for your vehicle depends upon the manufacturer's specifications. Although the front wheels are those most often in need of checking, proper camber in all four wheels is important for the best tire life and gas mileage. Camber helps the front wheels to keep from being forced outward, so a tire that rolls easily shouldn't require as much camber as one with more rolling resistance. Zero camber is best for gas mileage because the different parts of the tire will have the same rolling radius, thus reducing the amount the tire must flex.

Caster

A front-end angle that your mechanic may check when he's looking at the toe-in and camber is the caster angle. Caster makes it possible for you to lift your car (slightly, of course) just by turning the steering wheel. It's similar in function to the rearward tilt of a bicycle's front fork, and helps provide directional stability. It also produces the self-centering behavior of your steering wheel after you've completed a turn. While caster is not as important for gas mileage as the other front-end angles, incorrect caster can cause your car to wander and steer erratically—thus making it more difficult to maintain constant speed and directional momentum when you're driving for economy.

OTHER CHECKS
Air Conditioning System

If you have an air conditioner, you can minimize the amount of time it is on, and the energy it uses when engaged, by maintaining it properly. Using the sight glass to check for the need to recharge the system is one of the most important. With the engine idling and the air conditioning operating at its coolest setting, inspect the sight glass for foam or bubbles in the passing refrigerant. If they are present, the system's efficiency will be improved by having the refrigerant recharged.

Electrical System

Because the alternator uses fuel to produce electricity for various vehicle needs, fuel will be wasted if the alternator has to work harder than necessary because of a defect in the electrical system. Be sure that your battery is sound, will hold a charge, and has clean terminals and connectors which don't create unnecessary resistance for the alternator to overcome. If the battery is too old to hold a charge, the alternator will be working hard to pour electricity into a bottomless pit. Likewise, a defective voltage regulator may be forced to keep even a good battery at a higher voltage than the battery is capable of holding. If you do have a battery that you have to nurse along during cold weather, use a battery charger to lightly charge the battery using house current instead of vehicle current, which costs fuel dollars.

Shock Absorbers

If your shock absorbers are worn out, you may find your car acting like a small boat whenever you go over bumps or apply the brakes. While the effect on fuel efficiency may not be as important as safety considerations, weak shocks will result in your car presenting an unstable shape to the air through which it is passing. This will mean increased air resistance, variations in weight distribution, greater rolling resistance, and reduced driver control. Bounce each end of your car up and down several times to get it moving by itself, then let go. If the shocks are good, the car should not continue to bounce more than once.

Weather Sealing

Whether it's the air conditioner in summer or the heater in winter, you don't want to use fuel needlessly to help make the inside temperature more comfortable. Check the rubber strips around doors and vent windows for flexibility and tightness. If they are in good condition and you'd like to keep them that way, apply some rubber lubricant from time to time.

Exhaust System

Earlier in the chapter, we were primarily concerned with helping your engine inhale. However, engines, like people, have to breathe both ways. Check your car's exhaust system for dents and restrictions. A clogged exhaust system will increase engine resistance and lower your fuel mileage.

Wax

If you've ever waxed your car, you may have noticed how easily a rag slides over the waxed surface. Although surface friction is more significant for ships and airplanes, it applies to anything that's driven through a resisting medium. Besides helping to maintain your car's appearance, a coat of wax wouldn't hurt your gas mileage either. Naturally, don't expect your gas mileage to double.

MECHANICAL DEVICES

Many mechanical devices are advertised that are supposed to save fuel by modified air-fuel mixtures, regulated fuel pressures, intensified ignition sparks, and special spark plugs. Be suspicious of any approach which, by itself, promises extraordinary savings. Some test cars actually obtain better mileage without a device than with it. According to the U.S. Federal Trade Commission, there are approximately 100 gas-saving devices on the market that are advertised as offering great savings to consumers at very little cost. According to the FTC, not one of the devices tested so far has achieved the desired result of significantly improving fuel mileage, and some may actually cause damage to the vehicle in which they are installed. While not all available devices have been tested, the EPA has tested at least one device in each of the functional groupings it has established. According to the FTC, copies of the Environmental Protection Agency's tests on gas-saving devices may be obtained by writing to the EPA, 2565 Plymouth Road, Ann Arbor, MI 48105.Some devices are probably worth the money, but the prolific advertising and extraordinary claims make them difficult to identify. When evaluating fuel mileage claims, look for dynamometer tests and don't be too trusting of user testimonials. Most consumers are not in a position to measure accurately the effect of a particular device simply by measuring their own fuel consumption—there are too many outside variables involved. Use your own good judgment. Unfortunately for those who market bona fide fuel savers, suspicion is the order of the day. I'd rather take a chance on not mentioning a few items that *might* work instead of talking you into spending your hard-earned money on a lot of gadgets that *don't*.

Chapter 7
Planning for Efficiency

Now that you know the forces of nature you're up against, and are selecting, driving, and maintaining with efficiency in mind, it might seem that there's little room for improvement. Nothing could be further from the truth—planning when and how to use your car promises one of the biggest opportunities for improvement. In this chapter the emphasis will be on two things: (1) planning to obtain more miles from the gallons you do use; and (2) planning those occasions when you can get away without using any fuel at all.

Before we talk about your fuel efficiency game plan, let's take a look at where your fuel dollars are going right now. If you're a typical driver, you'll make about 1,400 trips each year, use around 800 gallons of fuel along the way, and spend approximately 15% of your household expense budget on the family automobile(s).[1] The kinds of trips, and the amount of fuel they will typically consume, are shown in Figure 7-1. As the diagram indicates, about one-third of your

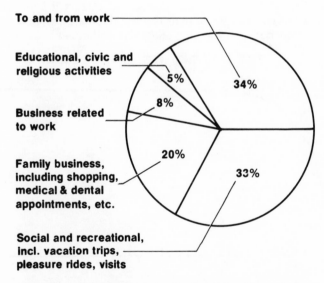

Fig. 7–1. Where does all that fuel go? If you're a typical driver, this diagram provides the answer. By applying the tips in this chapter, you should be able to reduce fuel consumption in each category. (Courtesy of American Automobile Association.)

fuel dollars are spent for traveling to and from work, another one-third for social and recreational driving, and one-fifth for family business.[2] These are the big consumers of our fuel, and thus hold the greatest potential for savings.

Because everybody tends to use fuel in a slightly different way, you can get the most benefit from this chapter if you consider the suggestions in light of your own usage pattern. When it comes to figuring out the best areas for you to save, chances are that *you* can be your best fuel efficiency consultant.

THE SHORT TRIP: ENEMY NUMBER ONE

In this land of seemingly endless interstates, it seems positively unimaginable that the most frequently made vehicle trip is only 1 mile long, but it's true.[3] Naturally, most of us consider such a miniscule distance hardly worthy of the label "trip." It is precisely because of this lack of respect that short-distance travel is a major consumer of our fuel dollars. As a matter of fact, trips under 5 miles comprise about 15% of the miles we drive, but consume 30% of all gasoline used by automobiles.[4] Figure 7-2 summarizes our national driving pattern in terms of trip length, and further illustrates the amazing frequency with which we make trips of very short length. As the chart shows, two-thirds of the trips we make involve distances of five miles or less.

Figure 7-4 shows how much fuel efficiency can suffer during a short, urban trip. In a two-mile trip with 70° F outside temperature, the average car delivers just 40% of the efficiency it would have delivered if fully warmed up. Thus, if a car capable of 20 miles per gallon under city conditions is started from cold and driven two miles, the result will be only 40% of its capability, or 8 miles per gallon! When the outside temperature is higher, at 70° F, things don't get too much better, with the fuel efficiency rising to only 60% of the car's fully warmed up economy.

Thus, when we consider the evidence of Figures 7-2 and 7-4, the short trip is bad news for two reasons: (1) we make a considerable number of them, and (2) our cars don't operate very efficiently during this type of driving. Although the short trip hurts in these two ways, it also means there are two different strategies we can use to reduce its considerable effect on our budget.

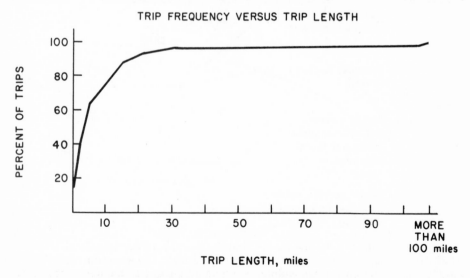

Fig. 7–2. As this chart indicates, we could probably plan our car usage a lot more efficiently. Two thirds of the trips we make cover five miles or less. (*Source:* Federal Highway Administration, U.S. Department of Transportation.)

Fig. 7–3. Short trips, such as this one for small grocery items, comprise 15% of all miles we travel, but use **30%** of the gasoline. Reason: Cars don't have a chance to operate at top efficiency under these driving conditions.

If it comes as a surprise that the short trip is so inefficient, remember that tires and lubricants don't tend to move very easily when you move away from a cold start. Also, during cold-engine operation, the operation of the automatic choke will cause the engine to run less efficiently because of the fuel-rich mixture which must be fed to the engine. Engine resistance, rolling resistance, along with the combined reluctance of all moving parts, results in the short trip being very undesirable from a fuel efficiency viewpoint. However, this isn't all—it has been estimated that 90% to 95% of all engine wear during a trip occurs

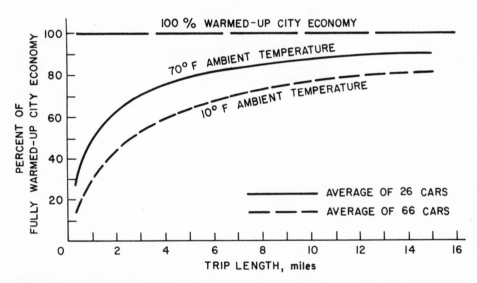

Fig. 7–4. As these test results show, the shorter the trip, the worse the fuel efficiency will be for a car started from cold. A two-mile trip, even in 70° F temperatures, will result in the average vehicle achieving only 60% of its fully warmed-up fuel mileage. (*Source:* Charles E. Scheffler and George W. Niepoth, *Customer Fuel Economy Estimated from Engineering Tests,* SAE Paper No. 650861, 1965.)

during the start-up and first 10 seconds of running. This is because oil has drained back down into the crankcase and requires a very brief (but expensive) period to circulate through the engine. As a result, a cold start to go to the corner grocery store will cause almost as much engine wear as a cold-start trip across the state.

So fuel savings and reduced engine wear provide two big incentives for us to eliminate as many of our short trips as possible. For those short trips which are indeed necessary, we will want to help our vehicle operate as efficiently as it can.

The No-Trip

Many local trips can be handled by using the telephone and mail facilities available in your own home. Checks can be sent to the bank, catalog orders can

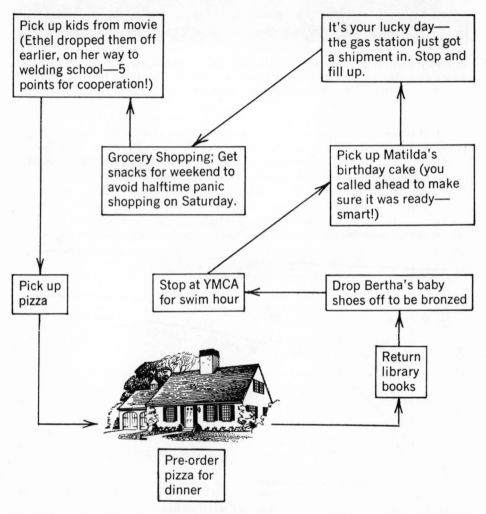

Fig. 7–5. While every day may not be as eventful as this one, those 1,400 annual trips average out to about four each day. By combining as many stops as possible into a single trip, you can make fewer trips and reduce your annual mileage and fuel consumption as well. Once out of the garage, the car will only have to warm up from cold one time during this well-scheduled trip, giving it the chance to operate more efficiently along the way.

be placed from the "wish book," you can mail Aunt Emily the hiking socks you knitted for her, and you don't have to be there to pound on the desk when you complain about your electric bill. While you can't use Railway Express to bring Johnny home from his tuba lesson, consider the dial-a-gallon possibility whenever you reach for the car keys.

Attacking Those Errands

One of the best ways to save fuel on short local trips is to combine as many of them as possible into a single effort. Not only will you travel fewer total miles, but you'll be getting more miles from each gallon while you're at it. As was demonstrated by Figure 7-4, a car's fuel efficiency increases considerably as the length of an urban trip increases. While it may take a little advance planning to schedule your errands, visits, and household business trips, it will pay off in fuel savings, as suggested by Figure 7-5.

Once you've combined a number of errands into a single trip, you can save further by deciding on the best order in which to make these stops. In the world of business, this has a counterpart called the "traveling salesman problem," in which the idea is to figure out the order in which the salesman should make his calls in order to minimize the total distance traveled. Depending on the number of places the salesman has to stop, the problem can become very complex in a hurry. While you may not want to apply the various mathematical solutions of the traveling salesman to your own situation, at least compare a few of the possible alternatives. With one-way streets, no-left-turns, and other obstacles, it might help if you made a little sketch of the routes you could take—if you have more than four places to visit, taking them in the best order can mean savings of both time and fuel.

A Household Engineering Approach

Because of the heavy toll short trips make on the average household budget (30% of all gasoline consumed), it would be a good idea to sit down and review your own short-trip driving pattern with an eye toward potential savings through consolidation, elimination or substitution. The steps outlined below will help to provide a framework for your planning. Whether you go through this planning process each week, or just keep its general ideas in mind when you anticipate the many household trips you require, the result should be fewer trips and less household money spent for automobile fuel and expenses.

1. Must you do it in person? If the answer is "no," consider using the telephone, mail, or other means to satisfy the purpose of the trip.
2. How flexible is the timing of the trip? Categorize frequent trips into the following groups:

DAY OF WEEK FLEXIBLE ?

	NO	YES
TIME OF DAY (AM vs. PM) FLEXIBLE ? NO	FIXED TRIP	DAY-FLEXIBLE TRIP
TIME OF DAY (AM vs. PM) FLEXIBLE ? YES	TIME-FLEXIBLE TRIP	FULL-FLEXIBLE TRIP

3. On a chart such as the following, mark each fixed trip with an X.

For example:

	Mon.	Tues.	Wed.	Thurs.	Fri.	Sat.	Sun.
AM	X		X			X	X
PM				X			

4. Try to arrange the Day-Flexible trips so that each occurs during a day and time period when a fixed trip is required. This may not be possible in each case—save the leftovers for step 6.
5. Try to arrange the Time-Flexible trips so that each occurs in a day and time period when a Fixed trip is required. This may not be possible in each case—save the leftovers for step 6.
6. Try to "cluster" the leftovers from steps 4 and 5 along with Full-Flexible trips so that each leftover will have plenty of company. If you have a large number of Full-Flexible trips, you may wish to cluster several of *them* together during a suitable day and time period.
7. Hopefully, the result of all this will be a distribution of trips like that below, which has the capability of satisfying a total of twenty-five different needs while requiring only six different trips:

	Mon.	Tues.	Wed.	Thurs.	Fri.	Sat.	Sun.
			OO				
AM	X		X			OOO	X
	OOO		OO			XO	OO
PM				XO	OO		
				OO	OO		

X = Fixed trip.   O = trip with time, day or full flexibility.

8. Whenever an unanticipated trip comes up, try to wait for the next "cluster" instead of running right out to the garage.

Drive the Hot Car

If you have more than one car, try whenever possible to carry out a short trip in a vehicle that is already warmed up. It doesn't make much sense to subject one car to the inefficiency and engine wear of a cold start when another is available and warm. If a trip is very short, it's possible that even a warmed-up large car may be more fuel-efficient than a subcompact that has been sitting out in the cold. This means that, for a multi-car family, it's wise to have vehicles that any driver can operate.

Use Your Garage

If you have a garage, use it. A car that's been sitting out all night is going to require a longer time to warm up. If you're driving only a few miles, it won't get warmed up at all. Even if you're using that efficient multiple-viscosity oil in the engine and manual transmission, every moving part of the car—from wheel bearings to universal joints—is going to require more horsepower than if the car had been in the warm garage.

If you already have an automatic garage door opener, you can gain even more efficiency by not having to let the car idle while you close the garage door upon leaving and open it on your return. By timing your "open" signal, you will be able to enter the garage without having to interrupt your momentum.

However, if you don't own an automatic garage door opener, don't run out and buy one for fuel savings alone. Of primary value for safety and convenience, the product would likely take more than half a century to pay for itself on the basis of fuel savings.

Fig. 7–6. A car that's been in the garage overnight is going to warm up more quickly and be more efficient than one which has been outside in the cold.

Shortcuts

If you frequently travel the same roads, you may sometimes tend to follow them even when you shouldn't. For example, if there were a breakdown delaying your morning traffic, would you have an escape route to avoid the tie-up and still get to work on time? Having commuted with a shortcut-conscious friend one day, I was so impressed with his contingency planning that I rode with him again the next day and took notes on each alley, side street, and back yard he used as he made his way into the city. If you don't happen to know someone with a Master of Shortcuts degree, do the next best thing and refer to a good map.

LONG TRIPS
Stay Off the Roof

Hauling 60 pounds can hurt your car's gas mileage more than hauling 1,000 pounds. Though hard to believe, it's true—if the 60 pounds happens to be a sailboat on your roof and the 1,000 pounds is a small camping trailer following behind. When you're cruising on a level highway, the boat is going to steal more gas than a trailer weighing fifteen times as much. Anything on your roof—be it a sailboat, foot locker, or grand piano—is going to increase the effective frontal area of your car, thus increasing the air resistance your engine must overcome. In addition, because of the disruption of air flow around your car, the car-plus-load combination is going to be less streamlined than the car alone, thus affecting the drag coefficient discussed in Chapter 2. A low trailer follows in your car's "wake" as the car breaks through the air. The trailer enjoys the same low air-resistance advantage which served the 138-mph bicyclist of Chapter 2. In highway tests at 55 miles per hour, the use of a roof-top carrier decreased the fuel efficiency of a compact sedan by 26%, while pulling a covered utility trailer of much greater capacity lowered mileage by only 15%.[5]

If you need the extra carrying capacity and often travel at steady highway speeds, opt for a small luggage trailer as your source of space. You'll get better gas mileage on the interstates, but may have to pay an extra fee on some toll roads. However, since we can travel practically anywhere without riding a toll road, this shouldn't prove to be too important. While the trailer will be an advantage on the open highway, it's not as practical in stop-and-go traffic where its extra weight makes it less economical than a load carried on the roof.

If you have no choice but to use a roof rack for carrying luggage or other

Fig. 7–7. If you're taking a highway trip and can't fit all of your baggage inside the car, this lightweight (200-pound) trailer can haul it for about half the extra fuel which the roof top carrier would require.

bulky objects, you can minimize the fuel penalty by properly arranging the items on top of the car. The air resistance will be less if you design somewhat of a "wedge" shape, with smaller objects placed in front, larger items at the rear.

Know Where You're Going

Intelligent use of a road map can go a long way toward reducing the frustration and wasted gasoline of trying to find your way around unfamiliar surroundings. When you're stopping every five minutes to ask directions, it's hard to maintain the smoothness that economical driving demands. Make your navigational notes before the trip, including approximate mileages between important decision-making points. Things look a lot simpler on the map than they do on the road, especially if you're traveling through a congested area where other drivers are more interested in getting home for supper than in welcoming you to their state. Maps of the areas you intend to visit or travel through will generally be available from gas stations, oil companies, Chambers of Commerce, and state agencies promoting tourism.

Besides knowing where you're going, it's handy to know when you're going to get there and, should gasoline stations be scarce, if you have enough fuel to make it without stopping. If you're calling ahead for motel reservations, it can be a good idea to make the call as soon as you're within cruising distance. Knowing your car, its gas mileage under different driving conditions, how to convert the gas gauge readings into gallons left, and how far you need to go can all be helpful in avoiding an out-of-gas emergency in the middle of nowhere. If you do run very low on gas, don't speed up so that you'll get to a station sooner. This is a natural tendency which only defeats your purpose. By going slow, you have a better chance of being able to stretch your gas until you reach a station.

Beating the Elements

The mailman might be able to get through wind, rain, snow, hail, and sleet, but he's not going to get good gas mileage while he's doing it. When faced with wet or snow-covered roads, take it easy for economy as well as safety reasons. Rolling resistance will be higher on these roads, and higher speeds will be even more expensive than they are under normal conditions.

Because higher temperatures favor more efficient combustion and better gas mileage, your miles per gallon will not be as good if you travel at night. In addition, night driving requires more use of the lights and heater, thus raising demands on the alternator and its supplier, the engine. One exception to this rule is late-night driving through heavily populated areas, by which you can avoid the usual daytime delays and traffic jams. Another exception is the driver who absolutely requires air conditioning whenever temperatures rise. For him, the best strategy is to travel from very early in the morning until early afternoon in order to minimize use of the air conditioner.

As discussed earlier, remember not to make up time while driving into a headwind. Driving 50 mph into a 20 mph headwind will make your engine think it's going 70, and it will drink gas accordingly. Recall also the resistance effects of various road surfaces. Try to make up time only when the elements are in your favor.

Avoiding the Crowd

There are two types of crowds that the economy-minded driver should try to avoid. The first type snarls the highways and tourist facilities by flocking to the most popular parts of the country at the most popular times. Two ways of avoiding them are: (1) go to a popular area in the off-season, or (2) go to an unpopular area anytime. Besides saving gas on the way, you'll also find that tourist accommodations are priced at a lower rate. You may not end up deciding to vacation in Maine in the winter or Florida in the summer, but at least consider the possibility of such off-season ventures.

The second type of crowd to stay away from is the breakfast, lunch, and dinner mob at roadside restaurants. By stopping for supper at five o'clock, you'll be doing the following to your gas mileage: First, because your car will be shut off longer, it'll take longer to warm up when you get back on the road. Second, having spent the extra time in the crowded restaurant, you may be tempted to make it up by rushing at uneconomical speeds for the rest of your trip. By stopping for meals either a half-hour before or after the peak periods, you'll be doing both your stomach and your gas mileage a favor.

Taking the Long Way

Sometimes the long way can be the short way, especially if your measuring stick is how many gallons of gas each alternative will take. A limited-access highway, even though part of a longer route, may actually save you gas compared to a shorter route to the same destination. With the more steady speeds it allows, the limited-access road will provide you with more miles per gallon, even though it does involve more miles. For example, you're better off traveling 15 miles at 25 miles per gallon than in traveling 10 miles at only 12 miles per gallon. Many stop-and-go routes that look short on the map are costly in terms of both time and gasoline. When you're considering alternative routes, measure distances in gallons, not just miles.

ANY TRIP
Before You Start the Car

There are a lot of things we do before beginning a trip of any length. However, we often start the car *before* taking care of these essentials, thus wasting fuel while the engine is idling and the car is stationary. Before you turn the igni-

Fig. 7–8. By stopping at fast-food restaurants during nonpeak hours, you'll get to your destination more quickly and efficiently. Long waits can allow engine to cool down and be less efficient after starting up and resuming trip.

tion key, be sure that you've already adjusted your seat, set the inside and outside rear view mirrors, checked to see that everyone is wearing his or her seat belt, and looked through your briefcase or purse to make sure you've got everything you need to take along.

Dress for Economy

Be aware that your fashion boots or steel-toed work shoes are going to affect the operation of that (hopefully, by now) sensitive right foot that feeds gas to your engine. Besides increasing the weight of your foot on the gas, awkward shoes will make it more difficult for you to smoothly move the throttle in order to keep the carburetor accelerator pump from squirting raw gas into your engine.

Avoid making unnecessary work for your air conditioner and heater. It's not efficient for you to wear your business suit while you drive, then expect the air conditioner to cool you off because you're hot. If possible, put your coat on a hanger and take a load off your air conditioner as well as your shoulders. Likewise, wearing light clothes while driving in the winter is not going to make your heater's job any easier. Both the air conditioner and heater use up energy that the engine must work to provide.

Lose Some Weight

For every 100 pounds added to the weight of a subcompact car, fuel mileage will drop by about .4 miles per gallon.[6] The lighter your car and the more stop-and-go driving you do, the more that extra weight will hold you back. For example, if you're driving under city conditions, rolling resistance and momentum are the greatest forces to overcome. Rolling resistance and momentum resistance are both proportional to the weight of the vehicle, so a 10% increase in weight could require as much as 10% extra fuel under extremely low-speed conditions involving frequent acceleration and stopping. Take a bumper-to-bumper inventory of your car and the extra weight it may be hauling around. Check your trunk for bowling balls, unnecessary tools, patio bricks, empty beer cases, snow tires or chains, vacation left-overs, and anything at all that isn't necessary for the safe operation of the car. Unless you want to chance being stuck with a highway flat, don't plan on losing weight by removing your jack and spare tire. While economy run drivers have been known to remove bumpers, hub caps, spare tires, jacks, tools, sun visors, ashtrays, glove compartment lids, and window washer fluid, don't go to this extreme.

Gasoline weighs 6 pounds per gallon. By carrying only a quarter of a tank on local trips, you can lighten your car by 40 to 120 pounds. In the winter, remove accumulated snow from your roof, trunk and engine lids, and fender wells. Wet snow can easily add 100 pounds to the weight you're hauling. If you have a removable luggage rack, take it off and save on both weight and air resistance.

If you use a metal tool box, you can save about five pounds by switching to a less professional looking cardboard box. If you absolutely *never* carry anyone in your back seat, this can also be removed for a reduction of twenty to forty pounds. However, never carry people in back if you have removed the seat.

If you don't mind the extra noise, soundproofing materials can be removed for a few pounds here and there. However, be sure that the padding doesn't serve other purposes, such as crash protection, or protecting the paint on the front hood from engine heat.

In the trunk, carry only the absolute necessities. Try to get by with a minimum of tools. For example, carry an adjustable wrench instead of a complete set of sockets and a ratchet, use a screwdriver that converts from standard to Phillips head on the same handle, and anything else that you may able to reduce from your rolling inventory of hardware and maintenance items. Don't carry extra oil or coolant unless you're having specific problems with your engine. With attention to these kinds of details, plus not allowing your car to become a mobile warehouse filled with books, clothing, and other fugitives from a garage sale, you should be able to keep your car at least fifty pounds lighter than similar models being driven by those who are less inspired.

Snow Tires

Snow tires, with their higher rolling resistance, require more gasoline than conventional tires. If you live in an area where you must have snow tires installed much of the year, consider radials instead of the normal variety. While radial snows still have a thick tread, their construction will facilitate easier rolling and the belts will minimize tread squirming on dry roads. Driving on snow tires, especially the studded type, can be a real waste of tires and gas in high-speed summer driving. In addition, it can be dangerous. The thick tread squirming against a hot road, combined with flexing of the heavy tire body, can raise tire temperatures above the critical 250° F level.

If you don't mind a few tire changes during the winter, have your snow tires mounted on their own wheels, which will enable you to put them on yourself and use them only when they're needed. By investing a couple of hours each winter into changing wheels, you can get better gas mileage as well as snow tire life far beyond the normal two years.

The View from the Driver's Seat

Driving for economy requires anticipation of what lies ahead and awareness of what is happening around you. If your visibility is poor, you'll tend to be more hesitant and less economical in your driving. Keep a rag handy for cleaning the

Fig. 7–9. This is the most efficient place for your snow tires. Their higher rolling resistance will increase fuel consumption unnecessarily if they are used in fair weather.

Fig. 7–10. Along with being a safety hazard, an improperly maintained wiper and washer system wastes fuel by requiring the wiper motor to work overtime, often when it isn't needed at all. (Courtesy of Car Care Council.)

headlights, mirrors, and windows. Maintain your windshield washer fluid at the proper level, including antifreeze in the cold months. If your windshield washer nozzles wash the roof instead of the windshield, use a straight pin to aim them in the right direction. Crack open a side window in the snow or rain to help prevent the windows from frosting up. Don't be one of those lazy drivers who only scrapes snow off the left side of the rear window.

Rush Hour

If you're forced to drive in rush hour follow the advice given in Chapter Four. But it's best to avoid rush hour traffic altogether by shortcutting, leaving your home or office at off-peak times, or by riding public transportation. Maybe your boss will allow you to start early and quit early or start late and quit late. If he doesn't go for that, climb the corporate ladder more quickly by offering to start early and quit late.

Parking

When you're about to park your car, think beyond just looking for an open space. In a jammed parking lot, some hopefuls circle the lot a dozen times while waiting for a space to become available. Others stake out a claim to an aisle, then idle their engines until someone happens to leave. Both strategies waste time and gas. In the meantime, there may be abundant parking just across a bridge 200 yards away. Don't be afraid to park a short walk from where you're going— after you've walked to your destination, the parking lot cruisers will still be going around in circles or tapping on their steering wheels.

When parking, look ahead to the conditions you'll face when you're going to leave. Pulling forward into a parking stall may seem harmless at the time, but when the ball game's over and everybody comes out at once, you're going to be at a gas-wasting disadvantage trying to back out into the rush. Avoid having to cross bumper-to-bumper lanes—favor parking lots from which you'll want to turn right when you leave.

That Sunday Drive

When you're Sunday-driving for family or personal relaxation, you may have a difficult time deciding which direction to turn when you reach the highway. The reason is simple—as long as the road is smooth and the scenery enjoyable, you probably don't really care which way you go. If so, here's another tip: go with the wind. By starting the day in the direction the wind's blowing, you'll cut air resistance and do your fuel mileage yet another favor. On the way back home, the wind will tend to be more calm, as it normally is in the late afternoon and early evening hours, and you'll have gained some free energy in the process.

Depending on other factors, such as the return of the masses to the city on a Sunday night, you may want to use a different strategy which is more appropriate to your situation. Keep in mind the various forces of nature and circumstances of man which combine to have an effect on your fuel efficiency. Anticipate them before you begin your trip and the result will be a more efficient Sunday drive.

RIDES YOU CAN SHARE

As kids, we often found that sharing was expensive—we usually ended up with only half a candy bar, part of a milkshake, or just one handful of sea shells. However, in sharing rides to work or for household business, it's possible to share and come out ahead at the same time. *Ridesharing* is a general term used to describe strategies in which we save money, fuel, and personal aggravation by sharing a car or van with others who also wish to save. For our discussion, we can break ridesharing into three main types—informal carpooling, work carpooling, and vanpooling.

Informal Carpooling

Wouldn't it be nice to be able to make your short trips in a car that got between 50 and 100 miles per gallon? It's easy—all you have to do is have a 25 mpg vehicle (that's not too difficult) and share the trip with one, two, or three of your friends. If you don't have three friends, even sharing the ride with one other person will raise the effective mpg to 50. Naturally, this assumes that the other

	YOUR FUEL BILL WILL THINK YOUR CAR GETS THIS MANY mpg	FUEL USED PER PERSON	TOTAL FUEL USED	
EVERYONE FOR HIMSELF	25 mpg	1 GALLON	4 GALLONS	
TWO RIDESHARE	50 mpg	$\frac{1}{2}$ GALLON	1 GALLON	
THREE RIDESHARE	75 mpg	$\frac{1}{3}$ GALLON	1 GALLON	
FOUR RIDESHARE	100 mpg	$\frac{1}{4}$ GALLON	1 GALLON	

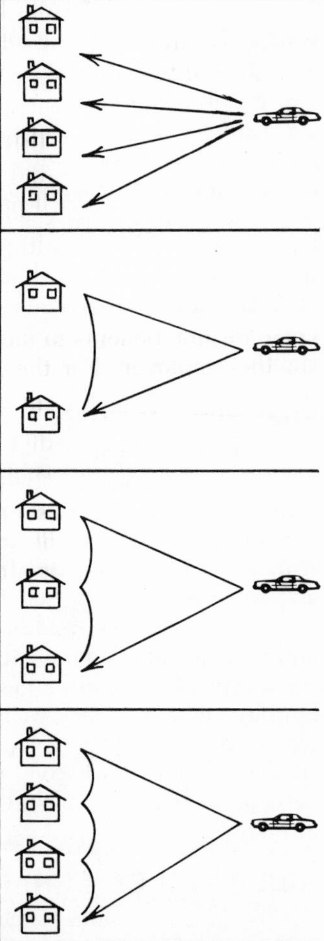

Fig. 7–11. Ridesharing is the quickest and surest way to reduce fuel costs without losing mobility. Finding just one person to rideshare with you will practically double your miles per gallon, provided you don't go *too* far out of your way.

person is going to drive his or her own vehicle next time so you can leave yours in the garage.

Figure 7-11 compares the efficiency of ridesharing with driving alone on a round trip of 25 miles in a vehicle getting 25 miles per gallon. As the number ridesharing increases, the fuel cost per person goes down proportionally and it soon seems very inefficient to drive by yourself. For example, if you're a real loner, you can beat the four-person rideshare trip only if you happen to have a car that will get you there and back at the rate of 100 miles per gallon!

While the other chapters provided sound information on improving fuel efficiency, it takes no imagination to see that ridesharing is by far the quickest way to decrease fuel consumption without limiting mobility. You can encourage informal carpooling and its savings by staying aware of what your friends and neighbors have in the way of transportation needs, then asking or offering to get things started. In an earlier section, we discussed a format you could use in scheduling your own household trips. If you expand this notion to include the "fixed" trips of others around you, it's likely that you will find that at least one person near you has a fixed trip nearly every day and time period of the week.

Work Carpooling

Because commuting to work is the biggest single category of automobile use, it can also offer the largest potential savings. As with any type of ridesharing, you save fuel dollars by sharing trips with others—however, in this case, it's a bit more structured than the informal carpool just discussed. In some instances, the carpool to work is started by a few people who live in the same neighborhood and happen to work in the same general location. In others, it may be the result of an effort by an employer to encourage and facilitate employees' participation in a company-sponsored program.

The savings from carpooling can be measured in many different dimensions, which include benefits to the individual, the local community, society in general, and the employer. For the sake of simplicity, let's assume that you don't care that (1) the air will be cleaner in the community through which you commute, (2) there will be more fuel to go around in the future as the result of your conservation, and (3) your workplace will enjoy less absenteeism, less tardiness, and more space in the parking lot. Again, let's look at the situation from *your* perspective alone.

In our example, we'll assume that you commute to work 250 days each year, 15 miles each way, that you have a compact car which gets 15 miles per gallon in commuter traffic, that it costs $2.50 each day to park, and that fuel costs $1.10 per gallon (which is more than I pay as I write this, but will probably be less than you pay as you read this). Depending on whether you drive by yourself or join a carpool with one to five other people, your annual costs will look something like this:

Commute by yourself:
  Your cost: $1100 (not including other running costs, such as oil, tires, and maintenance)
Commute with one other person:
  Your cost: $1100 ÷ 2 = $550 (you save 50%, or $550)
Commute with two other persons:
  Your cost: $1100 ÷ 3 = $367 (you save 67%, or $733)
Commute with three other persons:
  Your cost: $1100 ÷ 4 = $275 (you save 75%, or $825)
Commute with four other persons:
  Your cost: $1100 ÷ 5 = $220 (you save 80%, or $880)

Commute with five other persons:
Your cost: $1100 ÷ 6 = $183 (you save 84%, or $917)

As these figures indicate, the savings can be quite dramatic. By switching from single ridership to a carpool which includes just two other persons, your savings would be ($1100–$367), or $733 after taxes. As we discussed in Chapter 1, you don't pay taxes on this kind of efficiency savings, so this is the equivalent of giving yourself a $916 per year raise in salary (assuming you're in the 20% tax bracket). Naturally, savings such as these aren't without their risks, which can be minimized if you pay attention to the following points when you form and operate your carpool:[7]

1. Arrange a schedule of who will drive and when. Be sure you're always on time and that you let others know if you're going to be late.
2. If only one person is going to be driving, agree in advance on what the costs are and how they are going to be divided.
3. For both pick-up and return, make sure everyone knows the routes in advance. These may be at individual homes or at a central collection point.
4. Agree on how long you will wait for riders who are late.
5. Determine whether smoking, eating, or radio or tape deck playing will be permitted, and under what circumstances.
6. Check with your insurance company to see if any provisions need to be changed. You might even qualify for a premium reduction since you'll be driving fewer miles.
7. Even if you don't like the carpool at first, give it a two-week trial to iron out any problems which may arise.

If your trial run with a carpool works out to your liking, there is another benefit which you might be able to enjoy: the chance to avoid the hassle and expense of owning and maintaining a second car. If the carpool strategy allows you to own one car instead of two, your savings will suddenly include such significant expenses as depreciation, insurance, and loan charge, along with the money you save on direct operating expenses. As a result, it's quite possible that your carpool savings could amount to several thousand dollars per year.

Vanpooling

This type of ridesharing program is rapidly growing in popularity. It typically utilizes well-equipped vans with such amenities as reading lights, air conditioning, reclining seats, and stereo headsets. The driver of the van may have it on loan from a company and be free to use it as a second car, while riders pay a monthly fee for their privilege. In some cases, riders' fees may be supplemented by the company or community that supports the vanpooling program.

The vanpool is very much like a carpool, except you really travel first class, don't have to worry about driving your own car *at all*, have a lot more space in which to relax during the commute, and are likely to feel much better when you arrive at work in the morning and at home in the evening.

Because of greater seating capacity and the likelihood of corporate, community, or government support, the vanpool will generally offer greater individual savings compared to its cousin, the carpool. If one is available to you, consider it seriously. If none is available, write to the National Association of Vanpool Operators, 610 Ivystone Lane, Cinnaminson, NJ 08077, for information to help you get one started at your company.

Fig. 7–12. While it may not look like an economy car, this vehicle can be more efficient than a subcompact when it's the basis for a vanpool. Compared to a carpool, the vanpool tends to offer more space and more savings, along with a lot more comfort during the commuting trip.

Public Transportation

If it fits your schedule and your location, public transportation is likely to be the cheapest possible way to get back and forth to work or fulfill household trips. As with carpools and vanpools, you will have to be a little more dependent on others and structure your activities with them in mind. However, with increasing economic and governmental pressures—higher fuel costs as well as the penalizing of lone commuters with higher toll and parking fees, carpool, vanpool and bus-only lanes—abandoning a little bit of personal flexibility may be a great deal preferable to abandoning sizable amounts of your money.

ALTERNATE VEHICLES FOR SHORT TRIPS

During short trips, when the conventional automobile is most inefficient, a number of alternative devices for personal transportation are available. The first two are proven modes of transportation requiring little skill and investment; both have been around for many years. The third is increasingly popular because of its low operating costs and minimal ownership requirements. The fourth, an old-timer, has received renewed attention because it's both fun and efficient. The fifth is an old idea which high fuel costs and recent technology gains have once again made feasible. They are walking (yes, *walking*), the bicycle, the moped, the small motorcycle, and the electric car.

Walking

With the most frequent trip being a mile or less, the average person in good health could probably use this most primitive of all transportation modes to handle a lot of short trips during the year. At a brisk walking pace, it takes only about ten minutes to walk half a mile. If you're into jogging or tennis, it's a shame to think that you might jog four or five miles, then drive your car to the corner grocery for a loaf of bread. Depending on where you live and the kinds of short trips you make, it's not unlikely that you could use your feet instead of your car for 10% to 20% or more of your short trips.

Before proceeding to combine physical fitness with fuel efficiency, be sure that you have your physician's OK to undertake this type of activity, and that you don't overdo it when you begin saving this way. A good suggestion for the shopper-walker would be to increase carrying capacity and convenience by purchasing a backpack or similar device in which to carry small grocery items. If you have a small child, the type of baby carrier that puts little Johnny on your back is also worthy of consideration. For the serious walker, the backpack is the equivalent of a trunk, and is indispensable whenever longer walks require the carrying of even a few items. If you're automatically turned off by the prospect of walking, take a good look in the mirror just before your next shower or bath. If you don't like what you see, consult your physician for advice regarding your own program for burning calories instead of gasoline.

Bicycling

Depending on where you live, cycling may be able to replace many of the short trips of several miles or less. In addition, if the bicycle is used in a dual-mode trip (such as bike/bus, bike/train, or bike/car), longer trips are also possible at tremendous savings. For short household trips as well as more lengthy travel, luggage racks and other carriers are available to increase hauling capacity. In the case of the three-wheeled bicycle for adults, the vehicle comes equipped with a carrying basket larger than the trunks of many sports cars. The physical fitness and ecology movements are leading the way to commuter bicycle lanes and other means of helping to make bicycles even more practical as a method of local transportation.

To complement its energy efficiency, the bicycle is also beneficial in maintaining and strengthening your cardiovascular system, controlling body weight, and in otherwise providing valuable exercise in these sedentary times. As with walking or jogging, be sure to see your physician for advice before proceeding.

The Moped

With typical fuel efficiency of about 150 miles per gallon, the moped presents an attractive mode of personal transportation over short distances. The moped is a two-wheel (although some may have three) vehicle with an automatic transmission, a small engine producing between 1 and 2 horsepower, and having a top speed of approximately 20 to 30 miles per hour. Its weight will generally be about 100 pounds, making it easy to handle and convenient to store. In addition to the power provided by the engine, the moped has pedals which can allow the ambitious driver to increase performance by doing a little work on his or her own.

The moped is ideal for short trips, college campus travel, recreational use, and low-speed transportation in general. It's about as practical as a bicycle, but doesn't require any work on the driver's part and it is not necessary that you have a driver's license in order to operate the vehicle. In some states, even a twelve-year-old can legally drive a moped on public streets, and mopeds are generally free of the legal requirements, mandatory inspections, and other nagging expenses to which the motorcycle is subject.

The Small Motorcycle

A motorcycle of relatively small displacement and power can also be a suitable substitute for the automobile on short trips. However, compared to the moped, its initial cost will be significantly higher and its fuel efficiency (though impressive, with 80+ mpg possible) very much lower. In addition, operators must be licensed to drive on public streets, and the motorcycle itself will be sub-

Fig. 7–13. The moped is an attractive and fun alternative to using a thirsty automobile on a lot of short, low-speed trips. Fuel efficiency can exceed 200 miles per gallon.

ject to annual registration fees and state inspections. Despite these relative weaknesses versus the moped, the small motorcycle is likely to be more practical for longer trips, better able to keep up with highway traffic, and generally more satisfactory for use in a wider range of driving conditions.

Depending on your own short-trip and other transportation requirements, you may find that a small motorcycle will be able to replace the automobile on a sufficient number of trips to make its additional cost a worthwhile investment. This conclusion is especially likely if some of your short trips involve some travel over roads where vehicles are typically going at speeds greater than 30 miles per hour.

The Electric Car

By the mid-1980s, it may be possible to purchase an electric vehicle that is really practical for commuting, household business, and other short trips. In the past, electric cars have not been highly desirable because of their expense, the weight of their numerous batteries, short traveling range between recharges, and a very low top speed. The combination of these factors has hindered the use of the electric vehicle as suitable transportation for the masses.

However, continued research into the propulsion and power systems of electric vehicles has led to a high probability that such cars will be not only satisfactory, but also desirable for certain types of short trip applications. For example, General Motors recently announced a breakthrough in battery technology which could make the electric car both lighter and longer ranged. The

Fig. 7–14. With recent breakthroughs in battery and electric vehicle technology, the second-car of the 1980s may well be an electric model with batteries where the engine is usually found. (Courtesy of Firestone Tire & Rubber Co.)

improved battery, of the zinc-nickel oxide type, is said to be capable of storing between 2 and 2.5 times the energy of a conventional battery of the same weight. Recharging is accomplished by using a standard 110-volt outlet, with the battery's lifetime estimated at about 30,000 miles of travel. Top speed would be about 50 miles per hour, with a cruising range of about 100 miles.[8] As you read this, electric car technology may already have made even greater strides.

SURVIVAL DURING GAS RATIONING

During periods of gas rationing, there often isn't much you can do except drive less, drive more efficiently, make greater use of carpooling and public transportation, and employ any alternate means possible in making trips or substituting for them. The particular strategies you can best use will depend very much on your individual circumstances and the resources at your disposal. However, given that you're facing immediate or future gas rationing as a travel constraint, there are a number of general strategies which should prove helpful:

1. If you have two cars, try to arrange your license plate selections so that one will have an odd final digit, the other an even final digit. During odd-even rationing, this will enable you to buy fuel on any day of the week.
2. If you're traveling, find out in advance what restrictions exist in the states through which you'll be driving. Some states, especially those

which are tourist-dependent, waive the odd-even requirement for out-of-state motorists.

3. If there is a "minimum purchase" requirement, be sure that your car will hold the number of gallons for which you'll be charged. With such restrictions, you generally have to pay the minimum charge (usually $3 or $5) regardless of how little fuel you actually need.

4. Before entering a station with gas lines, drive by or observe from a distance in order to determine which line is likely to cause the least waiting time or frustration.

5. If possible, wait in a downhill gas line. This will reduce the number of times you'll have to restart your engine along the way.

6. Make friends with your local gas station owner and/or attendants. They can provide valuable information regarding availability, opening times, etc. Try to cultivate this friendship during a nonshortage period, since they'll have more than enough potential friends when the lines begin.

7. Remember that diesel fuel foams during filling, making it necessary to fill up very slowly if you really want a full tank. This is especially important if you're planning to travel a long distance on the new tankful. If necessary, check the oil or clean the windshield in order to create more time for the attendant to fill your tank all the way. A hasty fillup can leave you short by more than a gallon.

8. When topping up a half-full tank, buy in the morning and you'll have more fuel when you leave the station. Gas in the tank will be cold, thus taking up less space and allowing more room for the fuel being added.

9. If necessary, fuel up at two different stations for the complete fillup which restrictions may prevent at one alone. Plan these sequential purchases so that you'll be within the minimum and maximum purchase amounts at each station.

10. Don't store fuel in the trunk of your car (or anywhere else in your car, for that matter). Gasoline is very explosive—one gallon can have the explosive power of about forty-three sticks of dynamite.

11. If you have a large car and a small car, and both use the same type of fuel, keep the large car filled up and use it to help provide fuel for the smaller one. If you're going to store any gasoline, there's no better place than the fuel tank—after all, that's what it was made for.

12. If you're going to do any siphoning, be sure to use a hand-operated siphon. Don't try to save a little money by taking chances with sucking fuel through a hose, whether it's clear or not. A little gasoline in your lungs, and you're done.

13. Practice the strategies discussed earlier in the book for positioning your car to get a complete fillup instead of a near fillup plus an air pocket.

14. Before making a long trip, provide a little extra insurance by topping-up your tank with your lawnmower gas can just before you leave home. (Naturally, you should be sure that the fuel in the can matches that required in your car.)

15. Unless you want to take chances with the law, don't carry and use an opposite-numbered plate when traveling during periods of odd-even rationing. If you're stopped while you have the wrong plate on your car, you may be in serious difficulties with the law enforcement people. Likewise, don't pose as a physician, volunteer fireman, clergyman or other provider of essential services in order to get fuel. Such creativity may come into conflict with the law. If you have a real emergency,

don't hesitate to call the police or ambulance service for transportation to a hospital.

16. If you live near a turnpike where travelers are guaranteed access to fuel, get on the toll road for one exit and "travel" to one of the stations and back. This may cost a round-trip toll, but if you're desperate, it may be your only choice.

Chapter 8

Efficiency in Recreational and Commercial Vehicles

Air, rolling, acceleration, gravity, and engine resistance are universal forces that really don't care what type of vehicle is trying to fight them. For this reason, many of the buying, driving, maintaining, and planning guidelines offered earlier in the book will apply to the over-the-road truck as well as to recreational vehicles and 500-pound motorcycle and rider combination.

MOTOR HOMES

The buyer of a motor home interested in fuel efficiency should buy one that makes some attempt at streamlining and that has a small frontal area relative to the inside space. The weight of most motor homes necessitates a heavy chassis and the use of truck tires. For this reason, the addition of radial truck tires can add about 10% to the fuel efficiency of these vehicles. The sheer weight of a motor home makes it desirable to travel at steady speeds for the purpose of minimizing acceleration resistance. For this reason, a larger engine may actually provide better efficiency by allowing the driver to maintain speed on slight grades. Since most motor homes are equipped with automatic transmissions, which "lock up" and become more efficient at higher speeds, the momentum-saving ability of the larger engine becomes even more desirable. In addition, the fuel-saving advantages of a diesel over a gasoline engine can be even greater than with conventional vehicles.

The driver of a motor home can profit from most of the driving, maintenance, and planning strategies discussed earlier in the book. But there are a number of additional efficiency steps which may apply to your vehicle, depending on its features. For example, when traveling, don't carry any more water than you need. Each gallon of water weighs 8 pounds, and those gallons can add up to a lot of extra weight—a full 60-gallon tank will add 500 pounds to your vehicle. According to the Recreation Vehicle Industry Association, each 100 pounds of weight involves a 1% penalty on your fuel consumption.[1]

If you use your motor home for camping, consider the fuel cost and inconvenience of short trips at the campground—a bicycle, small motorcycle, or moped can be carried rather easily and uses a lot less fuel than having to move your entire "campsite" in order to go to the store for a quart of milk. However, be sure not to pack your auxiliary transportation on the roof. If possible, use the rear of the vehicle in order to avoid increasing your air resistance. If you have a refrigerator and your trip is not too lengthy, turn it off before you arrive at your destination. The insulation will keep things cool until you can hook up at the campground or remove the food at home.

Motor homes are especially thirsty vehicles compared to other travel alter-

Fig. 8–1. When buying a motor home, look for one that at least makes an attempt at streamlining. While not exactly a sports car, this model will have less air resistance because of its sloped front section. (Courtesy of Recreation Vehicle Industry Assoc.)

natives, but they have the advantage of being able to carry a lot of passengers. Hence they are able to deliver a high number of "people-miles" per gallon. To enjoy the convenience and comfort of these vehicles without undue fuel expenses, owners should consider the purchase of a fuel consumption meter of the type mentioned earlier in the book. While "the more you spend, the more you can save" applies to many everyday purchase decisions, it is especially valid for these big rigs.

TRUCK AND VAN CAMPERS

While more fuel efficient than the motor home, a truck or van camper will accommodate fewer passengers and afford fewer luxuries. If you intend to purchase one of these vehicles, first decide whether you can make do with a fold-up camping trailer which will be more efficient to pull and able to sleep as many persons without a lot of inconvenience. In deciding between a truck camper or a van, the ability to move about in a van may be an important factor on long trips or on shorter commutes. On the other hand, the camper truck is versatile; by removing the camper top, it becomes a pickup truck ready for use at work or on the farm.

As with any vehicle, look for a small frontal area combined with large interior space. The model shown in Figure 8-2 has a sloped front end and rounded corners for good aerodynamics, plus an interior that spreads backwards for good space without large frontal area. Likewise, the pickup camper shown in Figure 8-3 has a frontal area advantage because the top of the camping section can be collapsed to make the vehicle lower and more aerodynamic during highway travel.

If you're in the market for a van camper, seriously consider making it help pay for itself as a vanpooling vehicle during nonvacation periods. As discussed in Chapter 7, vanpool savings can be substantial, especially if you do all the driving and are able to attract a half-dozen enlightened commuters to make both your bank account and their work trip a lot more comfortable.

Fig. 8–2. For either camping or high-style commuting, this combination of small frontal area with long interior layout provides less air resistance for a given amount of passenger space. Note rounded corners and sloped front end. (Courtesy of Recreation Vehicle Industry Assoc.)

Fig. 8–3. The ability to lower the camper section helps this pickup camper to have a smaller frontal area and better fuel efficiency during highway travel. (Courtesy of Recreation Vehicle Industry Assoc.)

CAMPING TRAILERS

Like motor homes, pickup campers, and vans, camping trailers come in assorted shapes and sizes. The most efficient trailers to pull are those which fold down for less air resistance on the road, then expand for maximum interior space at the campsite. Some are cranked into position at the campground while others may require a bit of do-it-yourself in order to raise the roof. Figure 8-4 shows

Fig. 8–4. On the road, a fold-down camping trailer can help fuel efficiency by offering a low profile and slipstreaming through the hole the car has made in the surrounding air. In highway tests, models like the one shown here required extra fuel at the rate of about one gallon per 100 miles. (Courtesy of The Coleman Company.)

Fig. 8–5. The AMC Eagle is the sedan available with four wheel drive. It combines the pulling power of a vehicle with a larger engine and the lighter weight and comfort of a smaller sedan. It can be a more fuel efficient compromise, depending on your needs.

Fig. 8–6. Which combination is more fuel efficient? If you guessed "rooftop carrier," you're right, but not by much. Based on highway tests, a 300-mile trip with the camping trailer (weight about 1,000 pounds) would use only one more gallon of fuel than the same trip with the carrier. Aerodynamic drag reduces the carrier's weight advantage and makes it a close race at highway speeds. (And have you ever tried to sleep six in a rooftop carrier?)

a crank-up camping trailer on the road. The solid top and cranking system help to make set-up an easy job, while the aerodynamic ability of a low-profile trailer to "slipstream" behind even a small car provides good fuel efficiency on the highway.

The amount of fuel consumed by a camping trailer can be surprisingly small. For example, consider the two combinations shown in Figure 8-6. They show a Chevrolet Citation plus (1) a Coleman Ligonier camping trailer, and (2) a rooftop carrier. If you guessed that the camping trailer used more fuel than the rooftop carrier, you're right. However, the margin of victory is much smaller than you might imagine. In highway tests, the Coleman Ligonier (test weight: 1,050 pounds, including 160 pounds added to simulate camping gear) used fuel at the rate of 1.29 extra gallons per 100 miles compared to the Citation itself. The rooftop carrier (test weight: 120 pounds, including 80 pounds to simulate luggage) required extra fuel at the rate of .96 gallons per 100 miles. As an example of how efficient trailers can be compared to hauling even very light items on the roof, consider the difference between the two—for just .33 extra gallons per 100 miles, your car can pull a six-sleeper camping trailer which weighs nearly nine times as much as the rooftop carrier.

The moral of the story is that, for just 2 gallons of fuel on a 600-mile highway trip, you and your five friends can sleep in a camping trailer instead of in a rooftop carrier or its contents. The larger the towing vehicle, the less fuel penalty will be incurred by pulling the camping trailer. For example, in related highway tests using a Ford Fairmont, the Coleman Gettysburg (seven-sleeper) and Coleman Brandywine LTD (eight-sleeper) used extra fuel at the rates of just .82 and .96 gallons per 100 miles, respectively.

If you're in the market for a camping trailer, put the fold-down type at the top of your shopping list. However, should you opt for a nonfolding type, avoid showroom fever and buy one just large enough for your needs, preferably a unit with a small frontal area and at least token streamlining.

When pulling any trailer, remember that anticipation of stops, gradual acceleration, and steady speeds are even more important than when driving in the car alone. During a trip across the Midwest, our family station wagon pulled a collapsible tent trailer at steady 65 mph speeds (it was legal then) and delivered 27 miles per gallon in the process. During stop-and-start driving, the 4,000 pound weight of the car-trailer combination would have pulled gas mileage down to the teens or low twenties, but steady speed on a level road was very economically maintained.

For safety as well as low rolling resistance, keep the trailer tires inflated to the proper pressure. Since gas station tower gauges are notoriously inaccurate, carry your own pressure gauge in order to avoid improper inflation pressures that could damage either your tires or your fuel bill.

MOTORCYCLES

Motorcycles travel great distances on a gallon of gas, but they still benefit from proper maintenance, gentle riding, and reasonable planning. For prospective car buyers, a good question might be: "Can I make do with a motorcycle?"

Fig. 8–7. A touring type motorcycle with windshield and fairing attached. Besides streamlining, such devices add to driver comfort.

With the possible exception of installing a windshield, there is little that the motorcycle rider can do to reduce his already low air resistance. Rolling resistance may be higher for knobby tires than for the relatively smooth street tires, so the trail bike can be a little less economical than the street model. In addition, trail bikes usually have larger rear sprockets and are geared for higher engine speeds in any gear at a given road speed. For more miles per gallon from a vehicle that is already very good, get a street bike, then drive and maintain it for economy.

LONG-HAUL TRUCKS

Considering the loads they pull, long-distance trucks are already very fuel efficient. For example, if a truck with a 50-ton gross weight achieves just 4 miles per gallon, it has delivered 200 ton-miles per gallon—more than enough to win any economy run in which ton-miles per gallon is the criterion for performance. For example, to achieve this figure, I would have to obtain about 167 miles per gallon in my diesel Rabbit, about twice the already-impressive performance reported in the next chapter. However, despite its efficiency at hauling loads, the long-haul truck can be made to do even better.

Fig. 8–8. Long-haul trucks, though already relatively efficient at carrying heavy loads, can benefit from the modifications and driving habits noted in the text.

Engine

Three-fourths of the nation's long distance trucks are already diesel powered, with the proportion likely to increase in the future, so the Chapter 3 commentary on the diesel engine will apply to these vehicles as well as to passenger cars.

Engine Tuning

While the diesel engine doesn't require the periodic attention that a gasoline engine needs, there are two important checks which can help to maintain the truck diesel's efficiency—the air intake check and the overhead (valves and injectors) adjustment. The intake air restriction should be checked against restriction limits specified by the engine manufacturer. A dirty air cleaner or other blockage of the intake system can reduce fuel economy just as effectively as in a passenger car. In addition to checking the valves and injectors at recommended intervals, be sure that fuel pressure and governor settings haven't changed slightly over the miles. According to the Cummins Engine Company, a 10% increase in power caused by a too-high fuel pressure or governor setting can result in the consumption of 15% more fuel.[2]

Temperature Controlled Fan

As in a passenger car, the engine fan consumes a significant amount of horsepower even when it's not needed. At 60 miles per hour, it requires about

Fig. 8–9. This medium-duty truck diesel engine is manufactured in both naturally aspirated and turbocharged form, and produces about twice the fuel efficiency of a comparable gasoline version. Note temperature-controlled fan hub which reduces horsepower required by the cooling fan.

5% of the engine's rated horsepower just to turn the radiator fan.[3] Driving a 28-inch cooling fan at 2,300 rpm drains 14 horsepower away from the output of the engine.[4] Depending on the vehicle, engine, and gearing, the installation of a temperature-controlled fan can reduce fuel costs by 3% to 6%.[5]

Derate the Engine

If the engine already has power to spare for the job it's doing, fuel savings can be achieved by derating the engine to a lower horsepower. However, the engine should not be derated to the point where it will not be able to maintain a cruising speed in top gear. As an example of the fuel saving possible with the derating of an engine, the Cummins Engine Company found that fuel savings were 2.3% when a 290-horsepower engine was derated to 255 horsepower.[6] While derating the engine will usually increase fuel efficiency, it will also tend to

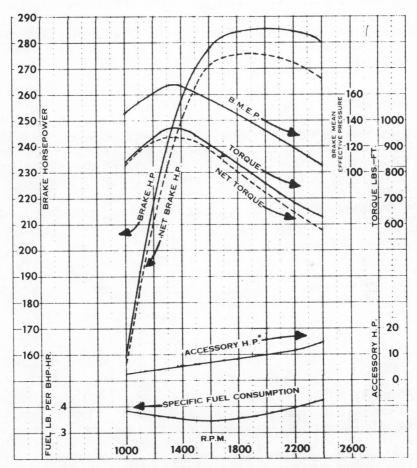

*NOTE: ACCESSORY HORSEPOWER CURVE SHOWN WITH THERMO-STATICALLY CONTROLLED FAN OPERATING AT MINIMUM POWER

Fig. 8–10. This chart shows the effect of derating a diesel engine from 385 hp to 325 hp. Both torque and horsepower are slightly reduced, but derated engines run more efficiently, longer, and cleaner than engines rated at full power. (*Source:* Mack Trucks.)

increase the time required to make a given trip. However, when derating is combined with other measures designed to reduce engine, air and rolling resistance, the same level of performance can be maintained.

Reduce Engine RPM

Because the engine is more efficient at lower speeds (down to 1,800 rpm), fuel economy will increase significantly provided that the truck has enough power to maintain cruising speed at the new rpm setting. However, the 8 to 10% fuel saving possible for some vehicle-engine-gearing combinations may be offset by 5% to 6% increase in time required for a given trip.[7]

Turbocharge the Engine

Besides raising engine performance, a turbocharging kit can reduce exhaust smoke, engine noise, and fuel consumption. The turbocharger pumps more air into the cylinder in order to allow a larger quantity of fuel to be burned in the combustion chamber. The energy of the exhaust gases is used to drive the turbocharger blower. As an example of the efficiency gained by this modification, Cummins found that installation of their turbocharger on one truck increased its miles per gallon by 4.2% and reduced trip time by .4%.[8]

Driving
Slow Down

Observing the 55 mph speed limit will be a big factor in minimizing fuel consumption on the highway. It has been estimated that each mph over 55 costs 2.2% in fuel costs, so even a few extra mph can make a significant difference.[9] The following table represents Cummins' findings on the effects of reduced speed on a 65,000-pound GCW, 13.5-foot van tractor/semi-trailer combination:[10]

Engine	Geared Speed at 2100 rpm	Cruise Speed Limit	Engine rpm at Cruise	Avg. Speed (mph)	Fuel Econ. (mpg)
Super-250	59 mph	none	2100	54.9	4.51
		55 mph	1950	50.9	4.86
		50 mph	1780	47.1	5.10
NTC-290	64 mph	none	2100	59.5	4.26
		60 mph	1970	56.9	4.60
		55 mph	1800	52.0	4.93
NTC-350	70 mph	none	2100	64.7	3.85
		65 mph	1950	60.4	4.35
		60 mph	1800	56.9	4.60

Minimize Idling

As with passenger cars, excessive idling will waste truck fuel. In addition to the loss of fuel, idling times in excess of five minutes may foul the injectors and cause the engine to be less efficient when returning to highway speeds.[11] In order to avoid valve and turbocharger damage, some idling of a diesel engine is necessary prior to shut-off. Five minutes of idling is sometimes necessary to cool down an engine which has been operated at full load. In order to avoid engine damage without using excessive fuel for idling, an "engine timer" may be purchased for the purpose of allowing the engine to idle for a predetermined amount of time without the need for personal attention. While some locales do not allow the idling of unattended vehicles, these devices can save fuel where their use is permitted.

Change Speed Gradually

Because of a truck's great mass, it is more important to maintain steady speeds, to anticipate stops and slow-downs, and to accelerate as gradually as possible. As with passenger cars, over-revving in the lower gears hurts fuel mileage more than it helps acceleration.

Progressive Shifting

When shifting, don't hit the governor on every shift and try to stay about 200 to 300 rpm below the governor at cruising speed. Keep engine speeds in the most efficient range, and gradually increase engine speed for each upshift, as shown in Figure 8-11.

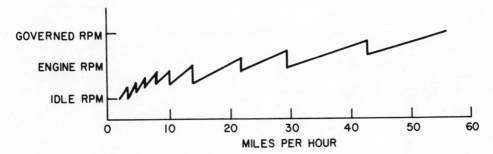

Fig. 8–11. By progressively shifting through the gears, cruising speed can be attained with a minimum of fuel consumption during acceleration. Note increased engine rpm at each shift. (*Source:* U.S. Department of Transportation, Voluntary Truck and Bus Fuel Economy Program.)

Lowering Resistances
Lower Air Resistance

A truck's large frontal area causes a proportionate increase in air resistance at highway speeds compared with an automobile. Truck trailers with over 100 square feet of frontal area are not unusual. In addition to the normal resistance of frontal area, the sudden change in shape between the cab and trailer and the gap between the cab and trailer both contribute to air resistance.

One device which can lower air resistance on present trucks is a wind deflector mounted on the roof of the cab. It redirects air toward the top of the trailer instead of allowing it to hit the trailer's box-shaped front. Another streamlining device is the "vortex stabilizer," designed to smooth the passage of air past the gap between the cab and trailer. With both devices added to a typical tractor-van combination, air resistance can be lowered by 20%, and fuel consumption reduced by about 5%.[12]

Since air resistance is proportionate to a truck's frontal area, reducing the height of the trailer hauled will increase fuel economy accordingly. This is especially promising when the trailer being used is rarely loaded to the top—a lower trailer can be used in these cases. In one study, lowering trailer height from 13.5 feet to 11.0 feet resulted in 4.7% lower fuel consumption.[13]

Lower Rolling Resistance

As with passengers cars, the use of radial tires will decrease truck rolling resistance by about 30% when compared to conventional bias-ply tires. The

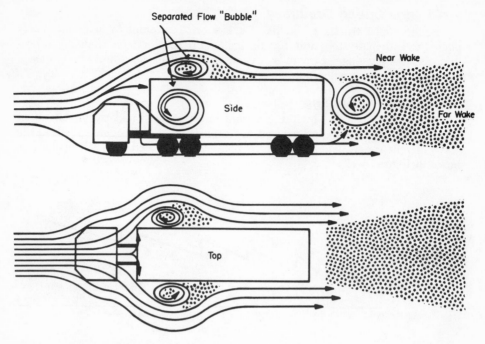

Fig. 8–12. These drawings show how a truck tends to displace the air through which it travels. Note the flow disruptions caused by the difference in size and shape between the cab and trailer. Aerodynamic add-on devices can help to smooth the flow and reduce drag at highway speeds.

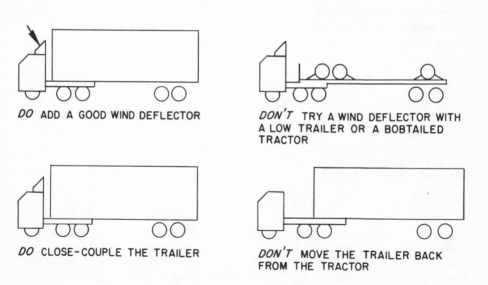

Fig. 8–14. These suggestions will help to reduce aerodynamic drag and improve fuel efficiency. At 55 mph, air resistance uses up about half of the horsepower required to move a typical truck down the highway. (*Source: Tips for Truckers,* U.S. Department of Transportation, Voluntary Truck and Bus Fuel Economy Improvement Program.)

Fig. 8–13. This truck is equipped with a wind deflector on the cab roof and a vortex stabilizer on the front of the trailer. This combination can improve fuel efficiency by about 8% at highway speeds.

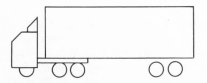

DO USE A SMOOTH-SIDED TRAILER

DON'T USE A VERTICAL EXTERIOR POST TRAILER

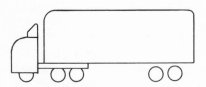

DO BUY ROUND CORNERED TRACTORS AND TRAILERS

lower rolling resistance of radial truck tires can deliver 8 to 10% more miles per gallon.[14] Proper vehicle wheel alignment and the use of wide-base single tires instead of duals are other paths to lower rolling resistance and better economy.

Other Economies

Another means of reducing truck fuel consumption is to use single drive axles whenever horsepower and traction requirements permit. Each drive axle will absorb about 5% of the total power being transmitted to the road. Choosing a single axle instead of tandems will yield fuel savings of about 3%.[15] These savings become even more significant when frequent curves and sharp turns are encountered.

When a truck is purchased, attention to the proper combination of engine transmission and axle ratio can ensure the best possible fuel economy for the driving conditions to be encountered. As a general rule, it's better to operate a larger engine at lower rpm than to run a smaller engine at full rpm in order to maintain the same cruising speed. Unlike conventional passenger car engines, truck diesels become more efficient at lower engine speeds. In order to cruise efficiently at 55 mph, a truck might be geared and powered so that it is able to cruise at 65. This gives top gear enough power reserve to enable it to maintain economical cruising speed on slight grades without frequent downshifting.

One important strategy for using less fuel is to increase a truck's payload and make fewer trips. This is where payload ton-miles per gallon becomes important. Consider the example of a truck required to shuffle 12,600,000 pounds of freight over a 200-mile route.[16]

Payload Pounds per Trip	Number of Trips Needed	Miles per Gallon	Gallons per Ton of Freight Hauled
25,000	504	4.64	3.46
30,000	420	4.55	2.93
35,000	360	4.45	2.56
40,000	315	4.36	2.30
45,000	280	4.28	2.08

As these figures indicate, the fuel savings from increasing payload are greater than those generated by other methods. Although miles per gallon performance decreases, the number of gallons used goes down a great deal faster.

Combined Measures

Applying any individual fuel-efficiency measure will save fuel dollars, but as emphasized throughout this book, it is combining several measures, however small, that will really make the difference your bank account will notice. The Cummins Engine Company has determined the combined effects of several fuel-saving steps as applied to a typical vehicle: a 6 x 4 tractor/13.5-foot van, 70,000 pounds, geared for 63 mph (4.11 axle, 10.00 x 22 tires), NTC-290.[17]

	Trip Time Saved		Fuel Saved	
Baseline Truck	Change	Total Change	Change	Total Change
Add steel-belted radial tires	+2.5%	=2.5%	+8.1%	= 8.1%
Add wind deflector/vortex stabilizer	+1.1%	=3.6%	+6.8%	=14.9%
Add temperature modulated fan	+1.0%	=4.6%	+6.2%	=21.1%
Derate to 270 hp @ 2100 rpm	−2.6%	=2.0%	+5.3%	=26.4%
Derate to 1950 rpm, use 3.70 axle	+1.0%	=3.0%	+4.1%	=30.5%
Use NTC-350, 3.55 axle; impose 64 mph max. speed	−3.0%	=0%	+5.5%	=36.0%

GASOLINE-POWERED TRUCKS

Smaller trucks, generally powered by gasoline engines, can also benefit from the air and rolling resistance measures described in the preceding section. As with any heavy vehicle, gasoline-powered trucks must be driven at steady speeds and with gradual acceleration if they are to deliver their best economy. The large frontal area of any truck causes sharply reduced mileage at higher speeds, during which the usual lack of streamlining becomes a greater consumer of horsepower. In addition, gasoline engines require more frequent checks and adjustments as described for passenger car engines in Chapter 6.

The prospective buyer would do well to consider a truck powered by a diesel engine. Depending on the application, the diesel can be a real fuel saver. The amount saved will depend on a number of factors, including loads, speeds, and amount of time spent idling. For example, a typical gasoline engine will idle for about 50 minutes on a gallon of fuel, whereas a diesel engine of the same horsepower will idle for up to four hours on the same amount.[18] The more time spent in stop-and-go operation and idling, the more fuel will be saved with the diesel engine. In tests conducted by the U.S. Post Office under postal operation conditions, a five-ton diesel truck had double the fuel mileage, and half-ton and one-ton diesel trucks had 50% greater fuel mileage than gasoline trucks of the same size.[19] Further discussion of the diesel engine is included in Chapter 3.

OTHER COMMERCIAL VEHICLES

Whether you operate a fleet of police cars, taxicabs, buses, or go-carts, the same general fuel-efficiency principles apply. Proper selection, driving, maintenance, and planning will go a long way toward reducing your fuel bill. For example, in taxi service, the use of a diesel-engined fleet is an obvious strategy for improved efficiency. Likewise, for police vehicles, substitution of subcompact vehicles for larger cars may be both efficient and satisfactory for many applications not involving high-speed pursuit or the transporting of disorderly football fans. As before, the *typical* use of the vehicle must be considered rather than the occasional use that may come up only once a year.

Fig. 8–15. As with private automobiles, proper selection, driving, maintenance, and planning will minimize the fuel consumption of commercial vehicles. And since the drivers usually don't have to pay for their own fuel, selection, maintenance, and planning take on added importance in commercial applications.

Chapter 9
Applying the Principles:
86 MPG on a Real Road

Having presented all the ingredients for fuel efficient driving, I would be remiss if I didn't provide a few examples of what can happen when these ingredients are combined in practice. Such demonstrations of the fuel efficiency "bottom line" can be a source of personal pride and enjoyment.

This chapter is presented in two parts. First is the description and results of a series of mileage demonstrations involving what is, at this writing, the most fuel-efficient vehicle available to the motoring public. Second, there is a slightly zany account of an economy run in which a family of five and a German shepherd squeezed into a small station wagon and managed to win first place over a variety of much smaller groups who ended up more than a little surprised at the standings.

86 MPG ON A REAL ROAD

By this time, you've probably been confronted with a myriad of fuel economy claims from various manufacturers and marketers, some of which have probably used the results of trips equivalent to traveling downhill from Pike's Peak. The trips in this section are very real, were repeated several times for reliability, involved a route that began and ended at the same altitude, and could have been accompanied by a state trooper whose traffic violation book would have gone unopened all the way.

The Participants

Naturally, the driver was Yours Truly. Three different passengers were carried on three different occasions, each with consistent results despite differing passenger weight. Obtaining willing observers for efficiency demonstrations is not easy because, for many individuals who have not achieved the motivation level which you and I now enjoy, fuel-efficient driving isn't as much fun as doing impersonations of Richard Petty in the Southern 500. Passengers included an auto salesperson, a retail store manager, and a retailing executive, all of whom were sober individuals and initially skeptical of the results I had promised they would see.

The Route

The route traveled consisted of a round trip over 86.4 miles of four-lane, country, and small-town driving in the Western Pennsylvania area. Terrain was generally hilly, road conditions ranged from good to atrocious, and average speeds were about 30 to 35 miles per hour for the total trip. Considering the country roads that made up a large portion of the route, such speeds were not much different from normal speeds over the same roads. In some cases, low speeds and pothole-dodging were necessary for safety purposes, and only individuals in a real hurry would have covered the route in much less time than the efficiency demonstrations required.

The Vehicle

The car selected for the demonstrations was a five-speed 1979 Volkswagen Diesel Rabbit (EPA combined city/highway mileage estimate: 41 mpg). Ours was a two-door custom hatchback equipped with standard steel-belted radial tires along with its fuel-efficient diesel engine. The car was stock in every way but one: the tires were inflated to 36 pounds per square inch, the maximum permissible pressure indicated on the sidewall, instead of the standard 27 psi. This provided a little less rolling resistance for the tests, but certainly couldn't be considered a major modification—anyone faced with gas lines or rationing might well decide to do the same. (Besides reducing tire life, such high inflation pressures might adversely affect the handling qualities of some cars, so be cautious about using the extra-pressure strategy in ordinary driving.)

Weather Conditions

On each demonstration run, temperatures were in the low eighties, winds were calm to moderate, and it was possible to maintain comfortable interior temperatures without having to use air conditioning, which was fortunate, since the car had no air conditioner. The front windows were opened by several inches and the flow-through ventilation used to counteract the summer temperatures.

The Driving

During the 86.4 miles of the testing, driving was in accordance with the advice provided in Chapter 4, and no laws were bent or broken during the course of each trip. As in ordinary driving, the car was in gear at all times (no coasting), with the exception of changing gears and arriving at stop signs and red lights. Generous use was made of the fifth gear overdrive capability of the manual transmission, and the trip was made with a minimum of rpm's as well as a minimum of fuel consumption.

The Results

In four trips around the test route, the results were as follows: 86.2 mpg, 86.5 mpg, and 88 mpg on the three trips with one passenger aboard, and 95.4 mpg on a solo trip with driver alone. At these efficiency levels, the mere addition or subtraction of a passenger can affect performance by about 10 mpg; on the basis of vehicle weight alone, a 170-pound passenger makes a difference in the vicinity of 7%. In addition, two occupants require more fresh air and ventilation than a single occupant, so aerodynamics of window positioning (or energy consumption of air conditioning, if present) becomes a greater drain.

The goal of the tests was to achieve 100 mpg without coasting or breaking any laws, and the results were agonizingly close—especially the 95.4 mpg solo run. The consistency of the two-occupant tests, along with the impressive solo run, suggest very strongly that the 100 mpg level can be realized.

Since the amount of fuel used was generally less than a single gallon, to measure fuel consumption a more accurate measuring device than the gas pump was necessary. For this purpose, a chemistry laboratory measuring cylinder was used to patiently fill and refill the tank. Remember that diesel fuel foams when poured, and that a true fill-up can take five minutes. Most gas station attendants would not have been very interested in having other customers wait for five minutes while they coaxed every possible cubic centimeter into the tank of a fuel-efficiency test car.

Unlike a lot of mileage demonstrations that bear no resemblance to the real world, these tests have very few "asterisks" associated with them. On any warm summer day, the author can take the same vehicle type and duplicate these test results for the benefit of any disbeliever weighing less than 250 pounds. The passenger will not be scared to death, will not witness dangerous driving habits, and, perhaps most importantly, will not have to push. The techniques in this book really do work, and the consistent mileage figures obtained during these tests show that the level of efficiency reported here is most assuredly achievable with present technology and the application of efficient driving practices.

THE WORLD'S MOST UNLIKELY ECONOMY RUN WINNER

"Hey, Pierre. There's a station wagon over there with two people, three kids, and a police dog. Do you think they want to enter the economy run?" "I don't know, Tim. But if they do, we'd better let them—that dog must weigh 100 pounds." So went the opening commentary as the Weiers family prepared for their local sports car club's annual economy run.

In case you've never heard of an economy run, it's a driving contest in which the fastest driver never wins. The idea is to travel as many miles as you can for each gallon of gas that you use. After you've filled up (and had your gas cap sealed) at the starting point, you drive as efficiently as possible over a prescribed route, then return to the starting point for a refill. When your car is refueled, the amount of gas is carefully measured, then your performance is converted into miles per gallon. (There's no "I can drive for two weeks on a tankfull" in this league.)

In order to allow all cars, large and small, to compete on an equal footing, economy run planners either group the contestants into classes or award trophies based on ton-miles per gallon. This is simply your miles per gallon multiplied by the number of tons your car weighs. Thus, if you can squeeze 25 miles per gallon from your 4,000-pound car, that's 50 ton-miles per gallon—enough to make you a trophy contender.

The rules for an economy run depend on the sponsor, but they always require that contestants obey all traffic rules. As a further control, competitors are faced with either actual or possible check points to ensure that they are following the prescribed course and staying within the law.

You can be disqualified for a number of reasons: (1) if your odometer reading indicates that you didn't travel far enough to complete the required route; (2) if your average speed is less than that required to get you back to the starting point on time; (3) if you tamper with the seal on your gas cap; (4) if you get out of your car for anything except an emergency; or (5) if you receive a traffic citation for any moving violation. Some economy runs even require the presence of an impartial observer to ensure that the driver complies with all the rules of the event and the state in which he is driving.

The economy run we entered used ton-miles per gallon as the method of evaluating the performance of all competitors, included all of the rules just described, and had an initial odometer check to discover if our odometer registered 10 miles after we had covered the first 10 miles.

Preparation

Our preparation for the economy run did not deviate much from the advice of the previous chapters. We had already bought for economy: our car was a subcompact station wagon weighing about 2,200 pounds, equipped with steel-belted radials and four-speed manual transmission. The car had always been pampered with the combination of proper-octane gasoline and frequent changes of top-quality engine oil. Just to help ensure that engine resistance was absolutely minimized, a can of anti-friction additive joined the brand-new oil in the crank-case.

Normal maintenance operations were carried out slightly ahead of schedule to provide every possible edge for the economy run. On the morning of the event, the following operations were performed: new spark plugs and ignition points were installed. Ignition dwell and timing were set. The front end was greased and the rear drum brakes were adjusted to eliminate even a hint of drag. Idle speed was lowered to the minimum required to keep the engine from stalling. Tires were inflated to their maximum allowable pressures as indicated on the sidewall. The car was washed with plain cold water in order to avoid removing that slippery wax. The air cleaner was rinsed out and topped up with fresh oil. Oil was changed (SAE 10W-40) and the oil strainer cleaned.

Before the Start

During the pre-start registration activities, most competitors stand around and converse while their cars stand around and get cold. The result is a car that has to warm up a little during the first part of the route—not desirable for efficiency. Until a few minutes before our scheduled starting time, we kept the car's moving parts heated up by driving in the vicinity of the filling station.

In fairness to the service station operator who is providing the facilities for the economy run, it's proper etiquette to show up at the event with a tank that needs some gas. To this end, our 10.6 gallon tank arrived at the pump with barely a half-gallon left. However, our purpose was not entirely altruistic. The day was unseasonably warm—over 70° F in early March isn't normal in Pennsylvania—and cold gasoline from the underground tank tends to expand as it is heated. As a matter of fact, ten gallons of gasoline will expand by about eight-tenths of a quart when the temperature goes up by 30° F. This is why your tank overflows when you fill up and park on a hot day, and is also the reason for our near-empty tank.

With our full tank of cold (about 40° F) gasoline expanding by nearly a quart during the afternoon, the fill-up at the end would require that much less, hence increasing our measured miles per gallon. Had the outside temperature been colder than that of the underground gasoline, our empty-tank strategy would have backfired, leading to shrinking gasoline which would have required a bigger fill-up at the end. If you're thinking about entering an economy run and applying this idea yourself, keep in mind that a quantity of gasoline will expand by seven-tenths of one percent for every 10° F increase in temperature. Thus, if the temperature of 20 gallons of gasoline were to increase by 10° F, the resulting volume of gasoline would be 20 x 1.007, or 20.14 gallons, an increase of .14 gallons—not much by everyday standards, but quite significant in a hotly contested economy run.

Knowing the route in advance provided an opportunity to take a practice run and made it less likely for us to get lost. In two of the preceding three years we had become hopelessly lost and either finished too late or had to drive inefficiently in order to return to the start on time. As it was, with a map and full set of instructions, I still managed to go off course twice during my solo practice trip.

Just before leaving the station, we double-checked the route instructions, then had our tank filled to the brim. During the filling process, the car was shaken from side to side in order to avoid the formation of costly air pockets in the tank. (You can't travel many miles on a gallon of trapped air.) Before starting our engine to leave the station, we waited until passing traffic was clear. This enabled us to move directly onto the road without losing momentum.

On the Road

As we turned right and headed up the hill, we accelerated at a rate that wouldn't have snapped a giraffe's neck. Taking advantage of the low speed, we lowered the radio antenna and folded back the side mirrors in order to lower air resistance (making these modifications back at the station would have been embarrassing—after all, who in his right mind would take three kids and a dog on an economy run, then lower the antenna to save gas?). The flow-through ventilation vents were opened wide on both sides of the dash. It was taken for granted that we would minimize air resistance by keeping the side windows up whenever the car was moving.

Having reached fourth gear and 35 miles per hour, we merged onto the four-lane section of the run. Along this route, the minimum speed was posted as 40 mph. Except for the times when gravity made us go faster, the speedometer was glued to 40 mph for the next half-hour. The best speed control device going is a steady right foot.

Finally leaving the four-lane road, we encountered gradually rolling hills and a string of traffic signals. The engine was always shut off whenever a signal didn't go our way, then restarted as we slowly accelerated back to our desirable cruising speed of about 35 mph. Whenever possible, the car was driven 25 to 30 mph in fourth gear. This is difficult for many small cars, but the combination of electronic fuel injection for engine smoothness and radial tires for low rolling resistance made it seem that we were moving almost without effort. However, since we had to average about 32 miles per hour in order to make it back to the starting point on time, speeds below 30 were a luxury we couldn't afford to enjoy for too long.

Continuing along the curvy back roads, it was possible to cruise smoothly without braking and to climb most hills without gearing down. Naturally, the brake was avoided as though it were a land mine. Having had the chance to make a practice run the week before, we were aware of the terrain and the various obstacles to our maintaining a slow and constant speed. For example, knowing in advance that a stop sign would be around the next curve made it possible to begin slowing down earlier and use less gas until we got there. In addition, knowledge of the conditions ahead made it easier to keep to 30 to 35 mph in fourth and to make gradual increases as we knew they would be necessary.

From time to time, our low but legal rate of speed would attract followers. Whenever possible, we pulled to the right to allow them to pass. Whenever impossible, we maintained speed while I pretended that my right foot was paralyzed. At these times, the presence of the dog in the back window helped to entertain the people behind and sustain their patience. (The kids' puppet show probably helped, too.) When pressured from behind, the temptation to speed up and waste gas becomes very strong. Feeling as though we had to do something about it, we sometimes pretended to be looking for a turn-off or house number as we continued along at a constant speed.

At times, we would come up behind other Sunday drivers who were either trying for super-economy or were in no hurry to reach their destination. But then, that's what Sunday driving is all about. We passed them as soon and as gently as we could. Although economy-run competitors were assigned to leave the starting point at three-minute intervals, we were passed by two or three who roared by as if they were less interested in winning than in the free gas provided by the sponsor at the end of the run.

About three-fourths of the way through the 96-mile route, we were directed to enter a weighing station in order to find out how many tons our car weighed. This was to be used in the ton-miles per gallon calculation to be made at the finish. Our station wagon, including driver and assorted occupants, weighed in at 3,010 pounds. While stopped on the scale, we relaxed and opened the side windows for some air. Because of our very constant speeds and the ability of the engine to pull smoothly, our extra weight (which included a 40-pound trailer hitch) seemed to be doing very little damage to our economy.

Throughout the trip, the family portion of the family drive was up to par, with the kids playing, eating, and looking for various farm animals along the way. Canine companion Schultzie was also interested in the farm animals, and would sometimes disrupt driving-for-economy with her loud challenges to them from the safety of her (slowly) moving car. Besides providing directions, the navigator planned different treats and games for the various legs of the course. The most popular diversion was the "it's my turn to get in back with the dog" game. The second most popular diversion was the "it's your turn to get in back with the dog" game.

At the Finish

We had just driven 96 miles at the most efficient speeds possible and had used every trick in this book to maximize our miles per gallon. Like many other Sunday drivers, we had covered a scenic route at a more relaxed pace. However, our arrival back home was probably a bit more tense than that of other families on the road that day. Back at the station, contestants were already beginning to cluster around the gas pumps to peek at the number of gallons required by their fellow competitors. Over the protests of drivers who claimed their tanks were already full, event officials squeezed in ever more gas in order to reach the generous pre-run tank level for each car.

Poke-alongs that we were, ours was one of the last cars to return. Stopping at the pump, we watched and took our turn objecting as officials unsealed the gas cap and filled the tank to its initial level. After an economy run, every drop spilled looks like a gallon. Considering the distance covered, nobody was surprised when the pump reading passed the one-gallon mark—after all this was a station wagon, not a motorcycle. What was surprising to onlookers and rewarding to us was that the tank satisfied its thirst after only 1.75 gallons, a quantity which indicated that we had obtained 54.7 miles per gallon.

When combined with our weight of 3,010 pounds (1.5 tons), our performance was calculated as 82.2 ton-miles per gallon—enough to put us in first place. The runner-up's aerodynamic Opel GT had actually delivered 2.5 more mpg, but its lighter (by 520 pounds) weight meant less bulk hauled around the course, leaving him with 71.1 ton-miles per gallon. The first-place trophy was accepted with thanks and apologies for not having done better—we suggested that we could have gotten another 5 miles per gallon if only the dog's harness hadn't broken just as we were clearing the top of a hill.

Notes

All SAE reports and papers are published by the Society of Automotive Engineers, Warrendale, PA 15086

Chapter 1
1. United States Department of Energy, Office of Conservation and Solar Applications, *To Help You Save Gas*, Washington, D.C., 1979, p. 4.
2. *Ibid.*

Chapter 2
1. "The Fastest Man on Earth," *Bicycling*, November, 1973, p. 20.
2. Jack C. Cornell, *Passenger Car Fuel Economy Characteristics on Modern Superhighways*, SAE Report No. 650862. Cited in Motor Vehicle Manufacturers Association of the United States, *Automobile Fuel Economy*, September 21, 1973, p. 7.
3. *Ibid.*
4. Thomas C. Austin and Karl H. Hellman, *Passenger Car Fuel Economy—Trends and Influencing Factors*, SAE Report No. 730790, 1973, p. 16.
5. Cummins Engine Company, *Answers to Questions about Diesels*, Bulletin No. 952760, August, 1970, p. 19.
6. Kent B. Kelly and Harry J. Holcomb, *Aerodynamics for Body Engines*, SAE Paper 649A, January, 1963.
7. Lloyd Nedley, *An Effective Aerodynamic Program in the Design of a New Car*, SAE Paper No. 790724, 1979, p. 2.
8. *Ibid.*
9. L. J. Janssen and H. J. Emmelmann, *Aerodynamic Improvements—A Great Potential for Better Fuel Economy*, SAE Report No. 780265, 1978, p. 7.
10. Nedley, p. 20.
11. A. L. Gutherie, *Fairmont/Zephyr—Engineered for Lightweight and Improved Fuel Economy*, SAE Paper No. 780134, 1978, p. 3.
12. William D. Bowman, *The Present Status of Automobile Aerodynamics in Automobile Engineering and Development*, Proceedings of the AIAA Symposium on the Aerodynamics of Sport and Competition Vehicles, April, 1968, p. 71.
13. Firestone Tire and Rubber Company, *Proper Tire Maintenance Can Roll Back Gas Costs*, Press Release, 1979.
14. Firestone Tire and Rubber Company, Promotional Announcement, 1973.
15. H. D. Tarpinian, G. H. Nybakken, and J. Mishory, *A Fuel Saving Passenger Tire*, SAE Paper No. 790726, 1979, p. 11.
16. Dieter J. Schuring, *Transient versus Steady-State Tire Rolling Loss Testing*, SAE Paper No. 790116, 1979.
17. S. K. Clark, et al., *Rolling Resistance of Pneumatic Tires*, United States Department of Transportation, DOT TSC-74-2, 1974.
18. Cornell, cited in Motor Vehicle Manufacturers Association, p. 7.
19. Donald A. Hurter and W. David Lee, *A Study of Technological Improvements in Automobile Fuel Consumption*, SAE Paper No. 750005, 1975.
20. Motor Vehicle Manufacturers Association, *Automobile Fuel Economy*, September 21, 1973, p. 4.
21. Carl E. Burke, et al., "Where Does All The Power Go?", *SAE Transactions*, 65 (57). Cited in Motor Vehicle Manufacturers Association, *Automobile Fuel Economy*, September 21, 1973, p. 10.
22. James A. McGeehan, *A Literature Review of the Effects of Piston and Ring Friction and Lubricating Oil Viscosity on Fuel Economy*, SAE Paper No. 780673, 1978.
23. United States Environmental Protection Agency, *A Report on Automotive Fuel Economy*, Washington, D.C., Government Printing Office, October, 1973, p. 30.
24. B. H. Eccleston and R. W. Hurn, *Ambient Temperature and Trip Length—Influence on Automotive Fuel Economy and Emissions*, SAE Paper No. 780613, 1978, p. 7.
25. United States Environmental Protection Agency, p. 30.

26. Chrysler Corporation, "Drive More, Pay Less," News Release, May 24, 1973.

Chapter 3

1. T. C. Austin, R. B. Michael and G. R. Service, *Passenger Car Fuel Economy Trends Through 1976*, SAE Paper No. 750957, 1975.
2. G. H. Huebner, Jr., and D. J. Gasser, "General Factors Affecting Vehicle Fuel Consumption" (Paper presented at National Automobile Engineering Meeting, Society of Automotive Engineers, Detroit, Michigan, May 15, 1973). Cited in Motor Vehicle Manufacturers Association, p. 6.
3. *Ibid.*
4. Jack C. Cornell, "Car Size Chiefly Responsible for Low MPG at High MPH," *SAE Journal*, April, 1966, p. 37.
5. United States Environmental Agency, p. 21.
6. Cummins Engine Company, *Answers to Questions About Diesels*, p. 7.
7. *Ibid.*, p. 8.
8. Neil Watson, *Turbochargers for the 1980's—In Which Direction Are We Going?*, SAE Paper No. 790063, 1979.
9. United States Environmental Protection Agency, p. 21.
10. *Ibid.*
11. Huebner and Gasser, cited in Motor Vehicle Manufacturers Association, p. 16.
12. Dennis J. Simanaitis, "Torque Converter Locks in Fuel Savings," *Automotive Engineering*, vol. 85, no. 11, November, 1977, p. 29.
13. United States Environmental Protection Agency, p. 14.
14. *Ibid.*
15. Cornell, cited in Motor Vehicle Manufacturers Association, p. 13.
16. Huebner and Gasser, cited in Motor Vehicle Manufacturers Association, p. 13.
17. Harold C. MacDonald, "Remarks" (speech presented to 1973 Engineering Meeting, Society of Automotive Engineers, Detroit, Michigan, May 15, 1973). Cited in Motor Vehicle Manufacturers Association, p. 5.
18. Cornell, cited in Motor Vehicle Manufacturers Association, p. 12.
19. Robert W. Donoho, *EPA MPG—How Realistic?*, SAE Paper No. 780866, 1978, p. 5.
20. F. C. Porter, *Design for Fuel Economy—The New GM Front Drive Cars*, SAE Paper No. 790721, 1979, p. 7.
21. Firestone Tire and Rubber Company, Promotional Announcement.
22. *Ibid.*
23. Kamei USA, Technical Research Report, October 6, 1979.
24. Bain Dayman, Jr., *Realistic Effects of Winds on the Aerodynamic Resistance of Automobiles*, SAE Paper No. 780337, 1978, p. 4.
25. United States Department of Energy, Office of Conservation and Solar Applications, *Gas Savers*, Washington, D.C., 1979, p. 2.
26. *Ibid.*

Chapter 4

1. Huebner and Gasser, cited in Motor Vehicle Manufacturers Association, p. 19.
2. United States Department of Transportation, Federal Highway Administration, *The Effect of Speed on Automobile Gasoline Consumption Rates*, Washington, D.C., October, 1973, p. 8.
3. California Highway Patrol, *What a Reduction in Speed Saves the Average Driver*, Press Release, May 24, 1979.
4. P. Hofbauer and K. Sator, *Advanced Automotive Power Systems, Part 2: A Diesel for a Subcompact Car*, SAE Paper No. 770113, 1977, p. 439.
5. Chrysler Corporation, cited in Motor Vehicle Manufacturers Association, p. 20.
6. Ronald M. Weiers, *Licensed To Kill*, (Philadelphia: Chilton Book Company, 1968), p. 35.
7. Huebner and Gasser, cited in Motor Vehicle Manufacturers Association, p. 12.
8. C. W. Coon and C. D. Wood, *Improvement of Automobile Fuel Economy*, SAE Paper No. 740969, 1974.
9. United States Department of Transportation, Federal Highway Administration, *The Effect of Speed on Automobile Gasoline Consumption Rates*, p. 8.
10. Cornell, cited in Motor Vehicle Manufacturers Association, p. 9.

Chapter 5

1. American Petroleum Institute, "Gasoline, Questions-Answers," Publication No. 1580, Washington, D.C., April, 1972, p. 5.
2. *Ibid.*
3. United States Department of the Interior, Bureau of Mines, *Thermal Properties of Petroleum Products*, Report No. M97, Washington, D.C., 1973. Cited in Motor Vehicle Manufacturers Association, p. 18.
4. Merrill L. Haviland and Malcolm C. Goodwin, *Fuel Economy Improvements with Friction-Modified Engine Oils in Environmental Protection Agency and Road Tests*, SAE Paper No. 790945, 1979, p. 1.
5. Walter E. Waddey, Harold Shaub, and Joseph M. Pecoraro, *Improved Fuel Economy via Engine Oils*, SAE Paper No. 780599, 1978, p. 11.
6. V. E. Broman, J. DeJovine, D. L. DeVries, and G. H. Keller, *Testing of Friction Modified Crankcase Oils for Improved Fuel Economy*, SAE Paper No. 780597, 1978, p. 5.

Chapter 6

1. Champion Spark Plug Company, *Tune-Up*, 1976.
2. Champion Spark Plug Company, *The Automobile Tune-Up*, 1977.
3. Joseph C. Brabetz and Donald S. Pike, "Engines Like To Be Warm," *SAE Journal*, January, 1965, p. 70.
4. *Ibid.*
5. American Petroleum Institute, "Gasoline Saving Tips," Washington, D.C., not dated.

6. *Ibid.*

7. *Ibid.*

8. Chrysler Corporation, cited in Motor Vehicle Manufacturers Association, p. 21.

9. P. N. Gammelgard, statement presented to U.S. Senate Subcommittee on Air and Water Pollution, Washington, D.C., June 26, 1973. Cited in Motor Vehicle Manufacturers Association, p. 14.

10. R. L. Bechtold and R. D. Fleming, *An Investigation of Fuel Economy Potential of Four 1977-Model Vehicles*, SAE Paper No. 770847, 1977.

11. B. M. O'Connor, R. Graham, and I. Glover, *European Experience with Fuel Efficient Gear Oils*, SAE Paper No. 790746, 1979.

12. P. A. Willermet and L. T. Dixon, *Fuel Economy—Contribution of the Rear Axle Lubricant*, SAE Paper No. 770835, 1977.

13. American Petroleum Institute, "Gasoline Saving Tips."

14. United States Department of Commerce, National Bureau of Standards, *Tires, Their Selection and Care*, Washington, D.C., March, 1971, p. 4.

15. Chrysler Corporation, cited in Motor Vehicle Manufacturers Association, p. 21.

Chapter 7

1. United States Department of Energy, Office of Conservation and Solar Applications, *Gas Savers*, Washington, D.C., 1979.

2. American Automobile Association, *Gas Watcher's Guide*, 1979, p. 2.

3. United States Department of Energy, Office of Conservation and Solar Applications, *Gas Savers*, Washington, D.C., 1979.

4. *Ibid.*

5. Tests carried out by author, 1979.

6. MacDonald, cited in Motor Vehicle Manufacturers Association, p. 5.

7. Based on discussion in American Automobile Association, *Gas Watcher's Guide*, 1979, p. 3.

8. Dick Wright, "GM Clearing the Way for Electric-Powered Cars by Mid-1980's," *Autoweek*, October 22, 1979, p. 2.

Chapter 8

1. Cummins Engine Company, *Trucker's Guide to Fuel Savings*, Bulletin 952880 (Columbus, Indiana: October, 1973), p. 5.

2. *Ibid.*

3. "Aerodynamically-Styled Paymaster Offers Tremendous Fuel Savings," *Diesel Equipment Superintendent*, October, 1973, p. 26.

4. Cummins, *Trucker's Guide to Fuel Savings*, pp. 11, 20.

5. *Ibid.*, p. 14.

6. *Ibid.*, p. 15.

7. *Ibid.*, p. 13.

8. United States Department of Transportation, Voluntary Truck and Bus Fuel Economy Program, *17 Tricks to Save Fuel and Save $$$$*, Washington, D.C., June, 1979.

9. Cummins, *Trucker's Guide to Fuel Savings*, p. 17.

10. *Ibid.*, p. 19.

11. *Ibid.*, p. 10.

12. *Ibid.*, p. 8.

13. *Ibid.*, p. 9.

14. *Ibid.*, p. 12.

15. *Ibid.*, p. 7.

16. *Ibid.*, p. 20.

17. Cummins Engine Company, *Answers to Questions About Diesels*, p. 8.

18. George C. Nield, "Light Diesels Give Promise in Mail Service," *SAE Journal*, July, 1966, p. 77.

19. Recreation Vehicle Industry Association, *Energy Saving Tips while RVing*, 1979.

Index

Page numbers in bold refer to illustrations